SOCCER
THE WORLD GAME

SOCCER

THE WORLD GAME

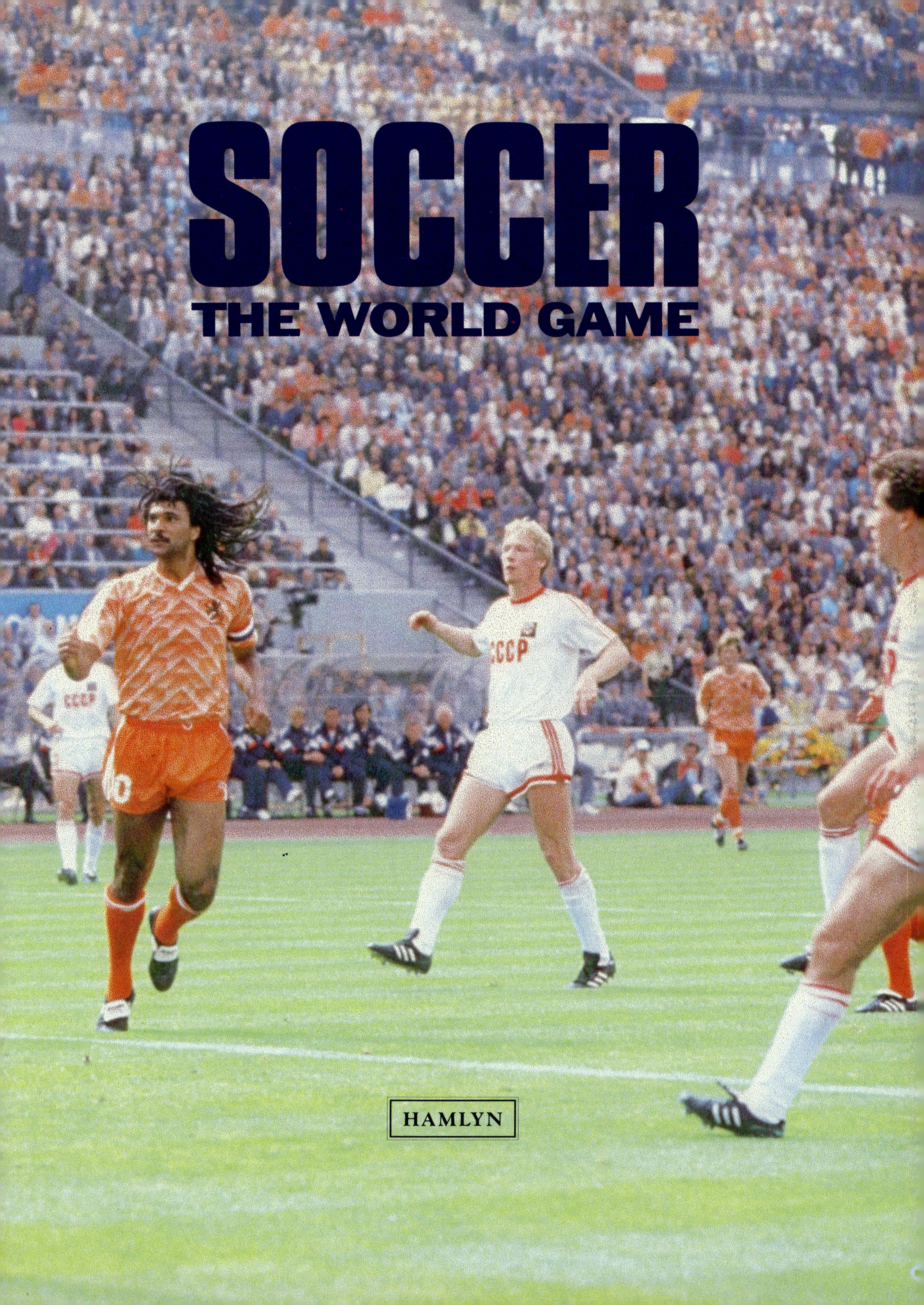

HAMLYN

Published in 1989
by the Hamlyn Publishing Group Limited
a division of the Octopus Publishing Group
Michelin House, 81 Fulham Road, London SW3 6RB

ISBN 0 600 56350 2

Produced by Mandarin Offset
Printed and bound in Hong Kong

Written by:
PETER BALL – Freelance sports reporter with *The Times* and the *Sunday Tribune*
BRIAN GLANVILLE – Football correspondent for the *Sunday Times*
KEIR RADNEDGE – Editor of *World Soccer*
STEVE TONGUE – Football writer for the *Sunday Correspondent*

PHOTOGRAPHIC ACKNOWLEDGEMENTS

Front Jacket (Ruud Gullit): Colorsport
Back Jacket (Gary Lineker): Colorsport

Abril Images/Ricardo Beliel 182; Action Images 127; AllSport 24 bottom, 71, 134 top, 136, (Simon Bruty) 21, 50, 113 bottom, (David Cannon) 17, 85 top, 134 bottom, (Russell Cheyne) 6, (Michael King) 175 bottom, (Steve Powell) 96, (Ben Radford) 20, 68, 108 (Vandystadt) 116, 171 bottom; Associated Press 74, 77 bottom, 80, 81, 163, 168, 178, 179 top; Colorsport 9 bottom, 11, 12, 13, 14, 16, 18, 19, 22, 23, 25, 26, 28, 29, 30, 31, 32, 34, 35, 37 bottom, 38, 41, 42 bottom, 43, 44, 45, 46 top, 47, 48, 49, 51, 52, 53, 54, 55, 57, 58, 59, 60, 61, 62, 64, 65, 66, 67, 69, 70, 72, 73, 76, 79, 83, 85 bottom, 88, 89, 91 bottom, 92 top, 93 bottom, 97, 100, 103 bottom, 105, 109, 110–111, 113 top, 114, 117, 118, 119 top, 120, 121, 122, 124, 126, 128, 131, 133 top, 137, 138, 139, 143 top, 145, 146 bottom, 149, 150, 151, 153, 156, 157, 160, 162, 166 top and bottom left, 167 centre and bottom, 169 bottom, 171 top, 172, 173, 174, 180, 181, 186, 187, 188 bottom; Glasgow Herald 42 top, 46 bottom; John Hillelson Agency/Presse Sports 82 bottom, 86 bottom, 92 bottom, 93 top, 95, 115, 135 bottom, 143 bottom, 144; Hulton Deutsch Collection 36, 106, 183, 184 top, 185 top; Olympia 98 top; Popperfoto 24 top, 140, 164, 184 bottom; S.A.M./Machette 177; Sporting Pictures 56, 86 top, 90, 141, 170 top; Syndication International 9 top, 101, 104, 111 bottom, 158, 165, 179 bottom, 185 bottom; Bob Thomas Sports Photography 27, 33, 39, 63, 75, 78, 82 top, 84, 87, 91 top, 94, 98 bottom, 99, 102, 103 top, 107, 110 bottom, 112, 119 bottom, 123, 125, 129, 130, 132, 133 bottom, 135 top, 142, 146, 148, 152, 154, 155, 159, 166 bottom inset, 167 top right, 170 bottom, 175 top and centre, 176, 188 top; Topham Picture Library 8, 10, 15, 37 top, 147.

CONTENTS

adidas

INTRODUCTION

It's always a pleasure to see informative, well-written books about football, and this one is all the more welcome for its colourful and detailed treatment of the game not just in Britain but throughout the world.

With the World Cup coming up, it's an exciting time for our sport, which will be under a huge global spotlight during the summer. The amount of interest created world-wide is a reminder of just how popular the game is, so let's hope that managers, coaches and players make Italy a month to remember.

We certainly had a dramatic climax to the last domestic season, with the Football League title not decided until the last minute of the last game. I was, of course, enormously proud that Arsenal emerged as Champions, but it was good for the public to be reminded what an exciting sport this can be: and also what a sporting one, for I thought that both teams and their supporters conducted themselves outstandingly well.

Enjoy your football, wherever you play it or watch it – and enjoy this book too.

George Graham

ENGLAND

Whether England can really claim to have invented football is debatable – the game's origins lie shrouded in the mists of antiquity – but it is unarguably the birthplace of the modern game.

An agreed set of rules was hammered out in 1863, the same year as the Football Association was founded. In 1871, when the Rugby Football Union was started by clubs who refused to outlaw hacking and tripping, the F.A. Cup was introduced. Professionalism soon followed, and in 1888 the Football League was established, with 12 founder members in the Midlands and North.

Professionalism was the key. In the early years the F.A. Cup was dominated by clubs based on the public schools and London society – Wanderers, Old Etonians, Royal Engineers, Oxford University. And the game's administration was dominated by players from those clubs – The Honourable Arthur (later Lord) Kinnaird, Major Francis Marindin and C. W. Alcock.

But as Scots came South to take up employment in the Lancashire cotton industry, and play football for their local clubs, providing there was some incentive to do so, power swung irrevocably. No longer was football a prerogative of the upper middle classes, it became the people's game.

The great Blackburn Rovers won the Cup five times between 1883 and 1891. Proud Preston were the first League champions with their famous centre-forward John Goodall and a bevy of Scots. They went through the season undefeated, a feat so far unequalled.

A year later Preston did the double, hotly pursued in the League by Lancashire rivals Everton and Blackburn. Everton won their first Championship in 1891 as Preston began a hat-trick of second places, but the 1890s was dominated by Sunderland, who won three League titles, and by Aston Villa who won four and did the double in 1897.

Fittingly the first full season of the 20th century produced Liverpool's first Championship, and Tottenham's Cup win the same season revealed that the South had recovered from the decline of the old amateur sides. The first decade of the century brought some familiar names to the fore, Newcastle United, Sheffield Wednesday and the two Manchester clubs claiming honours. But the old Lancashire teams still had their days, Bury and Burnley winning the Cup and Blackburn, under the great captain Bob Crompton, winning the Championship twice.

After the War power began to move, but Herbert Chapman's legendary Huddersfield side, with Alec Jackson and Clem Stephenson, won a hat-trick of championships, a feat equalled in the Thirties by Chapman's Arsenal. The immediate post-war period brought new names to the fore, Portsmouth with Jimmy Scoular, Jimmy Dickinson and Jack Froggatt winning the championship twice before the Wolves of Billy Wright, Bill Slater, Ron Flowers and Peter Broadbent emerged alongside Manchester United.

Burnley and Ipswich made final bids for the small clubs as the Sixties began, and the great Leeds side of John Giles, Eddie Gray, Jack Charlton and Billy Bremner also flourished before Liverpool's grip tightened.

For a long time international football

Tom Finney, the Preston winger with claims to be considered as England's greatest post-war player, scores against Scotland at Wembley in 1951. One of Scotland's greats, centre-half George Young, is for once caught in the wrong place.

was of rather less moment, only Scotland providing consistently testing opposition from the first meeting in 1872. It was an American politician who coined the phrase 'splendid isolation', but it was the English F.A. who practised it, disdainfully refusing to enter the World Cup, and ignoring evidence that Continental football was improving.

A 4–3 loss to Spain in Madrid in 1929 could be ignored when Spain were beaten 7–1 in London two years later. Superiority was taken for granted and the great post-War side which called regularly on such talents as Stanley Matthews, Raich Carter, Stan Mortensen, Tommy Lawton, Wilf Mannion and Tom Finney, beating Portugal 10–0 in Lisbon and Italy 4–0 in Turin, seemed to justify such attitudes.

A rude awakening lay ahead. England's first World Cup expedition, to Brazil in 1950, was a disaster, containing the ignominious scoreline 'U.S.A. 1 England 0'.

Even that was disregarded in some quarters, but there was no arguing with the next lesson, inflicted by the great Hungarians, who won 6–3 at Wembley in 1953, England's first home defeat by a foreign team, and even more humiliatingly, 7–1 in Budapest six months later. The teachers had become the pupils, and the road back was hard.

By 1966, however, as England staged the World Cup for the only time, it all came right, Sir Alf Ramsey's 'wingless wonders' overcoming some uninspired early matches to win a marvellous, gripping final 4–2 against West Germany.

Four years later in Mexico, two controversial substitutions helped West Germany gain revenge in the quarter-finals to begin another period of decline.

Recovery began again in the Eighties, the emergence of Gary Lineker and Peter Beardsley in Mexico in 1986 taking England to the quarter-finals and another controversial defeat, this time by Argentina, and subsequently to the 1988 European Championships finals.

But England's appearance in the European competition was a major disappointment. Defeats by the Republic of Ireland, Holland and the Soviet Union left them bottom in their group.

English football's proudest moment. Geoff Hurst completes his hat-trick in the last moments of the 1966 World Cup final, ensuring victory over West Germany.

England's re-emergence in the Eighties has been due in no small measure to Gary Lineker, stretching here to score against Paraguay in the 1986 World Cup.

ARSENAL

A club always more noted for competitiveness than flair, Arsenal in modern times have been the South's only consistent threat to Northern supremacy. And off the field their name has become a byword for efficient, and often far-sighted administration.

Although as Royal Arsenal they were early pacesetters, becoming the first Southern club to join the Football League, it was not always so. As Woolwich Arsenal, they found that corner of South East London almost as unresponsive as Charlton have done, but the move to Highbury, with its ease of access, in 1913, proved a masterstroke, whatever dubious manoeuvring by the club's rich and unscrupulous chairman, Henry Norris, was necessary to achieve it.

Norris's political deals also restored the club unfairly to a First Division place after the First World War, and their growing power was seen when they reached the 1927 Cup Final, going down 1–0 to Cardiff.

That was only a staging post on the way to success, which came with a rush when Herbert Chapman took over as manager to become the founder of one of the game's enduring great powers. Until the Liverpool of the present day, no club has dominated a decade in the 20th century as completely as Arsenal dominated the Thirties. They were League champions five times – in 1931, 1933–35, and 1938 – and runners up in 1932. And they were F.A. Cup winners in 1930 and 1936, and beaten finalists in 1932. If Alex James, the string-puller in midfield, was the supreme artist, from the cultured Eddie Hapgood at left-back, through the vividly contrasting wing-halves, the elegant Jack Crayston and the blue-chinned Wilf Copping, to the free-scoring forwards Joe Hulme, David Jack, Jack Lambert, his successor Ted Drake, and Cliff Bastin, there were outstanding players throughout the side.

But most important was the influence of Chapman, a dynamic leader in every way. Whether persuading London Transport to name the local tube station Arsenal or setting records on the transfer market, he made them the most forward-thinking club of the era. His impact on football was no less profound, pulling the centre-half back into defence to counter the change in the offside law, and building his side on defence and swift counter-attack, an approach which has stayed with the club ever since.

It has not been pretty, provoking opposition fans to christen the club first 'Lucky Arsenal', and more recently 'Boring Arsenal', but it has been effective. The Thirties' success survived both the death of Chapman and the War, Tom Whittaker taking over to guide them to further League championships in 1948 and 1953 and to the F.A. Cup in 1950. Joe Mercer, apparently approaching the end of a distinguished career, found a new one at Highbury to emerge as one of the game's true greats, well supported by Laurie Scott, Jimmy Logie and Alex Forbes.

Yet the greatest achievement was still to come. In 1970–71, at a time when the great Leeds team was at its height, and the two Manchester and two Merseyside clubs all provided formidable opposition, Arsenal did the double.

Ted Drake, the free-scoring Arsenal and England centre-forward, causes consternation among Sheffield United's defenders in the 1936 FA Cup final. He later scored the only goal of the game.

Rarely can a side have epitomised a club so perfectly, only the mercurial Charlie George and the elegant George Graham adding variation to the strict functionalism and competitiveness of their approach.

If Danny Blanchflower was the ideal representative of the Tottenham double winners, Peter Storey, a harsh tackler in midfield, embodied Arsenal. Yet the Gunners' achievement was arguably the greater, pulled off by a team whose whole was undoubtedly far greater than the sum of its parts.

Only when Alan Ball arrived a year later could the Arsenal side of that era claim to possess a great player. Its successors were more fortunate as Liam Brady, David O'Leary and Frank Stapleton came through the ranks and the splendid Irishman Pat Jennings arrived from Spurs to see Arsenal to three consecutive Cup finals.

The return of Graham as manager in 1986 and the emergence of a crop of talented young players led to two more Wembley visits in successive seasons, with a Littlewoods Cup victory over Liverpool achieved in the first by the enigmatic Charlie Nicholas's goals. Then, in 1989, London's first League title for 18 years was achieved against the odds when Michael Thomas scored the second goal required for a stunning victory at Liverpool in the very last moments of the season.

David Rocastle takes the ball past Tottenham's Gary Mabbutt during the North London derby at Highbury. Rocastle's form has earned the midfield player full international caps and he was also selected as the Barclays Young Eagle of the Year.

ASTON VILLA

When Aston Villa won the European Cup in 1982, startling as the achievement was, they were merely reclaiming a heritage some 80 years old. From well before the turn of the century until at least the First World War, the Villa were unquestionably the top club in England – and therefore the whole of Europe. If an understandable tendency to dwell on past glories continues to handicap them, they nevertheless remain among the aristocrats of British football.

The Football League itself was, after all, the brainchild of a Villa committee man. William McGregor, a Scottish draper, thought it ridiculous that three years after professionalism had been legalized, clubs were still playing only friendlies and cup ties, and brought a dozen of them together for the 1888–89 season.

Once Preston's 'Invincibles' had proved to be mortal after all, Villa overtook Sunderland, Everton and the F.A. Cup specialists Blackburn as the new giants, and in 1897 emulated Preston's League and Cup double. They won the Championship five times between 1894 and 1900, and the Cup five times before the First World War.

Decline, when it set in, was unexpectedly sudden. Always a top six team during the 1920s, Villa finished runners-up in 1931 (when Pongo Waring and Eric Houghton scored 79 League goals between them!) and 1933. But then the even more popular Billy Walker left to manage Sheffield Wednesday and before 1936 was out, the unthinkable had happened – Second Division football was being played at Villa Park.

Although they have always managed to achieve promotion quickly after relegation disasters, the post-war period would look dreadfully barren without the 1957 F.A. Cup success, which deprived Manchester United of the century's first double, and those remarkable years of 1981 and 1982. Even then, the team which Ron Saunders built, strong in defence and relying on Gordon Cowans and the more erratic Tony Morley for its flair, had only one good season in the League, pipping Ipswich to the Championship and setting up the following year's European triumph.

Tony Barton, Graham Turner, Billy McNeill and Graham Taylor have subsequently found it even harder to fulfil the massive expectations of Villa's demanding followers.

In 1988–9, Aston Villa depended on Alan McInally's goals to stay in the First Division.

DERBY COUNTY

Derby County, one of the founder members of the Football League, can claim one of the most chequered histories in the game.

Based in one of the most knowledgeable football areas in the country, and with a ground providing one of the most dramatic arenas in the country on big occasions, the club had to wait until 1946 for its first F.A. Cup final victory, and another 26 years until the coming of Brian Clough for its first League Championship. Even then nothing ran smoothly as Clough fell out with the chairman and departed amid mass protests. Dave Mackay replaced him to win another Championship and then resigned after being refused a vote of confidence, and sudden decline led to the Third Division and to within an inch of extinction as creditors closed in.

It all made the old story that the club was under a Romany curse all too easy to believe. Even at the turn of the century, an outstanding team, which at various times included the great Steve Bloomer and the Goodall brothers, John and Archie, reached the Cup final three times, only to fail at the final hurdle, while another fine team in the Thirties, with Sammy Crooks, who kept Stanley Matthews out of the England side for a time, Dally Duncan, Jack Barker, Jack Bowers and, briefly, Hughie Gallacher, could do no better than finish runners-up in the League in 1935 and reach the Cup semi-finals.

Things looked up immediately after the war as the club fielded two of the all-time great inside-forwards in Raich Carter and Peter Doherty and won the Cup in 1945–46. But though record fees were paid to recruit Johnny Morris and Billy Steel to replace them, and Derby remained a power, no further success came, and in the mid-Fifties they crashed to Division Three.

Brian Clough and Peter Taylor promised better things, leading them out of the Second Division to the Championship with a galaxy of star names – Dave Mackay, Roy McFarland, Colin Todd, Archie Gemmill and Kevin Hector – but Clough's departure set in train a disastrous decline. The millionaire publisher Robert Maxwell helped rescue the club from bankruptcy in 1984 and the efforts of Arthur Cox began an onfield recovery too, the side winning successive promotions to return to the First Division in 1987. The first season back was one of consolidation.

Scottish international midfielder Archie Gemmill, a key figure in Brian Clough's brilliant Seventies team.

PLAYER PROFILES

SIR STANLEY MATTHEWS

There will never be unanimous agreement on the name of the best player who ever lived, or indeed on the name of the best English player ever, but it is certain that Sir Stanley Matthews would figure large in the discussions.

On his record alone he is exceptional, making his debut for Stoke City as a 17-year-old in March 1932 and playing his last game for the club five days after his 50th birthday, having helped a virtually moribund club back to the First Division. The first professional to be knighted while still playing, the first 'Footballer of the Year' an award he won a second time 16 years later, and the first 'European Footballer of the Year', he was also among the most loved of all time.

When he fulfilled his great ambition, an F.A. Cup winners medal, at the third attempt in the 'Matthews Final' in 1953, one of the most dramatic in Wembley's history, the nation rejoiced. When he moved from Stoke in 1947 to Blackpool, where he spent 14 years before his dramatic return, there were public protests in the town.

He won 54 caps for England, the last as a 42-year-old, when there was little evidence that his gifts had declined. Even past 40 he was capable of 'skinning' such a respected full-back as Brazil's Nilton Santos. Had England not suffered an amateur selection committee, he would have been closer to 100 caps, even allowing for the war.

Every full-back knew what he was going to do – the left shoulder dropping to feint inside before the flick took the ball outside him and the killing burst of acceleration to take him clear – but very few knew how to stop him going it. He was a difficult man to play with or incorporate in a team pattern, and there have been doubts about how he would have coped in the modern game, when he would rarely have been left one-on-one with a full-back, and when he would have been expected to tackle back. He was regarded as one-footed and one-paced, he was no tackler, and he scored few goals, although when forced to play inside-right for England against Czechoslovakia he hit a hat-trick with his left foot. But for all those supposed limitations, he was a genius.

EVERTON

Like Tottenham in North London, purely in terms of results Everton might be regarded as Merseyside's second club, overshadowed by the machine-like efficiency of their powerful neighbour.

Football is not that simple, fortunately, and Everton are one of its aristocrats. No mere scraping for results will ever satisfy the fans at Goodison Park – style is equally vital. Football for Everton has always been 'the beautiful game'.

Until the 1970s, the Toffeemen had matched their rivals across Stanley Park, and could boast a much richer vein of great names running through the club. The senior of the Liverpool clubs, Everton were founder members of the Football League, and indeed had won their first championship (in 1891) playing at Anfield before Liverpool came into existence.

A year later a dispute over rent sent Everton to build a new ground at Goodison, the landlord and some remnants forming the new Liverpool club – and the rivalry began.

By the First World War, Everton led with an F.A. Cup win, while League honours were even with two titles each. Liverpool were faster out of the blocks after the war but Everton were the force in the late Twenties and Thirties, offering the most serious challenge to Arsenal's domination of that period, and unveiling two of the greatest English centre-forwards of all time: Bill 'Dixie' Dean and Tommy Lawton.

A year after Dean's arrival Warney Cresswell, one of the game's great full-backs, was captured from Sunderland and led the side to the Championship in 1928 as Dean revealed his full talents, scoring 60 goals.

Astonishingly, two years later Everton were relegated for the first time, the last of the 12 founder members to suffer the indignity. But the decline was momentary. With Wembley Wizard Jimmy Dunn arriving from Hibs and the club's great goalkeeper, Ted Sagar, breaking through, they swept back imperiously and a year later won the Championship, Dean this time scoring 44 League goals.

Bill Dean, universally known as Dixie, climbs above Arsenal's defence at Highbury, during a league match in the 1930s. Defenders are (left to right) Bob John, Eddie Hapgood and Herbie Roberts.

A year later, as the frail, talented Cliff Britton claimed a wing-half berth, the Cup was won, Manchester City brushed aside 3–0 in the final.

That flurry of success was not maintained, but as the Goodison club shocked the football world by paying Burnley £6,500 for the 17-year-old Tommy Lawton, a new team was on its way. With Joe Mercer also making his name, they emerged as champions in the last season before the Second World War.

The war, however, meant that potentially one of the greatest teams to represent the 'School of Science' never reached its peak. When it ended, the team were allowed to disperse, Mercer going to Arsenal and Lawton to Chelsea, and a penny-pinching approach saw Everton

Above: *Alan Ball, who formed one third of the celebrated Everton midfield with later Goodison managers Howard Kendall and Colin Harvey.*

fall into the Second Division in 1951.

The escape was quick, but a board of directors out of touch with the modern world were unadventurous, and it was not until the arrival of John Moores as chairman that things changed. Then they changed rapidly. Harry Catterick became manager to win their first post-war championship in 1963 with a team which brilliantly satisfied the requirements of the harsher modern game and Everton's great traditions. The combative Jimmy Gabriel, Tony Kay, and Roy Vernon provided the support for Alex Young, 'The Golden Vision' to those Goodison romantics.

Yet an even better team lay ahead – the 1970 champions. Built around one of the greatest midfields of all time, Alan Ball, Colin Harvey and Howard Kendall, and with Joe Royle potentially a centre-forward in the great Everton tradition, they were proclaimed by one Merseyside journalist a team to 'dominate the Seventies'.

Instead Catterick had a heart attack, Ball was allowed to move to Arsenal, and, wantonly, the team fell apart as Liverpool, bitterly for Evertonians, dominated that decade.

The return of Kendall as manager, however, brought renewed vigour, two championships in 1985 and 1987, the F.A. Cup, the European Cup Winners' Cup and three losing finals at Wembley. They became the only team in the Eighties capable of living with their neighbours.

With Neville Southall one of the world's great goalkeepers, a solid defence marshalled by Kevin Ratcliffe, and a midfield in Everton's great tradition organised by Peter Reid and, until his cruel injury, Paul Bracewell, and embellished by Kevin Sheedy's subtlety, they maintained the club's reputation.

In 1986 they came within a hair's breadth of denying Liverpool the double and three years later took them to extra-time in an even more emotional Merseyside F.A. Cup final.

Left: *Peter Reid, at the heart of Everton's Eighties revival, shields the ball from Coventry's Lloyd McGrath in the 1987 FA Charity Shield match. Everton won 1-0.*

PLAYER PROFILES

GARY LINEKER

Jimmy Greaves is generally regarded as the greatest modern English goalscorer, but the quicksilver Gary Lineker outstripped even his striking rate when he burst into the national team.

You have to go back even further, to the days of Nat Lofthouse, for a rate to equal Lineker's 23 goals in his first 26 internationals (four of them only as a substitute), achieved against meaner modern defences. Only after a debilitating bout of hepatitis in 1988, when he was below par at the European Championship finals, did the flow begin to dry up.

A keen cricketer and snooker player, and one of the nicest men in the game, Lineker began with his home club Leicester City. Even at a club usually found at the wrong end of the table he achieved a respectable striking rate of almost one goal in every two games. He had the speed to break clear from defenders, and was a lethal finisher, either one-on-one with the goalkeeper or inside the six-yard box, where he had the uncanny knack of being in the right place at the right time.

It was the move to Everton in 1985, soon after he had forced his way into the England team, which confirmed Lineker's outstanding qualities. In a team which had won the League and European Cup Winners' Cup the year before, Lineker thrived on a partnership with Graeme Sharp and on the service of Peter Reid, Kevin Sheedy, Gary Stevens and Trevor Steven, even claiming a batch of goals with his head – never previously his strong point – and earning his election as Footballer of the Year.

In the end Everton were shaded for the double by Liverpool, despite Lineker's 39 goals, but the player took his own thrilling form to the 1986 World Cup to emerge as the tournament's leading scorer, including a first half hat-trick against Poland which saved England's blushes in the first round.

That confirmed Barcelona's interest and at 26 he joined manager Terry Venables, making an immediate impression – especially on Real Madrid, against whom he scored a hat-trick. He also hit four goals for England against a Real-dominated Spanish defence in the Bernabeu stadium.

Even after Venables' departure and a change of style, he added 16 League goals to the 21 from his first season. After a less happy third year under Johan Cruyff he returned to England and to Spurs.

LIVERPOOL

It used to be a proud boast that English football was too competitive for any one side to dominate it continually. Liverpool have disproved that in the 1970s and 1980s, dwarfing their contemporaries as completely as Real Madrid have done in Spain, Juventus in Italy or the Glasgow duo of Rangers and Celtic in Scotland.

Their popular appeal too was enhanced even further by the dignified reaction of all at the club to the 1989 Hillsborough disaster in which 95 Liverpool supporters lost their lives, an event so nearly commemorated with another League and Cup double. They still had 10 championships since 1973 and 6 European trophies.

Those records alone stamp them as the greatest club in English football history. The only arguments are over which Liverpool side was the greatest, and whether Bill Shankly, Bob Paisley or Kenny Dalglish could claim to be the club's greatest manager.

Certainly there can be no doubt that Shankly, the folk hero, the man with the ability to communicate so effortlessly with the Kop hordes, was the man who built the modern Liverpool, even if his successors have surpassed his achievements. Shankly, inheriting a Second Division club in 1960, built a dynasty in a way that his great contemporaries Matt Busby, Stan Cullis, Alf Ramsey, Bill Nicholson and Don Revie were unable to do.

The F.A. Cup proved Paisley's bogey. Achieving the double was left to his protégé Dalglish, who not only did it in his first season, as player-manager, but was within 60 seconds of repeating it, astonishingly, six weeks after Hillsborough. Then Arsenal scored a second goal to snatch the League title.

The late Bill Shankly, Liverpool folk hero, gets a hand on the FA Charity Shield at Wembley in 1974. Emlyn Hughes, a player whose enthusiasm matched Shankly's own, shares the triumph.

PLAYER PROFILES

JOHN BARNES

John Barnes has a lot to thank his former Watford manager and mentor Graham Taylor for, but possibly the greatest of all was the fact that Taylor bullied him into joining Liverpool in 1987. Barnes felt he was stagnating at Watford, but was undecided over whether to move abroad or to a southern club. Taylor had no doubts what Barnes needed, although he later admitted that he had strained their relationship to breaking point in order to push the player north.

And how right Taylor was! Still only 24, Barnes gave even the great Liverpool team an extra dimension with his dazzling dribbling and finishing, some of his runs even provoking comparison with George Best. That is some claim to make for any player, but it is not far-fetched in the case of the son of the former Jamaican Military Attaché to London. Yet Barnes would be the first to admit that Liverpool have given him as much as he has given them. A natural athlete who represented Middlesex Schools at rugby and hurdling, Barnes is strong, fast, well-balanced and powerful.

He made an immediate impact when he was plunged into Watford's Second Division team months after being discovered on a park pitch. No-one who saw him destroying seasoned defenders could doubt that one of the finest forward talents for decades had emerged, and as Watford's run continued to second place in the First Division and the 1984 Cup Final there was little reason for a change of mind. Early appearances for England, including the goal in the Maracana Stadium, Rio, which any Brazilian superstar would have been proud of, only confirmed the impression.

But as Watford paused for breath, so did Barnes, and a lack of self-confidence coupled with uncertainty about his role with England left him on the fringe of the international scene, even though he had some memorable moments, notably when coming on as sub and nearly saving the World Cup quarter final against Argentina. However it seemed that he might never fulfil his potential – until Liverpool came to the rescue.

John Aldridge celebrates another goal. At the start of the 1988–9 season, his place seemed in jeopardy with the return of Ian Rush, but the latter's injuries meant that they rarely played together. Aldridge banished his nightmare of the missed penalty in the 1988 F.A. Cup final by scoring with his first touch in the 1989 game with Everton, though Rush's two extra time goals substituting for him proved decisive.

They were quick to make their mark, winning their first Championship in 1901, only eight years after their election to the Football League. Three years later they were stunned by relegation, but bounced back immediately, winning Second and First Division titles in consecutive years.

They were equally successful in the League immediately after the First World War, winning the Championship in 1922 and 1923, as their outstanding Irish goalkeeper Elisha Scott made his mark. But those were to be their last successes until after the Second World War. Then, with Paisley at left-half, the formidable Albert Stubbins at centre-forward and the flying Scot, the powerful Billy Liddell, on the wing they won the Championship in the first full post-War season, 1946–47, and reached the Cup final in 1950, their first appearance at Wembley.

With Paisley controversially omitted, the Cup continued to elude them as they lost 2–0 to Arsenal. The team were getting old, the club lacking drive and direction, and four years later they were relegated.

They were still there, an ailing giant, when Shankly blew in like a tornado. The Second Division was won in 1962, the First in 1964 and 1966, the Cup at long last in 1965 as Shankly's red machine, built around man-mountain centre-half Ron Yeats, with Gordon Milne, Willie Stevenson and, briefly, Jimmy Melia providing the midfield craft, Ian Callaghan and the dazzling Peter Thompson irresistible wing-play, and Ian St. John and Roger Hunt the goals, battered sides into submission.

Another Championship, a first European trophy and the F.A. Cup again were won before Shankly stepped aside and Liverpool really took off. Honours flocked in as Paisley, the shrewdest judge of players in the game, found one pearl after another in the transfer market. Graeme Souness, Alan Hansen, Mark Lawrenson, Ian Rush and Dalglish all merited that overworked description 'great' as they made Liverpool kings at home and abroad.

The F.A. Cup constantly proved Paisley's bogey and he could never achieve the double. That was left to his protege, Dalglish, who did it in his first season in charge – as player-manager. Another championship followed in 1987–88.

PLAYER PROFILES

PETER BEARDSLEY

Few players have enjoyed such a circuitous route to the top as Peter Beardsley, for whom Liverpool paid a record £1.9 million transfer fee in 1987. Enjoyed is the right word, for the quality which shines through everything Beardsley does, even more strongly than his sheer class, is his delight in his work.

It is probably just as well that he takes that attitude, or the early rebuffs that he suffered might have discouraged him and England would have lost a rare talent.

Born in Newcastle in 1961, Beardsley was turned down by his local club and went to Carlisle, quickly making a name for himself. He was taken to Vancouver, during the North American Soccer League's brief hour of success, by John Giles, who recognised the player's potential. Beardsley was loaned to Manchester United, but failed to get a game in the first team and for unaccountable reasons United allowed him to return to Vancouver.

Newcastle, however, were more fortunate, getting a second chance to sign the player who then formed a formidable partnership with Kevin Keegan and Chris Waddle as they won promotion to the First Division. Keegan retired and Waddle left for the bright lights of London, but Beardsley stayed to help Newcastle establish themselves in the First Division, and a clutch of injuries to other players brought him into the England 1986 World Cup party.

He grabbed his chance with alacrity, setting up the winning goal in a memorable victory in Russia, and although he did not begin the tournament in the side, he was brought in for the do-or-die match with Poland. He made a telling contribution, striking up an instant partnership with Gary Lineker, and has never looked back, his intelligent use of the ball, close control and eagerness to take on defenders in tight situations stamping him as a player of the highest class.

He resisted all blandishments to move abroad, but when Liverpool approached Newcastle with an offer United could not refuse, Kenny Dalglish recognising Beardsley as his ideal successor, he went eagerly.

MANCHESTER UNITED

The best supported club in the country, and probably the most loved, Manchester United's name is revered throughout the world, their commitment to colourful, attacking football finding a ready echo in an era increasingly dominated by method at the expense of flair.

There has, at least until recently, been no danger of United making such a choice. Under the direction of Sir Matt Busby, the club exemplified the best in football in three decades, setting new trends in the English game with its youth policy – the famous Busby Babes – and in Europe, becoming the first English club to enter European competition, against the Football League's advice. Climactically, in 1968, they were the first English club to win the European Cup.

In the Forties, Fifties and Sixties United could reasonably claim to be the country's most successful club, only Wolves in the early period and Liverpool and Leeds in the later offering consistent rivalry in terms of results, while the sweep and vision of United's football placed them far ahead of the opposition.

Great names were in the United tradition: Billy Meredith and Charlie Roberts played in the first outstanding United side, which won two Championships before the First World War, the second arriving almost immediately after their move to Old Trafford in 1910. But the period between the wars was a fallow time for the club, which fell into the Second Division while rivals City enjoyed a rare spell of supremacy in Manchester.

The arrival of Busby – a former City player – as manager at the end of the war proved the turning point. Busby inherited a shell, the ground having been bombed during the war, and they were forced to share Maine Road until 1949. But though there was little money, Busby was fortunate to have a talented group of players, many signed as youngsters by United's scout Louis Rocca before the war and

Sir Matt Busby's United win the European Cup at last. They beat Benfica 4-1 at Wembley in the 1968 final after 11 years of frustration.

PLAYER PROFILES

BOBBY CHARLTON

If not the greatest player to wear the shirts of Manchester United and England, Bobby Charlton was unquestionably the most honoured and best loved. If that owed something initially to sentimentality for the young survivor of Munich who came back to inspire United's scratch team to Wembley with some blistering goals, it owed more to the recognition of the mature man's stature. His perfect sportsmanship, along with his great gifts, made him the ideal representative for his club, country and the game itself. Born in 1937 into a footballing family in the North East – his mother was a Milburn, with four brothers and a cousin, the great Jackie, playing League football. His elder brother Jack was also at Leeds – Bobby's future was pre-ordained.

But he was to enjoy virtually three separate careers. Coming into the Manchester United team shortly before the disaster as a goalscoring inside-forward who stung goalkeeper's hands with the fierceness of his shooting, Munich forced him to take greater responsibilities.

For a time he lost his way, until a switch to the left-wing, offering him greater space to exploit his exhilarating body-swerve and the option of going wide or cutting in on his favoured left foot, rehabilitated him.

He played there to great effect in the 1963 F.A. Cup final victory which signalled the emergence of a new Manchester United, but it was the switch back inside to play in an advanced midfield role which was to prove the masterstroke.

Selected to play the same way for England by Alf Ramsey his was a crucial role in the World Cup victory in 1966, when he also won the Footballer of the Year and European player awards.

He would sweep eye-catching passes out to the wings, and burst past defenders from midfield into shooting positions. His two goals won the semi-final against Portugal. His brother Jack was England's centre-half.

Two years later Bobby led United to the European Cup, scoring two goals in the final against Benfica.

After 106 caps and a record 49 goals, his international career ended in Mexico in the 1970 World Cup in dramatic fashion. Substituted in order to keep him fresh for the semi-final as England led West Germany 2–0, Charlton could only watch as the Germans gained revenge for 1966, winning 3–2.

The incomparable Duncan Edwards, an England international at 18, who was one of eight players killed in the 1958 Munich air disaster.

now ready for first team duty. Led by one of the great captains, Johnny Carey, players like Stan Pearson, Jack Rowley, Henry Cockburn and Charlie Mitten, playing with the panache and flair which became the hall-mark of Busby teams, had the crowds flocking to watch them.

The cup was won in 1948 in one of the greatest finals, United coming from behind to beat Blackpool 4–2, and the League in 1952 after they had finished second four times in five years.

Greater glories lay ahead as Busby broke up that team to give his Babes their heads. Roger Byrne, a worthy successor to Carey, led a side containing the legendary Duncan Edwards, Eddie Colman, Tommy Taylor, Liam Whelan, Dennis Viollet and a young Bobby Charlton to consecutive League championships in 1956 and 1957. The world was at their feet, but then came Munich, the blackest day in English sport, their plane crashing on the way back from a European Cup-tie in Belgrade. Eight of the team including, after a brave struggle, Edwards, were killed.

Slowly the pieces were picked up again. Busby moved into the transfer market to acquire David Herd, Paddy Crerand and, above all, Denis Law, while the youth scheme continued to find gold with Nobby Stiles, John Giles and finally, thrillingly, George Best.

The League was won twice more. The second success in 1967, the club's last championship, paved the way for Europe to be conquered with the defeat of Benfica at Wembley in 1968.

Since then success has proved more elusive, with only three F.A. Cup wins in 1977, 1983 and 1985 adding to United's illustrious honours list, but the tradition for good football and star names has been maintained, with players like Martin Buchan, Stuart Pearson, Lou Macari, Arnold Muhren, Bryan Robson and Norman Whiteside taking their places in a glittering history.

For the second consecutive season Brian McClair was the leading goalscorer at Manchester United, but even with Mark Hughes' return from an unsuccessful spell in Europe, it did not bring the glory days back to Old Trafford. Manchester United had a very disappointing season in 1988–9, especially following the Red Devils' second place the previous year.

PLAYER PROFILES

BRYAN ROBSON

Bryan Robson, captain of England and Manchester United, was widely regarded as the one England outfield player of unquestionable world class in the 1980s. And this was in spite of injuries which prevented him from stamping his authority on two World Cups and also restricted his contribution to United's unsuccessful bids to recapture the League championship.

Those injuries have owed much to Robson's total physical commitment to the cause. His bravery in the tackle and in the penalty area has sometimes proved his undoing as well as being one of his greatest assets.

Born in that great soccer nursery, the North East, into a footballing family in January 1957, Bryan Robson grew up as a Newcastle fan, but elected to spend his formative years in a less hot-house atmosphere, joining West Bromwich from school.

There his talent was quickly recognised by John Giles, the great Irish international midfield player and then Albion's player-manager. Another Albion boss, Ron Atkinson, was equally impressed, and when he became manager of Manchester United he soon took Robson with him, paying a then British transfer record of £1.5 million in October 1982. By then Robson was an established international, but after a dominating performance in England's opening match against France in the 1982 World Cup, completely overshadowing Michel Platini and scoring two goals in a 3–2 win, he was injured in the next match and although he finished the tournament, some of his sharpness had been lost.

The 1986 World Cup was an even more bitter experience for him. A shoulder, dislocated when he ran into the electricity box controlling Old Trafford's undersoil heating system as he typically went full pelt after a centre, continued to let him down as United kept him playing in a vain attempt to claim the Championship.

Although both he and England manager Bobby Robson tried to play down the injury, it recurred against Morocco in the second match, and he was forced to sit out the rest of the tournament. He returned to the England side, however, and played in the 1988 European Championships.

NEWCASTLE UNITED

If volume of support and loyalty had anything to do with success – and in the modern world when finance is such a major factor it ought to – then Newcastle United would be a club to rank with the Merseyside giants, let alone those of Manchester and London.

Set in one of the most passionate football areas in the world, with a ready supply of young talent always available, cautious, and sometimes bad direction has seen Newcastle potter along on the fringes of the big time, their fans generally having to content themselves with worshipping glamorous individuals rather than great teams.

Only in three spells have Newcastle made an impact on the game's big powers. In the first decade of the 20th century, they won the League three times and the Cup once, with a team that included Colin Veitch, Peter McWilliam and the most famous exponent of the offside trap, Bill McCracken.

Between 1924 and 1932 they had more moments of glory, winning the Cup at either end of that period and, in 1927, with Scottish centre-forward Hughie Gallacher leading their attack, they won their fourth and last League title.

Their greatest Cup era was still to come – the 1950s, when they won the trophy three times in five seasons. Wembley reverberated to the sound of the Geordie anthem 'The Blaydon Races' as their hero Jackie Milburn – 'Wor Jackie' – led a side of thrilling talents to victories over Blackpool, Arsenal and Manchester City. Milburn was the star, but with little Ernie Taylor, the Robledo brothers, Joe Harvey, Jimmy Scoular, George Hannah, Len White and Bobby Mitchell also involved, the attacking talent was breathtaking.

White went on to form a dazzling partnership with Ivor Allchurch and George Eastham as the Fifties progressed, but only one more trophy – the European Fairs Cup in 1969 – lay ahead. Instead the fans had to content themselves with individual excellence, Malcolm Macdonald, Kevin Keegan, Peter Beardsley, Chris Waddle and Mirandinha all stirring their imagination with thrilling deeds to compensate for a lack of trophies.

'Wor Jackie' Milburn heads for goal in the 1955 FA Cup final against Manchester City. None of the illustrious successors to his number nine shirt have eclipsed his popularity.

NOTTINGHAM FOREST

Only three years younger than neighbours Notts County, the oldest club in the country, Forest, like bitter foes Derby County, had to wait until the arrival of Brian Clough to claim their first League Championship.

This time, however, Clough settled, and that first Championship proved just a stepping stone, Forest going on to win the European Cup twice, one of the few small provincial European clubs to achieve that feat, and establishing themselves as a major power in an English game increasingly dominated by the rich big-city clubs.

Until Clough's arrival, Forest's main claim to fame had been F.A. Cup final victories over Derby in 1898 and Luton in 1959, and a unique position as the only club, as opposed to limited company, in the Football League. They also had a reputation for good football, but a lack of direction saw them spending much of their League career in Division Two. The Fifties and Sixties saw Forest on an upsurge, as promotion in 1957 was followed by the F.A. Cup in 1959, a match which enhanced Forest's reputation for sweet football. Elton John's cousin Roy Dwight scored a brilliant goal before breaking his leg and Forest, inspired by Jeff Whitefoot, displayed some delightful passing in one of Wembley's most skilful finals.

That reputation was reinforced during the Sixties as players like Ian Storey-Moore and Henry Newton emerged to claim places alongside expensive signings Frank Wignall, Joe Baker, John Barnwell, Terry Hennessey and Alan Hinton.

In 1967 they pushed the Manchester United team of George Best, Denis Law and Bobby Charlton all the way for the Championship and reached the Cup semi-finals.

Progress however could not be maintained, and they sank back to the Second Division, which was where Brian Clough found them. Tony Woodcock, John Robertson, Viv Anderson and Martin O'Neill remained to reach the heights alongside Clough's imports John McGovern, Archie Gemmill, Peter Withe, Larry Lloyd, Peter Shilton, Kenny Burns, and two forwards costing respectively £2,000 and £1 million – Garry Birtles and Trevor Francis.

Subsequent purchases, as Woodcock, Withe, Shilton, Burns and Francis moved on, and others needed replacing, were initially less successful, but after the much publicised split with assistant Peter Taylor, Clough rediscovered his enthusiasm, building an exciting team around son Nigel, Franz Carr, Neil Webb and Stuart Pearce.

The goal which completed Forest's transformation from humble Second Division club to European Cup winners. Trevor Francis heads John Robertson's cross past the Malmö goalkeeper Jan Möller.

PLAYER PROFILES

PETER SHILTON

It is a measure of Peter Shilton's outstanding ability – and his longevity – that he was the most-capped England goalkeeper of all time, despite the challenge of Ray Clemence through most of his career.

To say Shilton is the greatest-ever England keeper would be a large claim, and admirers of both Frank Swift and Shilton's great predecessor Gordon Banks would have a lot to say on the subject, but it is unarguable that no previous incumbent had a rival to match Clemence, who was first choice for most of the 1970s and whose qualities persuaded Ron Greenwood to play the pair alternately in the run up to the 1980 European Championships. Shilton finally got the nod, and has been there ever since.

Shilton began his career at Leicester when Gordon Banks was the club keeper, and he was to follow Banks to Stoke as well as into the England team.

But Shilton was his own man, and had his own style. Big and broad, Shilton was a perfectionist to his finger-tips, spending hours working on every aspect of his game. He filled the goal more than any of his outstanding contemporaries, making it look almost miniscule to a forward left with only him to beat.

Not many succeeded in one-against-one confrontations. Not many succeeded at all during his great years with Nottingham Forest: Larry Lloyd, a big centre-half, covered his one questionable area, his ability with crosses, and Shilton threw up an almost impenetrable barrier as Forest raced to the 1978 League Championship and successive European Cups in 1979 and 1980.

Along the way he also picked up a League Cup winners medal in 1979, but it was his rare error which prevented Forest claiming another trophy the following year.

His performance in the 1980 European Final to deny Kevin Keegan's Hamburg more than made up for it. As Forest underwent a period of retrenchment, he was allowed to join Southampton, before moving to Derby in 1987, when at 38 he was still the England No. 1.

SHEFFIELD WEDNESDAY

The fifth oldest club in the League, Sheffield Wednesday have endured perhaps more than enjoyed an uneven history. Yorkshire's biggest club, possessors of one of the finest grounds in the country in Hillsborough, and inheritors of a great tradition, have in modern times rarely succeeded in punching their weight.

Like Newcastle, they should be able to challenge the best consistently, but too often have seemed to settle for respectability, their last major trophy arriving in 1935, when two goals from international left-winger Ellis Rimmer helped them beat West Brom 4–2 in the F.A. Cup final.

Their last League success had come at the end of the previous decade, an outstanding team including Tommy Leach and Jimmy Seed as well as Rimmer winning the Championship in successive seasons, 1928–29 and 1929–30, repeating the feat of another fine Wednesday side in 1903 and 1904, soon after the move to Hillsborough from Bramall Lane.

Two years after their Cup success they were relegated, staying in the Second Division until 1950, when they began a yo-yo existence, winning promotion four times and being relegated on three occasions within the decade. Jackie Sewell, a record signing at £35,000 in 1951, Albert Quixall and Redfern Froggatt were all exciting inside-forwards, and Derek Dooley, until he had a leg amputated after a freak accident, was the most talked about centre-forward of that era.

A lack of organisation cost them dear however, until the arrival of Harry Catterick as manager gave them more steel. In 1961 the side of Ron Springett, Tony Kay, Johnny Fantham, Peter Swan and David 'Bronco' Layne earned them their highest League position, second, since the Thirties. Then Catterick moved on to Everton, and the infamous bribes scandal broke, leading to the suspension of Swan, Layne and Kay, who by then had also gone to Goodison.

In 1966 they reached the Cup final, losing a memorable match with Everton, but then came decline, and a fall to the Third Division. Jack Charlton began the recovery, and Howard Wilkinson led them back to the top flight in 1984, but there have been few signs that they will recapture past glories.

Arguably the most popular of all Sheffield Wednesday players – Derek Dooley, whose leg had to be amputated after a freak accident against Preston in 1953.

A header by Wednesday's Albert Quixall beats two Welsh defenders in the 1953 international.

TOTTENHAM HOTSPUR

In terms of results alone, Spurs are London's second club. There is more to football, however, than the accountant's view of figures in wins and losses columns, as the club's most famous captain, Danny Blanchflower, realised.

The Irishman could have been speaking for his club when he said: 'The game is about glory. It's about doing things with style, with a flourish, about going out and beating the other lot, not waiting for them to die of boredom'.

Spurs have always done things with style, on the field at least. But then even the club's very beginnings under a lamppost in Tottenham High Street, and the choice of the name Hotspur, after the famous knight, sing of a romantic approach to life, and the club has been true to its origins. The cockerel strutting across the club shirts has plenty to be proud of.

From the start there was nothing ordinary about Spurs' successes. Southern League champions in 1900, in 1901 they became the only professional team outside the Football League to win the F.A. Cup, the first successful Southern challenge to the Midlands and North since the days of the Wanderers and Old Etonians.

Sandy Brown, their centre-forward, became the first player to score in every round as he set a competition record of 15 goals. Brown's successor, the stylish amateur Vivian Woodward, who scored 29 goals in 23 full internationals, was equally dynamic, seeing the club to the First Division only one season after their election to the League.

Like many newcomers to the senior division, Spurs found it a difficult transition and only the abandonment of competition during the First World War after one season (1914–15) saved them from relegation. The reprieve was only temporary, for by then they had new and unfriendly neighbours as Woolwich Arsenal moved across London to Highbury, in spite of the opposition of Tottenham, Clapton Orient and Chelsea. Arsenal's next move strained relationships even further, Tottenham finding themselves voted out of the First Division when the League restarted after the war. Arsenal, after some unscrupulous manoeuvrings by their chairman, replaced them.

A great team, however, was being

The first English club this century to complete the League and F.A. Cup double: Tottenham 1960–61.

PLAYER PROFILES

JIMMY GREAVES

Jimmy Greaves was probably the greatest finisher in the history of English football. He scored 357 goals in 516 games in the First Division between 1957 and 1971, and 44 goals in 57 internationals.

Many of them were tap-ins, a tribute to his ability to steal into the right spot for a rebound or for a pass threaded through a crowded area. But a good number also began on the half-way line, a mazy dribble leaving up to half a dozen defenders trailing in his wake, and finally the sidestepped goalkeeper clutching thin air too.

Greaves announced his presence as a 17-year-old on his Chelsea debut in August 1957, scoring ironically, against Tottenham at White Hart Lane. Goals came in all varieties – volleys, chips, drives, most struck with virtually no back-lift to give him that extra split-second which unhinged so many defenders.

A Londoner with the Cockney's irreverent humour, now seen in his television double act with the former Liverpool player Ian St. John, he was one of the most popular and respected of players, but ended his career with little to show for his great talents. A move to Italy from Chelsea proved misconceived, although he scored nine goals in 12 games for A.C. Milan, and a return to Spurs provided him with a more fitting theatre.

He arrived too late to enjoy the double season, and although the side went on to win the F.A. Cup and European Cup Winners' Cup in the next two years, the tragic death of John White, the broken leg suffered by Dave Mackay and the retirement of Danny Blanchflower meant the highest honours were denied him.

The 1966 World Cup was still more traumatic. A regular member of the side, Greaves missed the quarter-final against Argentina through injury. His replacement, Geoff Hurst, scored the winner and was not to be dislodged, Greaves watching the final from the bench.

His disappointment took its toll, and by the time he retired after an unhappy spell with West Ham, he was on the downward spiral into alcoholism. His subsequent recovery speaks volumes for the man.

Paul Gascoigne's transfer from Newcastle to Tottenham in July 1988, gave him the stage to show off his prodigious talent. Recognition has come in the form of full international honours.

formed, typically Tottenham: full of skill and exciting attacking play, with Fanny Walden and Jimmy Seed combining on one flank, the captain and driving force Arthur Grimsdell, and flying winger Jimmy Dimmock, down the other.

The team set a record points total of 70 (at two points for a win) as they won the Second Division. A year later the Cup was won again to start that surprising train of Cup wins 20 years apart (1901, 1921, 1961, 1981), and the following season Spurs made their most serious Championship challenge up to then, coming second.

Consistency has never been the club's strength, however, and by the end of the decade they were back in the Second Division where they stayed, apart from a break of two seasons, until 1950. The return this time was spectacular as Spurs won the Second Division and then their first Championship in successive seasons.

The football too was spectacular and typically innovative, Arthur Rowe developing a side who stroked the ball rather than battered it, covering the ground with quick, short, passing movements which left opponents chasing shadows.

From Ted Ditchburn in goal, Alf Ramsey at right-back, Bill Nicholson and Ron Burgess at wing-half and Eddie Bailey and Les Medley on the left, they were a team of outstanding talents playing wonderful and effective football.

The only question was whether they were as good as their successors, who also briefly lit up the game like a comet before they too went out suddenly. In between, in spite of the arrival of Blanchflower and in the presence of the sadly ignored genius, Tommy Harmer, things did not come together, but the appointment of Nicholson as manager paved the way for the formation of arguably the greatest English club side since the war.

With the brains, touch and subtlety of Blanchflower, with John White at the hub, Dave Mackay a rampaging force in midfield, the spring heels and electric pace of Cliff Jones and the classical battering ram centre-forward Bobby Smith, they were an awesome combination in 1961 as they became the first team to do the Cup and League double this century. A year later Jimmy Greaves arrived, the F.A. Cup was retained and in 1963 they became the first English club to win a European trophy, pulverising Atletico Madrid 5–1 in the Cup Winners' Cup.

Again, suddenly, the light went out. Blanchflower retired, White was tragically struck dead by lightning, Mackay twice broke his leg. Since then, the Championship has eluded them, although under Peter Shreeve they pushed Everton all the way in 1985.

Cup competitions at home and abroad have proved more fruitful: they won the U.E.F.A. Cup in 1972 and 1984, the League Cup in 1971 and 1973, and the F.A. Cup in 1967, 1981 and 1982.

But, more importantly, their football, fashioned by such stars as Alan Gilzean, Martin Peters and latterly Glenn Hoddle and Chris Waddle, has continued to excite.

Above all they showed their sense of adventure was unimpaired in 1978 when they brought Ossie Ardiles and Ricardo Villa to England. For that alone, English football is deep in Tottenham's debt.

Chris Waddle is yet another player who has gone on to greater things since leaving Newcastle United. His partnership with Paul Gascoigne brought great acclaim from football fans and journalists.

PLAYER PROFILES

GLENN HODDLE

The most gifted and perhaps the most controversial English player of recent years, Glenn Hoddle has always marched to the sound of his own drummer, refusing to compromise his beliefs in the way the game should be played.

Adored by Tottenham's fans, and an instant success when he went to Monaco in 1987, his abilities have been regarded more quizzically by the puritan north and by a series of England managers.

Born in Hayes in 1957, Hoddle won instant acclaim when he broke into the Spurs first team, helping them to win promotion back to the First Division at the first attempt. That summer Spurs bought the Argentinians Ossie Ardiles and Ricky Villa, and Hoddle quickly struck up a supreme understanding with Ardiles, but the prettiness of their football did not bring results, until the signing of strikers Garth Crooks and Steve Archibald provided the perfect outlet for Hoddle's unerring, defence-splitting long passes.

The Cup was won twice in successive seasons, and the U.E.F.A. Cup in 1984. But for all his vision and mastery of the ball – his sheer range of passing skills persuaded his captain Steve Perryman to liken his feet to a range of golf clubs – he was unable to command a regular England place, virtually sitting out the 1982 World Cup finals.

Spurs were also unable to make a successful assault on the Championship, a failing which persuaded northern pros that Hoddle's inability or reluctance to chase and tackle was a fundamental flaw. Hoddle retorted angrily that no one criticised the runners for not being able to hit 40-yard passes. He had a point, but his failure to impose himself on games that mattered both for England in the 1986 World Cup and, crucially, for Spurs in the 1987 Cup Final, his last game for the club, suggested that so did his critics.

By then the player was disillusioned with the English game and its stress on the athletic virtues at the expense of the artistic ones, and he moved to Monaco when still not quite 30.

WEST HAM UNITED

The pride of East London, West Ham have a popularity and an influence in football to rival the biggest clubs in the land. Originally formed as Thames Ironworks – hence their other nickname 'The Irons' as well as the more obvious 'Hammers' – they turned professional as West Ham United in 1900, moving to the Boleyn Ground, their current home, four years later.

Geoff Hurst gets in a characteristic twisting header. The long-serving Billy Bonds is in support.

Elected to the Football League in 1919, they made an immediate impact with an outstanding team, winning promotion in 1923, and the same year reaching the first Wembley Cup Final, where they lost to a David Jack-inspired Bolton Wanderers. It was the game primarily remembered for the policeman on the white horse controlling the crowds who had flocked on to the field as the terraces overflowed.

Five of the team – Ted Hufton, Jack Treasadern, Billy Moore, Vic Watson and Wally Brown – won England caps – but the club had slipped back into the Second Division by 1932.

Despite the efforts of Len Goulden, who on occasions kept Raich Carter out of the England team, they stayed there until 1958.

The side which won promotion that year became known as the 'Academy of Soccer', less for its undoubted merit on the field, where John Bond and Noel Cantwell proved precursors of the modern attacking full-backs, than for the training discussions involving Malcolm Allison, Frank O'Farrell, Bond and Cantwell, all subsequently notable managers and coaches.

The club's influence expanded with the arrival of Ron Greenwood and the development of the Sixties team which won the European Cup Winners' Cup in 1965 and provided the England World Cup winning team with its captain Bobby Moore and its Final goal heroes Geoff Hurst and Martin Peters.

West Ham's style, based on coaching which stressed the skills of the game, fluid movement and tactical awareness, was instantly recognisable, and brought them two more F.A. Cup final victories in 1975 and 1980, illuminated by the touch of players like Trevor Brooking and Alan Devonshire. The replacement of Greenwood by John Lyall also brought a greater awareness of the need for competitive players like the club's great servant Billy Bonds and David Cross, the 1980 Cup Final hero, and in 1986 the club achieved their best ever League position, third.

PLAYER PROFILES

BOBBY MOORE

'Calm', 'elegant' and 'unruffled' are the adjectives that spring to mind about Bobby Moore, captain of England's 1966 World Cup winners. Blond, with rarely a hair out of place even when the action was at its hottest, Moore's ice-cold temperament was one of his greatest assets.

He was marked for stardom early, proclaimed an England player in the making from his West Ham debut against Manchester United before a capacity crowd as a 17-year-old in September 1958. He did not take long to fulfil the prediction, claiming his place just in time for the 1962 World Cup.

Initially a midfield player, he found his true niche as the defensive wing-half turned into a second centre-half. In that position he has had few peers, his outstanding ability to read the game more than compensating for a slight lack of pace.

The fourth England goal in the 1966 World Cup final illustrated his great talents and his unflappability, Moore ignoring his team-mates' pleas to kick it anywhere as he waited for the right moment before striking a perfect long pass to send Geoff Hurst away for a goal labelled 'West Ham'.

Yet if Moore's demeanour disguised a ruthless streak from the watchers, it was not hidden from his colleagues or opponents.

'Bobby Moore was hard,' testified Hurst, and opponents took liberties at their peril. The World Cup was Moore's third successive Wembley victory, following West Ham's 1964 F.A. Cup and 1965 European Cup Winners' Cup triumphs.

Sadly it was also to be his last trophy, the club failing to build on the presence of Moore and his two England colleagues, Hurst and Martin Peters, but refusing bids that would have taken Moore to more fashionable, and successful surroundings.

He finally left in 1974, not long after the last of his then record 108 caps for England, joining Fulham to help the Second Division club to the 1975 Cup final, where, ironically, they lost to West Ham.

SCOTLAND

Even patriotic Scots are forced to admit that they followed England's lead in giving football its structures. Queen's Park, the leading Scottish club of the time were a member of the Football Association, and playing in the early F.A. Cups before they instigated the setting up of the Scottish F.A. and a Scottish Cup competition in 1873.

But in the playing of the game they were soon to surpass their Southern neighbours. Indeed, the early leaders of the professional game in England, the Lancashire teams Blackburn and Preston in particular, based their sides on Scots lured over the border by pay or promises of jobs.

The same pattern was soon seen on the international field. The first match between the two countries, in 1872, when Scotland were represented by the entire Queen's Park team, ended goalless, but for the rest of the next two decades Scotland's dominance was unarguable. 'Another season has passed without a single defeat to mar our brilliant record', crowed the Scottish F.A. Handbook in 1879. 'It is now six years since an international was lost.'

Nemesis lay just around the corner. Scotland continued to enjoy spells of superiority over the English even if the early almost total supremacy could never be repeated, but the self-congratulatory insularity which surpassed even that south of the border paved the way for some terrible humiliations on the wider international front.

Like England, Scotland refused to enter the first World Cups, not taking part until after the Second World War, and even then declining to go to Brazil in 1950 as runners-up in the Home International Championship, which was the qualifying tournament. Scotland insisted they would only go as winners, and so England endured that embarrassment alone. Scotland would surely have fared little better then, for their game, like England's had become obsolete.

What results the Scots side of the Twenties would have commanded in European competition, if they had entered, can only be guessed at, but the Wembley Wizards, the outstanding 1928 team who won 5–1 at Wembley with a forward line of Alec Jackson, Jimmy Dunn, Hughie Gallacher, Alex James and Alan Morton would surely

Scotland's finest hour? Hughie Gallacher (dark shirt) watches as Alec Jackson's shot flies in for the first goal in the sensational 5-1 victory by the 'Wembley Wizards' in 1928.

Left: *Alex James, the link between attack and defence for Scotland and Arsenal, who paid Preston £9,000 for him in 1929.*

That national capacity for self-delusion and their other great talent for self-destruction were to undermine the sides of Willie Ormond and Ally MacLeod when they did qualify in 1974 and 1978, the latter trip to Argentina suggesting that the country had learned nothing since 1954.

The appointment of Jock Stein in the aftermath of Argentina offered hope that things would change, the great Celtic manager setting himself to conquer the pervasive myth that beating England was all that mattered. 1982 suggested that he was making some progress, but his death before the 1986 World Cup left Alex Ferguson as a temporary successor and once again Scotland fell by the wayside.

Andy Roxburgh, the new manager, is faced with a considerable rebuilding job and with the loss of Kenny Dalglish and Graeme Souness, the famous Scottish creative ability looks thin on the ground.

Below: *Bruce Rioch, 24 caps for Scotland in the Seventies.*

have done better than any of their modern successors.

The talent in that era was immense, with Davie Meiklejohn, Jimmy McGrory, Bob McPhail and Alec Cheyne also available, and a little later the arrival of those excellent wing-halves Bill Shankly and Matt Busby, later even more famous as managers, ensured the standard was maintained. Yet already there had been warnings for those who would heed time, 1931 producing a 5–0 thrashing by Austria and a 3–0 defeat by Italy in rare ventures abroad.

The first trip to the World Cup, in 1954, was to yield rather more bitter evidence of Scotland's decline as an international force. A lack of preparation was suitably punished, Austria beating them 1–0, and Uruguay 7–0. 1958 was little more successful, Scotland losing to Paraguay and France, and drawing with Yugoslavia.

The 1960s saw a flowering of Scottish talent as players like Jim Baxter, Denis Law, Pat Crerand, Dave Mackay, John White, Bobby Murdoch, John Greig and subsequently Jimmy Johnstone and Billy Bremner all appeared. Once again a spell of supremacy over England was achieved, including a victory over the 1966 World Cup winners which persuaded some that Scotland were the rightful world champions. It overlooked the point that they had failed to qualify for the finals.

ABERDEEN

British senior football's most northerly outpost had a team from 1903, but it was not until the coming of the oilrigs that Aberdeen became a force to challenge the Glasgow supremacy.

They began to compete seriously after the Second World War, winning the Scottish Cup for the first time in 1947. The 1950s saw the challenge sustained as they reached the 1954 Cup final, losing to Celtic's double-winning side, then won the League for the first time a year later with a distinguished team containing Graham Leggat and Paddy Buckley, two dangerous forwards in front of a sound defence. A year later they were runners-up and won the League Cup for the first time, but that side grew old and the Sixties brought little success.

Glory for the Granite city: Aberdeen win the European Cup-Winners' Cup in the rain of Gothenburg. Skipper Willie Miller doesn't mind the weather.

Then Eddie Turnbull, once a member of the famous Hibs forward line, took over and his firm direction began the new era. In 1967 they again reached the Cup final, and again succumbed to Celtic, who were the all-conquering team of the year, but three years later they were back again with a young team under the captaincy of the youthful, elegant defender Martin Buchan, and this time they beat the Glasgow team.

As well as Buchan, players like Arthur Graham and Joe Harper caught the eye. Aberdeen were unable to keep them, but the foundations had been laid. As oil money brought prosperity to the town the football club at last could hold their own with the big city outfits.

Pittodrie became unrecognizable, setting standards for the rest of Britain as it was transformed into an all-seater stadium. Turnbull did not stay to see the job through, moving to his old club Hibs. He was replaced by his coach Jimmy Bonthrone, and then as the side failed to fulfil expectations, Ally MacLeod.

MacLeod was immediately successful, the team winning the League Cup before he moved on to take over as Scotland manager from Willie Ormond. In his stead came Billy McNeill, the imposing former Celtic centre-half who had served an apprenticeship with Clyde.

Rangers came between him and a prize, Aberdeen finishing second to the Glasgow club in both the League and the Cup, but they were clearly now a major force. Willie Miller had already claimed his position; during the season Steve Archibald and Archie McLeish began to make their marks, and Neale Cooper, Gordon

PLAYER PROFILES

ALAN HANSEN

If ever there was a British player who might have stood comparison with Franz Beckenbauer as a sweeper with the ability to attack, it was Alan Hansen. But even when Kenny Dalglish flirted with the position, never a popular one in the English game, Hansen was not given the task.

He was no more fortunate with Scotland: manager Jock Stein believed in the position, but often preferred the Aberdeen captain Willie Miller.

Hansen's failure to win more recognition for Scotland – he was even omitted from the 1986 World Cup party by Alex Ferguson – has been one of football's great mysteries. As an orthodox centre-half he has had few peers, his excellent reading of the game being supported by firm tackling and more-than-adequate ability in the air.

Yet it is his ability on the ball which marks him out as a player of the highest class, his runs forward from defence as he accelerates past people as smoothly as a Rolls Royce gave Liverpool's attacks an extra dimension.

All in all the university-educated Scot, who was born in Alloa in 1955, has proved one of Liverpool's greatest players since he was signed from Partick Thistle. He has helped them to seven League Championships, three European Cup wins, four League Cup triumphs and two in the F.A. Cup, forming a wonderful partnership with Mark Lawrenson until the latter's enforced retirement. Hansen has played more than 400 Football League games for the Anfield club – and his record of consistency and quality defending set him alongide the greatest names in Liverpool's glittering modern history.

And that would seem to be more than ample compensation for the fact that he was allowed to make only 26 appearances for his country in eight years. Hansen's constant rejection by his country's national team selectors may well go down as one of the great blunders in Scottish football. Surely he would have been a fixture in almost any other international side of the modern era.

Aberdeen beat Real Madrid in the 1983 European Cup-Winners' Cup final. Eric Black runs in the first goal.

Strachan and Doug Rougvie also got a taste of first team action.

McNeill, however, did not stay to enjoy success in the Granite city, the lure of Celtic proving irresistible, and instead Alex Ferguson came in to take the club to glory.

Between 1980 and 1986 the Championship was won three times, the Cup four, with the League Cup thrown in for good measure along with two runners-up spots in the Championship. Above all there was Europe. European competition suddenly became Aberdeen's by right, and in 1983 they won the Cup Winners' Cup, beating the most famous European team of all, Real Madrid, on a filthy but memorable night in Gothenburg, Peter Weir and Strachan destroying the Spanish team on the wings, the only decent part of the pitch, for Eric Black and his replacement John Hewitt to score the goals.

If not as outstanding a performance as Celtic's in Lisbon in the senior competition 15 years earlier, it showed the same qualities of attacking football, individual ball skills and a sheer determination to overcome adversity which is characteristic of Scottish football at its best.

Ferguson's side had all that, and if at times they sometimes showed too much physical commitment, notably in some bad-tempered tussles with Celtic, that too was a reflection of the Scottish game, and also of their new standing, with other teams as eager to defeat them as they were to beat Rangers and Celtic.

The change, though, could be seen in Aberdeen's success in holding on to some of their best players, Miller and McLeish remaining even though the oil boom declined. Nevertheless Aberdeen were still forced to reconcile themselves to the loss of Archibald, and subsequently Strachan and Ferguson himself.

PLAYER PROFILES

STEVE NICOL

In every great side, there is an unsung hero – a grafter quietly going about his job amidst better-known (and probably better-paid) superstars. Managers tend to know their real value and at Liverpool Kenny Dalglish has publicly identified his fellow-Scot Steve Nicol as just such a reliable stalwart.

Born in Irvine on 11 December 1961, Nicol does have one natural advantage: the enormous size of his feet. Size 12 boots mean that he has a better chance than anyone else of getting a toe-end to the ball at crucial moments. Bob Paisley saw more orthodox signs of quality in the teenage Ayr United full-back who had already played for Scotland's under-21 team, and paid £300,000 for him in October 1981.

In the next two years, he made only two League appearances but midway through the 1983–84 season Nicol was given a European debut as Phil Neal's deputy and then a long run in midfield.

The next season brought a full international debut, Scotland preferring to use him at right-back, where he alternated with Richard Gough. Paradoxically, he had just displaced Neal at last in the Liverpool number two shirt when the Scots switched him to midfield. He finished the memorable Liverpool double season in 1986 by playing in every Scotland game at the World Cup finals.

A cool head and occasionally devastating shot have also brought Nicol more than 30 goals for Liverpool, where he added another string to his bow in 1988–89, helping to solve serious injury problems by playing just as efficiently in central defence. The Football Writers' Association were sufficiently impressed to vote him Footballer of the Year.

CELTIC

Marginally less successful than their great rivals Rangers in terms of volumes of trophies won, and undeniably less influential in the corridors of power, Celtic have the greater world-wide respect and affection.

They are loved not because they are the only Scottish winners of the European Cup, although they did strike a blow for every football lover whatever their nationality or religious affiliation by beating the negative, defensive approach of Inter-Milan, but because throughout their history they have stood for football as art and passion, rather than the physical functionalism of their deadly rivals.

The club was formed in order to provide money for the soup kitchens of the East End of Glasgow in 1888.

Their first game at the original Celtic Park was, needless to say, against Rangers. The Protestant club had been going for 15 years, but Celtic won 5–2, an auspicious beginning. Among the players in that game who had been persuaded by the commitment of the club's driving force, Brother Walfrid of the Marist Teaching Order, was William Maley. He went on to become the club's first great manager as they dominated the first two decades of the 20th century.

Jimmy McGrory (right) against Partick Thistle in 1935, averaged more than a goal per game in 16 seasons with Celtic.

By then they were already well established, having joined the Scottish League on its formation in 1890, and having won their first four Championships in the 1890s along with the first of their record 27 Scottish Cups. That same decade saw the club's charitable concerns thrown out of the window as hard-headed businessmen replaced the Catholic priest, forming the club into a limited company. Maley's team, however, was to set a new standard for Scottish football as they dominated the League, winning it six times consecutively between 1905 and 1910, a record which survived until the 1960s and 1970s.

As important as the achievements was the manner of them, Celtic laying a new emphasis on football as a team game. They did so without sacrificing individual skills or entertainment, their passing game being rich in both, but now the talents of wingers Alec Bennett and Davie Hamilton, and the inventiveness of the clever inside-forward Jimmy McMenemy, had a pattern and purpose–much of it to provide openings for the mighty Jimmy Quinn.

There was one notable change as the team won those six consecutive titles,

Jock Stein . . . an ordinary player but an extraordinary manager.

PLAYER PROFILES

JIMMY JOHNSTONE

Few players have encapsulated the dual nature of Scottish footballers so well as 'Jinky' Jimmy Johnstone, who combined prodigious talent, a fiery temper and a self-destructive streak in equal proportions.

His capacity for getting into scrapes, on and off the pitch, followed him around throughout his career. Early in his days at Celtic, Johnstone was suspended for a week by manager Jock Stein for lunging at an opponent; in 1974 as Scotland's preparations for the World Cup were undermined by constant stories of indiscipline, Johnstone was found drifting in a rowing boat without a paddle in the small hours of the morning.

Yet no-one doubted his ability. His contribution to Celtic's European Cup triumph in 1966–67 was immense, particularly in the final, where he destroyed his marker Tarcisio Burgnich, as he did many a top class full-back in his career. In the first ten minutes in Lisbon, Johnstone left his marker totally bemused on four occasions, doing much to swing the crowd on to Celtic's side from the start.

Defenders watched, and took note. Subsequently Johnstone was to be tested at his most vulnerable point, his hot temper, by the hard men of two Continents. A year later in the World Club Championship, against the disgraceful Argentinian team Racing Club, Johnstone, who had been sorely used, retaliated and was sent off, the first of three Celtic players to go in a farcical third match.

In the notorious European Cup semi-final in 1974 against Atletico Madrid, managed by the Argentinian Juan Carlos Lorenzo, Johnstone was the principal target of the hatchet men. Continually tripped and hacked, he showed stoical resolution – and was kicked in the stomach as he left the field.

In the second leg, in Madrid, he was given two black eyes by Spanish elbows, yet still kept his head when retaliation would have been only too human.

But in the end what stays in the memory are the jinking dribbles of the red-headed player whose ball control once persuaded a Scotland manager to abandon training early. 'Nobody had a kick. They couldn't get the ball off Johnstone,' he explained.

In all he won 23 caps, the last in 1977 against Spain, when he was 30 years old.

Leader of Celtic as player and then manager – Billy McNeill.

Bennett moving to Rangers, to be replaced by a former Rangers player, David Kivlichan. The bitterness of the Irish uprising and partition had yet to be felt in Scottish football.

As the League continued into the War, the great Patsy Gallagher took his place in the side and, after Rangers won a hat-trick of titles, Celtic recovered the ascendancy with four more straight wins. But as Rangers reorganised under Bill Struth, Celtic were to be forced to content themselves with second best as the men from Ibrox dominated the Twenties and Thirties, Celtic claiming the League just four times and the Cup six in spite of the goalscoring heroics of Jimmy McGrory.

The post-war decades were even less successful, a Cup and League double in 1954 not withstanding, fans finding solace only in inspiring individuals like Charlie Tully and Neil Mochan.

Then came Jock Stein, an ordinary player but a quite extraordinary manager. Giving the club a new discipline and organisation, but retaining the historic commitment to clever, attacking football, Stein built a dynasty as his team won the League nine years running between 1965 and 1974, did the double four times, the treble of League, League Cup and Cup twice, and in 1967 won everything they entered, including the European Cup.

Billy McNeill, Bobby Murdoch, Tommy Gemmell, Bertie Auld, John Hughes, Steve Chalmers and Jimmy Johnstone made them one of the finest club teams of all time. As the run reached its end, players like Davie Hay, Lou Macari, Danny McGrain and George Connelly had joined the throng, and so, finally, did Kenny Dalglish.

Eventually McNeill became manager and retained Celtic's pre-eminent position, the club winning the new Premier League on five occasions. McNeill then moved to England, but returned to his first love in 1987 to meet the challenge as Graeme Souness gave Rangers renewed vigour.

Celtic's reward was immediate as McNeill took them to the League and Cup double in 1987–88 – for the tenth time in their history.

PLAYER PROFILES

DANNY McGRAIN

Possibly one of the best full-backs ever to play for Celtic or Scotland, for whom he won 62 caps, Danny McGrain's story is as much a tribute to his character as his ability.

Many players have to overcome injury at some time in their careers. Few have to overcome a fractured skull. But McGrain came back from such an injury to take his place in the Scotland party in the 1974 World Cup.

Fate had not finished with him, a serious foot injury ruling him out of the 1978 trip to Argentina, but once again he showed his resilience, bouncing back to reclaim his place and take part in the 1982 World Cup with distinction.

Ironically he grew up supporting Rangers as he learned his football in the Glasgow backstreets, the home of so many great Scottish players of earlier eras, and hoped to play for the club. The scout who ran the rule over him however decided that Daniel Fergus McGrain could only be a Catholic, and so Rangers did not approach him.

It was their loss. McGrain, a Protestant, instead went to Celtic, then at the height of their powers, and grew up with the next batch of young lions – Lou Macari, Kenny Dalglish, George Connelly and David Hay. But while Connelly dropped out of the game and the other three moved to England, McGrain devoted his career to the Parkhead club, developing into a stirring leader.

A solid, hard-tackling defender, he had the attacking skills demanded of full-backs in this era too, his surges up the line proving an important attacking outlet for both club and country.

With Celtic he won every domestic honour, including five League Championship and six Scottish Cup medals, and became the club's most capped player. Fittingly he ended his international career on the grand stage, making his last appearance in the 1982 World Cup, as a substitute against Russia. Without his talents – and the wisdom he brought to their defence because of his vast experience – Scotland then struggled to make an impression.

RANGERS

Willie Waddell added a touch of class to a physical post-war side.

Rangers are the most powerful club in Scotland, on and off the field. Whether their influence has always been healthy is debatable: the club's religious bigotry – no Catholic has been allowed to play for them – and preference for physical power football rather than skill both qualify admiration for their achievements.

Their new manager, Graeme Souness, who is married to a Catholic, has committed himself to end the club's anti-Catholic policy, but the side's appalling disciplinary record since he took over still means that their reputation is less than spotless.

Their record, however, is indisputable – 35 First Division championships, four more in the new Premier League, giving 39 in all, while they have been runners-up 23 times. The Cup has been won 24 times, the League Cup 16 times. The European Cup Winners' Cup was won in 1972 after Rangers had lost in the finals of 1961 and 1967. Only the European Cup has escaped their grasp.

Formed in 1872, they were overshadowed by amateur club Queen's Park in the early years, as was every other club in the country. But they soon established themselves and when Queen's Park refused to join the League when it was set

Alan Morton, the 'Wee Blue Devil' responsible for much of Rangers' success in the Twenties.

PLAYER PROFILES

JIM BAXTER

'Slim' Jim Baxter may not have been the greatest Scottish wing-half of all time – although it is difficult to think of a better one – but there can never have been one so quintessentially Scottish.

A strolling player of exquisite touch, Baxter gloried in his art for its own sake, displaying all his extravagant gifts with an almost contemptuous disdain for the opposition.

Born at Hill O' Beath in Fifeshire in 1939, he began with Raith Rovers after a brief spell as a coal miner, but was clearly destined for greater things.

In 1960 a dazzling display at Ibrox, where he scored one of the goals as Raith beat Rangers 2–1, an almost unprecedented feat in those days, persuaded Rangers to buy the slender left-half with the glorious left foot.

It was the start of a brief but sparkling spell as Baxter became the creative influence in the great Rangers team of that period, supplying the ammunition for Alex Scott or Willie Henderson, Ian McMillan, Jimmy Millar, Ralph Brand and Davie Wilson. He was equally influential in a Scottish team of rare fluency, combining with Pat Crerand to inspire the team of Denis Law, John White, Ian St. John and Wilson to great performances.

There was nothing that group enjoyed better than displaying their superior skills to the 'Auld Enemy', and Baxter was a central figure in a period of marked Scottish ascendancy. In his five games against England, Scotland won four, the last in 1967.

By then, however, he was past his peak. A broken leg and the subsequent enforced idleness after he had overdone the trickery in a European Cup tie in Vienna in December 1964 took something away, and as the years progressed he had an increasing weight problem which a taste for alcohol did not help.

A £72,000 transfer to a poor Sunderland team in 1965 was followed by a spell at Nottingham Forest, but at the end of the 1968–69 season he was given a free transfer by the club which had paid £100,000 for him 18 months earlier. He then ended his days back at Rangers.

Ally McCoist essays an overhead kick during Rangers' match with Hamilton at Douglas Park in August 1988. Rangers won the Scottish League title by a large margin and, having won the League Cup earlier in the season were only deprived of a domestic clean sweep by Celtic in the F.A. Cup final.

up in 1890, Rangers and Celtic became major influences.

Rangers won the first Championship, shared with Dunfermline, although ironically they were regarded as too soft in the season previously when they opened Ibrox Stadium, the show game for the occasion resulting in a humiliating 8–1 defeat by Preston North End.

They soon found the necessary hardness, producing a run of four consecutive League titles around the turn of the century, the first in 1898–99, when they scored maximum points, 36 from 18 games. They were soon to be surpassed by the great Celtic side of the 1900s, but when that paused for breath Rangers took their opportunity with a hat-trick of League wins before the First World War as Glasgow's monopoly became established.

It was the Twenties and Thirties which saw Rangers take over almost completely, under their great manager Bill Struth. His accession was almost accidental – he took over when the previous incumbent Willie Wilton, was drowned.

Struth, a professional runner, had been employed as trainer, and as manager he left the tactics to the senior players while giving them a fitness which outstripped their rivals. He knew enough to buy Alan Morton, however, and in the powerful Davie Meiklejohn had a captain and leader to whom it was easy to delegate. Between 1919 and 1939 they won the Championship 15 times.

After the Second World War Rangers began in much the same vein with an even more functional approach built on burly defenders George Young and Willie Woodburn, with only Willie Waddell adding a touch of class to a direct, physical side.

But old age was catching up on Struth, and the Fifties were less successful until Scott Symon signed Jim Baxter at the end of the decade to produce one of the most attractive skilful Scottish club sides of all time. They won the League four times in six years, reaching the semi-final of the European Cup in 1960 and the European Cup Winners' Cup final a year later.

That side had quality throughout, but the side was given direction by Baxter, and when he left the genius went with him. Even though Sandy Jardine and the great competitor John Greig strove manfully to keep them at the top, the emergence of the great Celtic side of 1965–74 began a period of decline for Rangers.

The appointment of Graeme Souness as player-manager and the recruitment of Terry Butcher, Chris Woods and Graham Roberts from England to bolster the native talent was quickly rewarded with the 1986–87 League Championship, and with money apparently no object the club seem poised to reassert their pre-eminence north of the border.

However, they had to play second fiddle to Celtic in the 1987–88 season as their oldest rivals performed the League and Cup double.

PLAYER PROFILES

GRAEME SOUNESS

Few players have rivalled Rangers player-manager Graeme Souness for having a major influence on an era. The abrasive Souness has played dominant roles in the Liverpool and Scotland midfields, and has set the tone as player-manager of his new club on and off the field.

It is almost impossible to believe that in his youth at Tottenham Souness was regarded as a 'Fancy Dan' type of player, enjoying life to the full off the field and full of tricks on it, but lacking hard professionalism. His own head-strong quality was shown when he left Spurs to join Middlesbrough in pursuit of first team football.

At Middlesbrough he came under the influence of Jack Charlton, and the straight-forward Geordie gave Souness a new, more professional approach to the game, although he retained his enjoyment of the good things enough to keep his 'Champagne Charlie' nickname.

With Middlesbrough, Souness established himself as one of the top midfield players in the country, and his move to Liverpool to link up with Kenny Dalglish in 1977 was the foundation stone for the club's domination of the next ten years.

The pair dove-tailed perfectly as Liverpool won everything, Souness even providing the pass for Dalglish to score the winning goal in the 1978 European Cup final, and Souness was to stamp his influence on crucial games for both club and country, even if his tackling sometimes evoked resentment from opponents.

The dominant personality in the Scotland team in the 1982 World Cup, he saw Liverpool to five League Championships, four League Cup final victories and three European Cups before moving to Italy, for tax reasons. Two quiet years there were followed by his appointment as player-manager of Rangers in 1986. His sending off in his first game set an undesirable precedent, and the club's disciplinary record under him is far from good, but he showed great vision in reversing a trend by signing English internationals Chris Woods, Terry Butcher and Graham Roberts and won the Championship in his first season.

DUNDEE

For most of their history, Dundee were the senior club on Tayside, but until the arrival of Bob Shankly as manager that seniority was strictly relative.

Formed in 1893, they soon made their mark by winning the Cup in 1910, and coming second in the First Division three times in the first decade of the 20th century.

Thereafter, apart from an unsuccessful Cup final appearance in 1925, the club ticked over, even being relegated briefly to Division Two, until the end of the Forties.

Then, like Hearts and Hibs, Dundee emerged as a national power. They first gave notice of their intentions in 1948–49, coming second to Rangers by one point. The League Cup, however, was to be the start of their success, Dundee winning the trophy in both 1952 and 1953, while finishing as beaten finalists in the 1952 Scottish Cup. The side was inspired by the return of Billy Steel from Derby County, some compensation for the departure of Alec Forbes to Arsenal.

But it was the beginning of the Sixties with Bob Shankly, once a junior player with Glenbuck Cherrypickers, and showing that he had some of his brother Bill's flair, that Dundee's name rang through Europe. With former Liverpool goalkeeper Bert Slater, solid full-backs in Alex Hamilton and Bobby Cox, a powerful centre-half in Ian Ure, workmanlike wing-halves in Bobby Seith and Bobby Wishart, they had a sound base.

They also had a formidable attack, with veteran Gordon Smith providing the passes for Alan Cousin and Alan Gilzean, one of the most devastating headers of a ball in the game's history. In 1962 they won the Championship for the only time, Smith thereby gaining a medal with three different clubs. In itself that was remarkable, but to do so with neither Celtic nor Rangers, was almost incredible.

The Championship was just the prelude to the side's European Cup campaign, beginning in unbelievable fashion with an 8–1 win over Cologne in the first round, first leg. Sporting Lisbon and Anderlecht were also dismissed but in the semi-final, they fell to A.C. Milan, over-confidence letting them down in the away leg. Soon the side disintegrated as Ure and Gilzean went to London and Smith retired.

Like their Edinburgh counterparts, Dundee found the advent of the Premier League a testing time, and adding to their tribulations as they yo-yoed between Premier and First Divisions was the rise of Dundee United.

Iain Angus in possession for Dundee at Celtic Park. Angus showed his versatility during the 1987–8 season by playing at both left wing and left back.

PLAYER PROFILES

KENNY DALGLISH

It used to be a matter of some debate whether Scotland's most-capped player was better in midfield or at the front. The way things are going, 'behind the desk' will soon become the answer to queries about Kenny Dalglish's best position.

His record as manager already suggests that he will prove the equal of his predecessors Bill Shankly, Bob Paisley and Joe Fagan. But Dalglish the player was a major influence in Dalglish the manager's first successes – the League and Cup double in 1986, his first season in charge. Most still would sooner see him playing rather than wielding his influence from the touchline.

In spite of supporting Rangers as a boy, Dalglish made his name with Celtic, playing with considerable flair both in midfield and as an out-and-out attacker, scoring 112 League goals for the club, and rapidly becoming a central figure in the Scottish sides which went to the 1974 and 1978 World Cups.

But it was his move to Liverpool, where he settled into a forward spot as Kevin Keegan's replacement, which brought him to his peak. Lacking a yard of pace, he more than made up for that deficiency with his brain which almost always took him into the right place at the right time.

A sound enough finisher to share the Scottish international scoring record of 30 with Denis Law, and claim more than 100 goals in the Football League too, thus achieving a rare double, his greatest attribute was his contribution to the all-round team play. A focal point for attacks, desperately difficult to dispossess when he had his back to goal, his awareness of play and his colleagues' positions was exceptional, and his passing deadly accurate.

He was the consummate team player, eschewing personal glory as he helped Liverpool to six League championships, four League Cups, three European Cups, scoring the winner in 1978, and one F.A. Cup triumph. Graeme Souness, his room-mate and friend, compared him favourably to Diego Maradona and Michel Platini, and the judgement is hard to dispute. Born in Glasgow in 1951, Dalglish made more than 550 Scottish and Football League appearances, and won 102 caps between 1972 and 1987.

DUNDEE UNITED

Few footballing transformations have been as remarkable as that effected on Tayside in the last two decades as the balance of power transferred dramatically from Dens Park to Tannadice.

Very much the second side in the city until then, United are now one of the powers in the land, a club to rank alongside teams like Aberdeen, Celtic and Rangers.

Much of that achievement is down to one man, Jim McLean. When McLean took over, the club he inherited was, in his own words, little more than a run-of-the-mill Division Two 'corner shop'.

Formed as Dundee Hibernians in 1909, becoming Dundee United in 1923 when Irish associations were not too desirable in Scotland outside of Glasgow, their only honours were the Second Division championships in 1925 and 1929, and a Scottish Cup final appearance in 1974, when they lost 3–0 to Celtic.

There were some good players coming through, however, and McLean, an inspirational coach, gave them the organisation and tactical framework they needed. In front of veteran goalkeeper and longest serving player, Hamish McAlpine, Paul Hegarty and David Narey helped provide a solid defence, and Eamon Bannon and Paul Sturrock a useful attack.

In 1980 came the breakthrough, the club beating Celtic to win their first major honour, the League Cup. United retained it a year later and in 1983 won the Championship, paving the way for European adventures. The tightly-packed little ground proved a frightening cockpit as United raced to the semi-finals of the European Cup. However, not even the emergence of Richard Gough to strengthen the defence still further enabled them to hold out against Roma in Rome.

But the experience was invaluable, and in 1987 Mclean's rebuilt side chalked up notable victories over Barcelona and Borussia Moenchengladbach to reach the U.E.F.A. Cup final and also their third Scottish Cup final in the Eighties. However, tiredness caught up with the players and they lost both finals in the course of four depressing days.

Later, McLean became Scottish footballs' first manager-chairman of modern times.

Dundee United's most capped player, defender David Narey, beats Maurice Johnston, just before the latter's move from Celtic to Nantes of France.

PLAYER PROFILES

DENIS LAW

'Law, Best and Charlton' – how the names trip off the tongue! It was this trio who gave Manchester United their image for football of breathtaking beauty in the Sixties.

George Best was probably the greatest in terms of sheer natural ability; Bobby Charlton was the great sportsman respected throughout the world; but Denis Law was the fans' favourite. The focal point of the side, first at Huddersfield, then at Manchester City, he dominated their strategies with his quick, eager one-twos. Indeed, he was so good an organiser that Harry Gregg, a stern critic, likened him to the great Alfredo Di Stefano.

But goals in football as a whole were increasingly at a premium as the Sixties wore on – and Law could score goals. He settled into a forward role when he joined Manchester United for a record £115,000 in 1962 after a brief, unhappy sojourn in Italy with Torino.

At Old Trafford he found his natural spiritual home, and his goals lit up a decade for United and Scotland. A crossfield pass from Charlton, some sorcery on the wing from Best and then a centre, a sudden blur of red and blond, a leaping header or a bicycle kick, and the ball was nestling in the back of the net.

Law rounded off a superb first season by scoring twice at Wembley as United won the 1963 F.A. Cup. Soon his goals, in between lengthy bouts of suspension as he rebelled against the increasingly harsh treatment he was receiving, were inspiring United to two League championships, but he was to watch their European Cup triumph from his hospital bed after a knee operation.

He was never to reach the same heights again, but as United declined he enjoyed an Indian summer, returning to Manchester City to make another Wembley appearance, and at the close of his international career at last enjoying a trip to the World Cup – in Germany in 1974, by which time he was 34.

He shares the Scottish scoring record with Kenny Dalglish, 30 goals but in 55 appearances against Dalglish's 102, while ironically his last League goal, a typically cheeky back-heel, consigned United to the Second Division. Never had he taken less pleasure in a strike.

HEART OF MIDLOTHIAN

Edinburgh's senior club by one year, Hearts were quick to establish the capital's ability to compete with Glasgow, winning the League Championship twice in its first seven years.

However, they were not to win it again until 1958, a gap of 61 years. Then, as great rivals Hibs declined, Hearts took over to provide success for the East coast under their outstanding manager Tommy Walker, winning the title again in 1960.

Cup success came hand in hand with their League wins, the Scottish Cup reappearing in the Tynecastle Park trophy cabinet for the first time for 50 years in 1956. The League Cup was won for the first time in 1954–55, and by the end of the decade had been won three times in five seasons.

It was a list of successes which either of the 'Big Two' would have been happy with, Walker putting together a formidable team which allied determination to the club's traditional artistry.

If the deadly inside-forward trio of Alfie Conn, Willie Bauld and the club's record aggregate goalscorer Jimmy Wardhaugh caught most of the attention, there were outstanding talents elsewhere. Gordon Smith had moved from Hibs to add his wing-play to the mixture. Bobby Parker was a forceful full-back, Dave Mackay and John Cumming a powerful pair of wing-halves. Waiting to come in as age caught up with Bauld and Wardhaugh was Alex Young, a forward of delicate skills.

But financial pressures and age overtook the club. Mackay and Young went to England, Smith to Dundee. For a time Hearts held their own, but the early years of the Premier Division proved a severe test, Hearts slipping into the First Division three times.

Recent years have been more promising under the management team of Alex MacDonald and Sandy Jardine. In 1986, after dominating the League for most of the season with an unbeaten run of 27 games and after reaching the Cup final, they saw the double slip away in the last week.

Needing only a draw to win the title, they were beaten by two goals in the closing stages by Dundee's substitute Alex Kidd and then, their spirits low, were well beaten by Aberdeen in the Cup final. But those reverses could not disguise the club's return to better health, confirmed by second place in the 1987–88 Championship and a brave run in the following year's U.E.F.A. Cup.

Sandy Jardine, the Edinburgh club's player-coach when Hearts had the League title wrenched from them at the end of the 1985–86 season, holds off Aberdeen's John Hewitt.

PLAYER PROFILES

DAVE MACKAY

A rumbustious, hard-tackling wing-half, Dave Mackay played football as if he had the claymore in hand going into battle to the sound of the bag-pipes, his broad chest pushed forward until it almost burst out of his shirt.

In the great Spurs double side of 1961 he was the perfect complement to Danny Blanchflower, his great physical drive balancing the cunning, cerebral approach of the Irishman.

Sometimes he was too physical for his own and other people's good. Twice he broke his leg as his impetuosity got the better of him. On other occasions his tackling was too fierce to be within accepted limits. But always he met challenges head on, with hardly a cynical or a sly action to his name.

And he was more than a physical force. His control was good, his passing sound, his shooting when he charged forward provided a good share of goals and, in his later years, he became an excellent reader of the game as he played alongside centre-half Roy McFarland to help Derby to the First Division.

But above all he was a leader. That quality shone out even in his youth with Hearts, where he caught the eye of the new Spurs manager Bill Nicholson. It is not too much to say that the signing of Mackay was the key to Tottenham's transformation from an entertaining side to a team of winners. With Mackay a crucial figure, Spurs did the double, won the Cup the following year and the European Cup Winners' cup the year after that. He was the natural replacement for Blanchflower as captain, but soon came his broken legs.

He returned to lead Spurs to their F.A. Cup final win over Chelsea in 1967 before joining Derby as Brian Clough transformed the club. Mackay saw them established in the First Division before moving to Swindon as player-manager.

He returned to Derby as manager, winning the Championship in 1975, but resigned a year later on a point of principle, and worked abroad until his return as manager of Doncaster Rovers in 1987.

He won 22 caps for Scotland between 1957 and 1965, but was less successful on the international stage than in club football, Jim Baxter and Pat Crerand claiming the wing-half spots in the early Sixties.

HIBERNIAN

Not the least of Hibernian's claims to fame is that the club provided the original inspiration for the formation of Celtic. Hibs, as the name suggests, were formed, in 1875, by a group of Irishmen based in Edinburgh.

Although the capital was a rugby stronghold, Hibs' policy of attracting players from the West of Scotland made them successful enough to persuade the Glasgow Irish community to follow suit. Celtic's success meant that Hibs were less able to attract players from the West, and their own reputation for rough play resulted in their first application for membership of the Edinburgh F.A. being turned down.

Even though they were the first Eastern side to win the Scottish Cup in 1887, they were not founder members of the Scottish League, but were elected to the Second Division in 1893 and won the competition in 1894 and 1895. Their second success saw them promoted, and they won the First Division in 1903.

Like every other club except Motherwell, they were overshadowed by Rangers' monopoly in the Twenties and Thirties, but the post-war period saw a rare flowering on the East coast, with Hibs leading the way.

They had a forward line known as 'The Famous Five' – Gordon Smith, Bobby Johnstone, Lawrie Reilly, Eddie Turnbull and Willie Ormond. The defence, though, was not of the same calibre – Ormond tells a story of Reilly demanding: 'Have we got to score four again today?'. But the power of their attack was enough to win the League championship in 1948, 1951 and 1952.

As that team faded, the arrival of Joe Baker, the prolific English centre-forward, kept Hibs in respectable positions, but the Sixties and Seventies saw decline set in, the new Premier League in particular testing the club and finding it wanting.

Hibs were relegated in 1980, returned in 1982, but are still a far cry from the side which led the challenge to Glasgow.

Hibernian reached the semi-final of the Scottish F.A. Cup in 1988–9, but they went out to Celtic at Hampden Park. It is now ten seasons since Hibs have played in the F.A. Cup final, and three since they reached the League Cup final. In the last few seasons they have lived in the shadow of their cross-city rivals Hearts.

PLAYER PROFILES

BILLY BREMNER

The face of an angelic schoolboy could not disguise the occasional low boiling point of a fierce competitor.

In midfield for Leeds and Scotland, Billy Bremner, Footballer of the Year in 1970, will be remembered above all for his part in making Leeds the outstanding side in an era of great teams.

He was both captain and an ideal partner for John Giles, the most influential midfield player of his day. Giles was the controlling genius, but Bremner's scurrying combativeness and considerable passing ability was almost as important, and his ability to pop up and score vital goals was a major factor in Leeds' success.

The club won two Championships and were runners-up four times between 1966 and 1974, as well as winning the F.A., League and European Fairs Cups and reaching the finals of the European Cup and European Cup Winners' Cup. As that record showed, they came second a lot, possibly because of the fear which gripped manager Don Revie, but there was no doubt that Bremner was a winner.

Sometimes his competitiveness overflowed the bounds, and his quick temper got him into trouble, most notoriously in Brian Clough's first match in charge, the 1974 F.A. Charity Shield at Wembley when he was sent off along with Kevin Keegan. Both players were fined and suspended for six weeks.

The summer of 1974 was an eventful time for Bremner, for he had captained Scotland in the World Cup, the highlight of his career, but had nearly missed the tournament after breaking curfew along with Jimmy Johnstone in Brussels. Fortunately the Scottish Football Association decided not to send the players home.

His play in the World Cup, when he was one of Scotland's successes, was perhaps his best for his country, for whom he gained 54 caps. He finished his career at Hull and had a spell as manager at Doncaster before returning to Elland Road in 1986 and taking his former club to a promotion play-off replay and an F.A. Cup semi-final but not back to the First Division. He was sacked in 1988.

NORTHERN IRELAND

Soccer was slower to make its impact in Ireland than in mainland Britain. The rival claims of rugby and nationalist interests impeded its progress, although the first recorded soccer match, played by two Scottish teams in Belfast, was sponsored by Ulster rugby clubs.

With its strong Scottish influence, Belfast was the centre for the Irish F.A. and Irish League even before the country was split, Cliftonville and Linfield following the traditions of Queen's Park and Glasgow Rangers.

After the country was divided, Linfield became the dominant club, but the national team was based on exiles who moved to the English and, less frequently, Scottish leagues, Belfast offering a rich vein of talent for the scouts.

Below: *Billy Bingham, manager behind Northern Ireland's international revival.*

Below Left: *Peter McParland, outside-left for Aston Villa and Northern Ireland's 1958 World Cup team.*

From the days of Bill McCracken, the master of the offside trap, a steady stream of outstanding Irish players enhanced the Football League. There were rarely enough to create a powerful international side, but the 1950s saw a sudden flowering of talent, giving manager Peter Doherty, one of the country's greatest players, some compensation for his own fruitless struggles with little support.

With Danny Blanchflower an inspiring captain, Jimmy McIlroy almost his equal as a scheming midfield general, a heroic goalkeeper in Harry Gregg, and two excellent wingers in Billy Bingham and Peter McParland, they were the sensation of the 1958 World Cup, beating Italy to qualify and twice upsetting the powerful Czechoslovakia side to reach the quarter-finals before going down to France.

Like Wales, they then went into decline as if the effort had exhausted them to leave players of the quality of George Best and Derek Dougan to play out their international careers in a morass of mediocrity, but the appointment of Bingham as manager at the end of the Seventies heralded a new, equally successful era.

With the peerless Pat Jennings in goal behind such solid defenders as John McClelland, Chris Nicholl, Jimmy Nicholl, and Mal Donaghy, and inspired midfield leadership from Martin O'Neill and Sammy McIlroy, supported by the tireless David McCreery, the side was always hard to beat. They lacked goals however, for all the work of Gerry Armstrong, until the arrival of Norman Whiteside, the latest in the list of the country's greats. Two British Championships were won, the side reached the quarter-finals of the World Cup in 1982 before going down again to France, and in 1986 again qualified for the finals.

As impressive was their ability to conjure unexpected results, beating the immensely powerful Germans twice in the 1984 European Championship qualifiers, and winning in Rumania to reach the 1986 World Cup. It was the most successful era in the country's history.

PLAYER PROFILES

GEORGE BEST

'Georgie, Georgie, who is this Georgie?' cried a beleaguered American tourist caught up in a surging mob pursuing the Irishman to his Spanish hideaway.

The American was probably the only person in the country who needed to ask that question, for if the Beatles could claim at the height of their popularity that they were more famous than Jesus Christ, George Best, the first footballing Beatle, could have claimed that he was more famous than John, Paul, George (Harrison) and Ringo.

The outstanding British talent of his generation, possibly of all time, Best was a player to rank with Pele and Johan Cruyff as the greatest in the world. Small, but immensely powerful, with dribbling ability to match Stanley Matthews or Tom Finney, speed which left defenders for dead, a bravery which allowed him to withstand the regular assaults which marked one of the most brutal eras in the game's history, finishing power which brought him a large quota of goals, and surprising heading ability for someone of his height, he was almost the complete footballer.

He was also the game's first modern superstar, arriving in the swinging Sixties to catch the mood of the times.

For a time he held other distractions at bay, playing a decisive role in Manchester United's re-emergence as the glamour team of the Sixties. With Best on the wing they won two League championships, and finally, in 1968, the European Cup. It was the climax of all the club had wanted for a decade, and subsequently a decline set in.

It was a tragedy for Best, who was only 22 and still had his best years to come. A poor Northern Ireland team offered little solace, and as things went wrong his frustration began to show as he retaliated against harsh treatment to earn himself a reputation for indiscipline, while his taste for wine and women, if not song, began to undermine his consistency. After a series of absences, he walked out on United in 1972.

A year later he returned briefly before leaving again for the North American Soccer League, and then Fulham, then finishing his career making brief appearances almost as a circus turn at a variety of clubs.

PLAYER PROFILES

DANNY BLANCHFLOWER

Real success came late in his career to Danny Blanchflower, which was probably how that great iconoclast would have wished it.

'People think that football is about winning,' he once remarked. 'But it isn't. It's about glory.'

That was how Danny played it, and at the end he was proved right as he ended his career in glory, leading the fine Northern Ireland team to the quarter-finals of the World Cup in 1958, and then enjoying his role as captain and guiding light of the Tottenham double side, possibly the greatest British club side of the 20th century.

A meticulous passer of the ball, a player who caressed it as he persuaded it to do his bidding, Blanchflower was the natural playmaker of every team he played in from his best position of wing-half. Not a strong tackler, nor a player of great speed, his brain took him into position to make vital interceptions defensively as well as telling him where the probing pass would do most damage.

And his early career at workaday Barnsley and at a Villa Park still dwelling on the glories of the distant past brought him only frustration. His move to Spurs in 1954, when he was already 28, was not the immediate panacea it had promised to be as the push-and-run side fell apart and a sick Arthur Rowe was replaced by Jimmy Anderson, who found Blanchflower too strong and stripped him of the captaincy.

Peter Doherty proved a kindred spirit as manager of Northern Ireland and the team's success in 1958 demonstrated Blanchflower's supreme qualities in the right environment. Almost immediately that environment was created at Spurs and the side gelled as Bill Nicholson restored Blanchflower to the captaincy, after for a time leaving him out of the side, and John White and Dave Mackay arrived.

The double was done in 1961, the Cup won again in 1962 and the European Cup Winners' Cup, the first European trophy to be won by an English club, in 1963.

It was a fitting finale to a distinguished career. In all he played 553 League games for his three clubs and was capped by Northern Ireland 56 times.

PLAYER PROFILES

PAT JENNINGS

It is almost impossible to believe it now, but in his early years at Tottenham, Pat Jennings was regarded as erratic, like Bruce Grobbelaar a goalkeeper whose acrobatic brilliance was betrayed by impetuosity and lack of judgement.

Perhaps in those days, Jennings arriving at Spurs after only one year with Watford to be plunged into the First Division, there was some truth in the criticism, but with the dedication and professionalism he showed throughout his career, Jennings quickly set out to repair his deficiencies.

How well he succeeded. Possibly there have been goalkeepers as good as the quiet, immensely strong man from Newry – of his British contemporaries Gordon Banks, Neville Southall and Peter Shilton can be mentioned in the same breath – but none surpassed him.

Tall, powerful and athletic with a huge pair of hands, his trademark of the leaping one-handed catch gave inspiration to his team-mates and sapped the confidence of opposing forwards. He was a trend-setter in the increasing use of legs and feet by goalkeepers both in coming out at opponents' feet and in covering the area of the goal, while his positional sense became superb as his experience grew.

A pillar of the Tottenham side which won the F.A. Cup, the League Cup twice and the U.E.F.A. Cup between 1967 and 1973, he was Footballer of the Year in 1973. 'How could I help winning it playing behind our defence?' he joked with typical modesty, but he was certain of his own worth for all his quiet self-effacement, and when Tottenham decided he was expendable in 1977 he was delighted to prove them wrong.

In fact his greatest moments were ahead of him as he saw Arsenal to three consecutive Cup finals from 1978 to 1980 and helped Northern Ireland to the World Cup finals in Spain and Mexico.

Mexico provided the perfect end to his career: after he had returned to Tottenham to keep in trim for the occasion, Jennings made his record 119th and last appearance against Brazil. He was 41 years old.

PLAYER PROFILES

JIMMY McILROY

Burnley were noted for their ability to find stars without breaking the bank, but they can rarely have made a better investment than the £7,000 they paid Glentoran for Jimmy McIlroy in 1950.

McIlroy, then 19, became the brains of their team at the height of the club's post-war success, guiding and prodding them to the League Championship in 1960.

A classical scheming inside-forward, McIlroy was a clever dribbler when the occasion demanded, but he always saw himself as first and foremost a passer of the ball, finding the opposition's most vulnerable point and sending the ball to it with deadly precision.

An intelligent playmaker, he enjoyed splendid partnerships with the wing-halves behind him, Jimmy Adamson for Burnley, and his creative equal as player and thinker for Northern Ireland, Danny Blanchflower. With Peter Doherty as an inspirational manager, Blanchflower and McIlroy took Northern Ireland to their greatest heights, masterminding the 1958 World Cup quarter-final side, in which McIlroy formed a devastating partnership with Peter McParland.

The high points of their club careers lay ahead, but even after guiding Burnley to the championship and a Cup final appearance two years later, McIlroy had more glory left. The part played by Stanley Matthews in the revival of Stoke City has been well documented. Matthews, however, was always dependent on a good inside-forward to supply him with the ball and McIlroy proved as adept as Raich Carter or Ernie Taylor.

Matthews and McIlroy helped see Stoke back into the First Division, and that success led to McIlroy's recall to the international arena in 1966 after a three-year gap. He played three times then, taking his total to 55 full international appearances, which brought him ten goals, including one in Northern Ireland's historic victory at Wembley in 1957.

After finishing his career back in Lancashire, with Oldham at the age of 36, he returned to Burnley to become a sports journalist, a post he still fills.

PLAYER PROFILES

SAMMY McILROY

The last of the Busby Babes, Sammy McIlroy made a sensational debut for Manchester United, scoring in a tense derby with Manchester City. He then played an important part in United's brief flowering under Frank O'Farrell before George Best went off the rails and everything fell apart.

United was not an ideal place for a young player trying to learn his trade in the early Seventies, and McIlroy perhaps never quite lived up to the great expectations he had aroused, especially as a goalscorer.

But a move back into midfield in the exciting mid-Seventies side gave him a new career, and he thrived, his close control and weaving runs finding plenty of scope in his new position, while his ability to take people on in tight situations made him a dangerous man when he moved up in support of his forwards.

Perhaps his most memorable goal came in the 1979 Cup final, a jinking run through a packed Arsenal penalty area and a curling shot past his international team-mate Pat Jennings bringing United back into a game which seemed lost beyond recall.

By that time his international career, which has brought him 88 caps, had begun to blossom again, and he played an important role in Billy Bingham's team which was to become the most successful in the country's history. He was virtually an ever-present as Northern Ireland twice won the Home International Championship, and went to successive World Cup final rounds in 1982 and 1986, captaining the side in the second tournament.

By then he had left United, Ron Atkinson dropping him to make way for Bryan Robson. McIlroy's reply revealed the man, signing off with a hat-trick on the day Robson was presented to the Old Trafford fans.

He moved to Stoke and then returned to Manchester to join City. That proved a mistake, City fans regarding him as a United player, and he was allowed to move to Bury at the age of 33.

Sammy is no relation to Jimmy McIlroy (see previous page).

PLAYER PROFILES

NORMAN WHITESIDE

Few youngsters have shown such composure on the big occasion as Norman Whiteside, who made his international debut when barely 17 in the 1982 World Cup finals, with only two Football League appearances to his credit, and emerged as one of the star players of the tournament.

Whiteside, a powerful, intelligent striker or midfield player, has gone on from that auspicious beginning to confirm a maturity beyond his years. As a teenager he was, Billy Bingham was fond of remarking, '19 going on 30', and the sheer ice-cold calculation of his football is nothing short of breathtaking.

He scored on his full debut for Manchester United, and although not a prolific goal-scorer, he has made a habit of hitting the target on the big occasion, for both United and Northern Ireland. In his first full season he scored United's only goal in the League Cup final defeat by Liverpool, the winner in the F.A. Cup semi-final against Arsenal, one of the four in the final against Brighton, and above all the brilliant goal curled round Neville Southall which won the Cup in 1985 when United had been reduced to ten men with the sending-off of Kevin Moran.

His performances for his country have been equally telling. He scored the goal in Ireland's astonishing defeat of West Germany in Hamburg in 1983 and laid the groundwork for Jimmy Quinn's goal in Bucharest which gave Northern Ireland qualification at Rumania's expense for the 1986 World Cup.

As well as scoring vital goals, Whiteside has been an important creator of them, whether playing at the front or in midfield. His lack of pace tells against him, but his ability to hold the ball, and the vision of his flicks has led Bingham to compare him with Kenny Dalglish, while his sheer power makes him an uncomfortable opponent for even the best defenders.

At times he can allow his tackling to get out of hand, but if age and experience teaches him to temper his aggression he will have little else to learn.

WALES

A small country hampered by the challenge of rugby's popularity, and by North and South rivalries, Wales have nonetheless held their own as a footballing country.

In the early years of the organised game they proved formidable opponents for England, winning the third and fourth games between the countries, 1–0 at Blackburn in 1881, and 5–3 at Wrexham a year later.

As rugby took hold, soccer's progress could not be maintained, despite the incomparable presence of Billy Meredith. In the 1920s, however, the international team again became a force to be reckoned with, based at Cardiff and on the powerful Cardiff City side which lost the 1924 Championship on goal average, but in 1927 became the only team to take the F.A. Cup out of England. With first Fred Keenor and then Bryn Jones as a major influence in midfield, they were teams to be reckoned with.

The post-war side, with Cardiff's Alf Sherwood and Trevor Ford, who still shares the goalscoring record with Ivor Allchurch, and that driving wing-half Ron Burgess, were slow to make an impact. But the arrival of a thrilling generation from Swansea and the valleys soon changed all that, producing the greatest Welsh side of all from Jack Kelsey in goal to the flying outside-left Cliff Jones.

Ivor and Len Allchurch, Mel and John Charles, Terry Medwin, Derek Tapscott and Mel Hopkins all helped Wales reach the quarter-finals of the 1958 World Cup in Sweden. When they lost, it was 1–0 to eventual winners Brazil – and without their hero, John Charles, the victim of some disgraceful Hungarian tackles in the first round play-off.

That high-point has yet to be equalled. As the team grew old and Cardiff declined from the First Division to the brink of extinction, Welsh football lost its way, a scattering of fine individuals like Mike England, Leighton James and John Mahoney failing to cover the deficiencies.

The appointment of an English manager, Mike Smith, however, steadied the ship, and the emergence of a new Swansea team led by John Toshack, which did briefly reach the First Division with players of the calibre of Robbie James and Alan Curtis, helped the recovery. But though the current squad with Ian Rush, Mark Hughes, Neville Southall, Kevin Ratcliffe and Pat van den Hauwe is undoubtedly the strongest since 1958, success has so far eluded them.

One of the very best of Welsh inside-forwards: Ivor Allchurch of Swansea, Newcastle and Cardiff.

Mark Hughes takes on the Czech defence in Cardiff, where a 1–1 draw proved costly in the 1986–88 European Championships.

PLAYER PROFILES

JOHN CHARLES

Few would quarrel with the description of John Charles as the greatest Welsh player of all time. Many Welshmen would go further and describe 'the gentle giant' as the greatest player of all time.

At 6 ft 2 in tall, and nearly 14 st, Charles was a giant in stature, but he had small, quick feet, a beautiful touch and control and a deceptive turn of speed which unhinged the unwary defender.

Born near Swansea in 1931, a member of the outstanding generation from the Valleys which included the Allchurch brothers and his own brother Mel, it was a matter of some bitterness locally that he was lured away to West Yorkshire by Major Frank Buckley, who described him simply as 'the greatest footballer I have ever seen'. Many were to echo those words.

Put into the Leeds United side at 17, Charles made an immediate impact as a centre-half. A year later he moved forward to start a debate which has never been resolved – was his best position centre-half or centre-forward? With his powerful frame, awesome heading ability and feet which were equally good at tackling or shooting fiercely, he could adapt to either with alacrity, while his one possible weakness, a lack of aggression, was an equal handicap in either role. Yet scoring goals is harder than preventing them, and it is as a goalscorer that Charles will be remembered.

His goals helped guide Leeds into the First Division and keep a mediocre side there as long as he stayed. He scored a club record of 42 in one season, 38 in his first season in Division One, and contributed 150 in all before the football world was stunned by a £65,000 transfer to the Italian giants Juventus, a staggering fee at the time.

He had found a new home, proving as popular and as successful in Italy as he had been at home. The move limited his international appearances to 38, which brought him 15 goals even though half his caps came as a defender.

He took part in Wales' most successful World Cup campaign in 1958, but the savage treatment he received ruled him out of the quarter-final against Brazil. The last of his caps came in 1965, when he was winding down his career at Cardiff, following a second spell at Leeds and an equally short stay with Roma.

PLAYER PROFILES

MIKE ENGLAND

Like George Best for Northern Ireland, Mike England was unfortunate to play his football during a low ebb in his country's fortunes. Born a few years earlier or later both would have been formidable additions to sides which made a considerable impact internationally.

There the resemblance ended, however, for there was little of Best's genius or self-destructiveness in the Prestatyn-born defender.

Big, hard-tackling and a powerful header of the ball, England was a natural defender, an uncompromising, no-nonsense player, although he enjoyed revealing occasionally that his touch was not to be sneered at by bringing the ball out of a crowded area.

Born in 1941, he began his career with Blackburn Rovers, coming into the side of Ronnie Clayton, Bryan Douglas and Peter Dobing in its declining years.

When Rovers were relegated in 1965–66 it was obvious that they would have to sell their most viable asset, and England was linked with Manchester United before joining Tottenham, where he enjoyed a rewarding career. He played in two European finals, an F.A. Cup final and two League Cup finals, his heading power proving a formidable additional weapon in Spurs' armoury when he moved forward at set-pieces alongside Alan Gilzean and Martin Chivers. These were his peak years.

On occasions Tottenham were tempted to play him at centre-forward, but he was never given an extended run in the position, his defensive qualities proving too important.

He won 44 caps for Wales before, disheartened by Tottenham's abrupt decline, he retired in 1975. Possibly the decision was hasty, and after a summer in America he made a brief return with Cardiff City before moving back to the U.S.A.

When the game's short resurgence in America petered out he returned to Britain to take over as manager of Wales. In spite of the presence of a core of outstanding talents in Neville Southall, Kevin Ratcliffe, Ian Rush and Mark Hughes, however, they continually fell just short of qualifying for the finals of major competitions, and in early 1988 England was sacked.

PLAYER PROFILES

MARK HUGHES

Mark Hughes, like his partner in the Welsh team Ian Rush, found problems when he left the Football League for European club football, and was equally delighted to return at the same time, in the summer of 1988. Nevertheless, with his penchant for dramatic goals and for upsetting defenders with his muscular agresssion, he was a player of top quality.

Born in Wrexham in 1963, Hughes began his career with Manchester United as an apprentice midfield player, but it was his conversion to a forward, partnering Norman Whiteside in United's successful Youth team, which stamped him as a star of the future.

Unlike Whiteside he had to wait to make his impact, but when he did break through, in season 1984–85, he burst on the scene thunderously, winning the P.F.A. Young Player of the Year award in his first full season.

The choice was almost inevitable, not only for the number of goals he scored – 22 in League, FA and Milk Cups – but for the style of them. The glorious leaping volley which flew past Luis Arconada in a World Cup qualifying match against Spain in 1985 will linger long in the memory.

He not only scored superb goals that season, but vital ones as well – that goal against Spain, and the winner in the F.A. Cup semi-final against Liverpool, when he broke clear to beat Bruce Grobbelaar with a perfectly placed low shot.

Unquestionably brave, sometimes like Whiteside too fierce, with a powerful, technically excellent shot, good dribbling ability and surprising success in the air for a man of 5 ft 8 in, he is as strong as his powerful thighs suggest.

It seemed the football world was at his feet after that first season, and when he began the following season in the same vein as United made their marvellous start, the offers flew in.

By Christmas his move to Barcelona was already in progress, but as United lost their way so did Hughes. The move to Spain, where he did not learn the language as easily as new clubmate Gary Lineker, looked a disaster. He was dropped and after joining Bayern Munich on loan, jumped at the chance to move back to United, quickly regaining his form and popularity.

PLAYER PROFILES

BILLY MEREDITH

From 1895 to 1920, Billy Meredith was an automatic selection on the wing for Wales, setting astonishing standards of longevity, consistency and quality. One critic has called him 'a Matthews, Finney and Best of his day rolled into one'.

His style was forceful and direct, committing defenders by running at them and often coming inside to shoot.

Born in 1875, Meredith's first cap came within a year of leaving Northwich Vics, who had failed to gain re-election to the Football League in 1894. For ten years he starred for Manchester City, leaving under a cloud after allegedly offering a bribe to an opponent. Manchester United were eventually allowed to sign him, for a £500 fee.

They were League champions in his first full season and he did much to help establish the club over the next decade. When he returned to City in 1921, aged 46, United were immediately relegated.

His last competitive game was in 1925 at the age of 49, leaving him with a total of 857 career matches and 470 goals – a staggering return for a winger.

Meredith's international appearances would have been even more numerous but for the number of occasions on which either Manchester club refused to release him. It is estimated that he was actually chosen for 71 games, appearing in only 48, plus two war-time Victory internationals.

He later set up as a publican in Manchester, as well as helping United with coaching and scouting and died in that saddest of years for the club, 1958, just two months after the Munich air disaster.

PLAYER PROFILES

IAN RUSH

With 'Dixie' Dean and Tommy Lawton playing for Everton, Merseyside can claim almost a monopoly on the greatest British centre-forwards, but whether even his predecessors quite match up to Ian Rush may be doubted.

He is not in the classical mould. Tall, but built like a whippet rather than a lion or a bull-dog, Rush did not power through the air to bullet headers past goalkeepers, nor sweep defenders aside with physical abandon. Instead his speed and the sheer cold-eyed ruthlessness of his finishing reduced the most physically brave defender to a quivering wreck.

Those who did not watch him carefully would have you believe that Rush did little until he suddenly burst into the action to score a goal.

Nothing could be further from the truth. As he matured, and particularly in his last season at Anfield when Kenny Dalglish's appearances were sporadic, he increasingly became the focal point as Liverpool built up their attacks, collecting the ball out of defence and laying it off simply but effectively before speeding off to a new position.

Even more important, he was the first line of defence, the speed and pointedness of his harrying forcing several teams to abandon their usual practice of playing the ball out from the back in favour of safer methods when he was around.

The number of goals he made for himself or a partner by pouncing on and robbing an unwary defender is unascertainable, but in one Cup tie against Ipswich, he twice embarrassed such a solid defender as England's Terry Butcher.

But above all, Rush was a goalscorer, and the sight of him breaking free to leave defenders in his wake before slotting the ball home will live with all who saw him in his glory with Liverpool. He scored 139 goals in 224 League games, and over 200 in all for the Merseysiders as the club won the European Cup, four League titles, four League Cup finals and the F.A. Cup in his time with them before transferring, when still short of his 26th birthday, to Juventus for over £3 million in 1987.

Rarely looking fully fit in Italy (although he was the club's top scorer with only 8 goals in 29 League appearances), Rush thrilled Liverpool's supporters by rejoining them after just one season abroad.

PLAYER PROFILES

NEVILLE SOUTHALL

When he won the Player of the Year award in 1984–85, Neville Southall became only the fourth goalkeeper to do so, following in the footsteps of Bert Trautmann, Gordon Banks and Pat Jennings.

He was quite at home in that august company, for his performances as Everton pursued the treble and won both Football League Championship and the European Cup Winners' Cup, were quite inspirational.

One save from Mark Falco, which effectively ended Tottenham's challenge, had experienced writers going back to Banks' famous save from Pele in the 1970 World Cup for a comparison. His colleagues were more blasé, saying that 'Nev' made saves like that every week. 'He is the best keeper in the world', Peter Reid insisted.

Of all Howard Kendall's signings for Everton, getting Southall for only £150,000 from Bury must rank with the 'steals' of all time. Kendall however recognised that the former dustman was still raw, and bought his former goalkeeper Jim Arnold from Blackburn to fill the gap while Southall learned his trade.

Not everyone understood the reasoning, particularly when Southall, after 40 First Division games, found himself back in the Fourth Division on loan to Port Vale. Goodison inmates were aware of the potential however, Martin Hodge moving to Sheffield Wednesday because he saw that Southall presented too formidable opposition for the place. And since Southall finally claimed it, only injury has shifted him. In his absence, caused by torn ligaments, Everton saw the 1986 League and Cup double dashed from their hands by Liverpool, but his return in October helped see Everton to their second League Championship in three seasons. His agility, command of his penalty area and phenomenally sound pair of hands have inspired one of the most solid defences in the League.

A late developer, not reaching the First Division until the age of 25, he was soon rivalling Jack Kelsey as his country's finest goalkeeper ever.

AUSTRIA

Austrian football has a much more distinguished history than many young enthusiasts might imagine.

From 1902, when they defeated Hungary 5–0 in the first official international played outside Britain, until the mid-Fifties, they were a major Continental power. The 'Viennese' school had even become an accepted and distinctive style of soccer, based on the short-passing Scottish game but even more artistic and skilled. It was practised by a national team honed by Hugo Meisl, the father-figure of Austrian football, and his chief coach Jimmy Hogan, one of the many leading British coaches who had to go abroad to achieve recognition.

In 1932 the Austrians might have become the first foreign country to win away to England, 21 years before Hungary did so. They lost 4–3 in an epic game at Stamford Bridge, one of only two defeats suffered in 27 games between May 1931 and May 1934, when they took fourth place in the World Cup.

By the time Hitler's Nazis overran the country in 1938, this 'Wunderteam' was past its peak, but had achieved a famous 2–1 victory over England in Vienna on 6 May 1936.

A new generation of players with the same commitment to skill, like Ernst Happel, Ernst Ocwirk and Gerhard Hanappi formed another outstanding national team in the early Fifties. Not entered for the 1950 World Cup by the Austrian F.A., they became the first Continental side to win in Scotland but were just on the wane by the 1954 competition. After scoring five goals in seven minutes while defeating Switzerland, the host country, 7–5, they lost the semi-final to West Germany 6–1, missing the opportunity to confront Hungary in the final.

International success since then has been confined to reaching the second stage of the 1978 and 1982 World Cups. Keeping the best players at home has become almost impossible as average League gates fell to little more than 4,000, and national team manager Branko Elsner warned sadly as he resigned in 1987: 'We are third-rate. I can see no future for Austrian football.'

Strasser of Austria (dark shirt) challenges West Germany's Manny Kaltz during a 3-2 win in the 1978 World Cup finals.

THE CLUBS

F.K. Austria

Founded in 1911, having grown out of a club of obviously English origin, the Vienna Cricket and Football Club, F.K. won their first national title in 1924.

Rivals Rapid already had eight Championships under their belt by that time, but F.K. could claim by the mid-1930s to have become one of the leading clubs in Europe, twice winning the prestigious Mitropa Cup, the pre-war predecessor of today's European tournaments. Either side of the Second World War, they produced two of the country's greatest-ever players in Matthias Sindelar and then Ernst Ocwirk.

The team of the late Seventies overshadowed Rapid, and everyone else, winning the championship four times in a row (1978–81); and a new star, striker Toni Polster, helped produce another hat-trick (1984–86) before leaving for Torino. Even the best Austrian clubs continue to suffer financial worries, which in F.K.'s case have led to a bewildering number of name-changes after amalgamations and sponsorships. Now officially known as F.K. Austria Memphis, they were called Austria/W.A.C. when losing to Anderlecht in the 1978 European Cup-Winners' Cup finals.

Rapid Vienna

Twelve years older than their neighbours F.K., Rapid shared with them the distinction of supplying many of the players for the two 'Wunderteams' of the Thirties and Fifties.

They achieved an unusual feat by winning the German Cup in 1939 and the German Championship in 1941, after Hitler had annexed their country, and were prominent in the early days of the European Cup – once defeating Real Madrid with a hat-trick by Ernst Happel, only to lose the subsequent play-off.

Rapid have won the Austrian title in every decade except, strangely, the Seventies: all the odder since they had the formidable Hans Krankl to score goals for them. But Krankl was able to inspire a run to the European Cup-Winners' Cup final of 1985, in controversial circumstances. The tie against Celtic was replayed in Manchester after crowd trouble at Celtic Park, Rapid winning against the odds before eventually losing to Everton.

The Rapid side beaten by Everton in the 1985 European Cup-Winners' Cup final.

PLAYER PROFILES

GERHARD HANAPPI

Born in 1929 and first capped in 1948, the versatile Gerhard Hanappi's career should have encompassed no fewer than four World Cups, which would have provided a platform for his talents to be even more widely appreciated. Instead, because of the Austrian F.A.'s decision not to enter in 1950 and 1962, it was restricted to two; and a row with national team manager Karl Decker in the early Sixties left him four short of the magical 100 caps.

The majority of those were won at wing-half, where his ball-playing and passing abilities in the best Viennese mould served him well. Intelligent too (his part-time job was as an architect), he could fill in elsewhere, notably at left-back, as he did in marking Stanley Matthews with considerable success when picked for the Rest of Europe against England at Wembley in 1953.

Remarkably, he might have become a Football League player. In 1956 Sunderland offered Rapid £20,000 for him, but the Austrian F.A. blocked the deal. Wearside's loss was Vienna's gain and the Rapid ground is now named after him.

HANS KRANKL

The only Austrian player of the Seventies to achieve an international reputation, Hans Krankl proved irreplaceable as a goalscorer for the national team until the young Toni Polster began to make an impression.

Born 14 February 1953 in Vienna, Krankl joined Rapid at an early age and was loaned to Wacker, then recalled in a hurry after scoring eight times in one game. His 36 League goals in 1973–74 equalled the championship record set in 1951, and brought the first of many caps.

Gerhard Hanappi (bottom row, third from the left) with the 1954 Austrian World Cup Team.

Hans Krankl, a world star in the late Seventies.

A strong centre-forward, adept on the ground and particularly good in the air, he was at his best before and during the 1978 World Cup, when more than one critic named him in a 'World XI'. In April 1977, the Salzburg crowd saw him score six against Malta, and in the finals his two goals defeated the holders, West Germany.

Barcelona decided they must have him as replacement for Johan Cruyff, but apart from scoring the winner for them in the 1979 European Cup-Winners' Cup final, it was not a terribly happy partnership. He returned to Rapid, later managing another Viennese side, Wiener S.C.

ERNST OCWIRK

Three years older than Hanappi, Ocwirk was his senior partner in most of the outstanding games played by Austria's exciting post-war side. His eminence as the last of the great attacking centre-halves and, later, as wing-half or inside-forward, was recognised too by selection for the European XI in matches like the 4–4 draw against England in 1953 and in Belfast against Britain two years later (when Hanappi had to withdraw and a British team containing Danny Blanchflower, John Charles and Stanley Matthews was thrashed 4–1).

Ocwirk, whose principal club was F.K. Austria, was in fact a total footballer, capable of playing in any position, and liable to pop up in any during the course of a game. Winning the first of 62 caps in 1947, he played in the London Olympics the following year and the 1954 World Cup, scoring in the successful third-place match against Uruguay.

In 1956 he moved to Sampdoria in Italy, returning to F.K. in 1961 as player, and later coaching them and also Cologne. He died in 1980.

MATTHIAS SINDELAR

The death by suicide of Austria's most gifted pre-war player, Matthias Sindelar, at the age of only 36, is a grim reminder of how the country's 'Wunderteam' played its extravagant football in the shadow of Nazism. Believed to be partly Jewish, he gassed himself in his room in 1939.

Although Germany, having annexed his country, had used four Austrian players in the 1938 World Cup finals, Sindelar, fortunately for his self-respect, was by then considered too old. His prime had been around 1932, when he played and scored in the epic 4–3 defeat by England in London.

Nicknamed the 'Paper Man' because of his deceptively lightweight build, he relied even more than his team-mates on ball skills, balance and body-swerve. His club was F.K. Austria, whom he helped to two Austrian Championships and two Mitropa Cup wins.

BELGIUM

Fourth place at the 1986 World Cup indicated that Belgium might at last be emerging from the shadow of neighbours Holland, West Germany and France.

The period which began with Anderlecht contesting the 1970 Fairs Cup final against Arsenal has certainly been the most successful in their long football history. The Brussels club subsequently reached three successive finals of the European Cup-Winners' Cup (from 1976–78); Bruges and Standard Liège also reached European finals; while the national team took third place in the 1972 European Championships, went one better in 1980 and qualified for the World Cups of 1982 and 1986.

Success in Mexico was particularly sweet in that Belgium had at last eliminated the old enemy Holland to get there. They began quietly, improving with a thrilling extra-time victory over the U.S.S.R. by 4–3, then eliminating Spain on penalties before falling to Maradona's brilliance in the semi-final.

What might have been a much stronger challenge for the 1984 European Championship was ruined by a bribes scandal involving Standard Liège, which resulted in six players missing the finals. Although Tottenham's Nico Claesen was easily the top scorer in the 1988 qualifying group, a 2–0 defeat by Scotland prevented them getting through.

In earlier times, Belgium staged and won the 1920 Olympics (opponents Czechoslovakia walking off after having a player dismissed) and later were one of only four European teams to travel to Uruguay for the initial World Cup.

Nico Claesen, later to play for Tottenham, beats Maxime Bossis of France to score in the 1986 World Cup third-place match. France won 4-2 after extra-time.

THE CLUBS

Anderlecht

Founded in 1908, Anderlecht did not win the Belgian championship until 1947 but have more than made up for lost titles since then, establishing themselves as one of Europe's most respected clubs.

Between 1947 and 1968, a period which began under the guidance of Englishman Bill Gormlie, they won 14 national titles, including five in succession from 1964. Their dominance of domestic football was illustrated that same year when a substitution against Holland meant that all 11 players in the Belgian team on the field were from Anderlecht.

The prolific scoring feats of Jef Mermans, hero of the Fifties, were emulated later by Paul Van Himst, but Dutch players too have had their part to play – notably Jan Mulder, Arie Haan and Robbie Rensenbrink, who scored two goals in each of the winning European Cup-Winners' Cup finals in 1976 and 1978. U.E.F.A. Cup winners under Van Himst in 1983, they lost the following year's final to Spurs.

Standard Liège

Like Anderlecht, Standard came to prominence late, playing second fiddle in their own city for several decades to F.C. Liège, who were the first Belgian champions in 1896. By the late Fifties, however, they were spending boldly on foreign players and coaches, with considerable success.

Whereas Anderlecht were often outclassed in the early European Cups (once losing 10–0 in Manchester to Matt Busby's babes), Standard enjoyed good runs, reaching the quarter-final in 1958 and the semi-final four years later, after Irishman Johnny Crossan helped destroy Rangers in Liège.

A European Cup-Winners' Cup semi-final appearance in 1967 was followed by a hat-trick of Belgian titles and in 1982 a place in the Cup-Winners' Cup final against Barcelona. That was unfortunately scheduled to be played on the Spaniards' own ground, where Standard lost 2–1, playing, though we did not know it at the time, with troubled consciences.

They had bribed Waterschei to lose a critical Belgian championship match, which gave Standard the title. The club's president, coach and captain Eric Gerets were among those banned when the scandal broke two years later.

Anderlecht's Frankie Vercauteren (white shirt) on the attack against Yugoslavia in the 1984 European Championship.

PLAYER PROFILES

JAN CEULEMANS

Tall, blond and elegant, Jan Ceulemans spanned the successful Belgian teams of 1980 and 1986, though his role changed somewhat in between times.

An out-and-out striker early in his career with Lierse, he remained a prolific goal scorer after joining Bruges in 1978, claiming 29 as they won the 1980 League title. It was his goal which frustrated England in the opening game of the European Championship finals, though his subdued performance in the final was one of the reasons why Belgium did not push West Germany even harder.

In later seasons he moved deeper, exerting a greater influence on the whole of the match while still capable of coming forward to score. As captain in 1986 he was largely responsible for holding a young side together, especially after his great friend and former Lierse team-mate Erwin Vandenberg was injured early on. Ceulemans led by example and was able to shepherd the team through to an unexpected fourth place.

Right: *The Italians wanted Vincenzo Scifo – but Belgium capped him first.*

Below: *Jan Ceulemans in full stride at the 1986 World Cup finals.*

VINCENZO SCIFO

Born in a Belgian mining town, the son of Sicilian parents, Vincenzo Scifo's principal footballing ambitions for many years were to play for Italy and a top Italian club.

At the age of 18, already an established Anderlecht midfielder, it was clear that he had the ability to do both. But as the Italians hesitated, Anderlecht and Belgium's desperate

Paul Van Himst eludes Arnold Muhren's tackle in the 1973 meeting of old enemies Belgium and Holland.

desire to keep him won the day, and in between the two legs of the U.E.F.A. Cup final against Tottenham in 1984 he declared that he would sign a new contract with the Brussels club and seek Belgian citizenship. Belgium duly thrust him straight into the European Championship finals.

The lira eventually talked loud enough, however, when in 1987 Inter took him to Milan for around £1.5 million. Dark, Italianate looks as well as the name hint at his origins: so, in a sense, does his style – artistic but with a scorer's instinct which brought him literally hundreds of goals as a junior at La Louvière.

PAUL VAN HIMST

Succeeding Jef Mermans as the goalscoring hero of Anderlecht and Belgium, Paul Van Himst went on to become his country's most-capped player (with 81) and, many would say, its most distinguished. He achieved success as a manager too, winning the 1983 U.E.F.A. Cup with Anderlecht, who were runners-up the following season.

Capable of playing at centre-forward or inside-left, he was both skilful and powerful, forming a particularly telling partnership with bespectacled Anderlecht team-mate Jef Jurion. Van Himst came into the national team right at the start of the Sixties, when it was at a low ebb – losing all four qualifying games for the 1962 World Cup despite his goals.

Belgium improved thereafter, while Anderlecht went on to dominate domestic football. Van Himst left the club amid some controversy in 1975 for Racing White, just before the hat-trick of European Cup-Winners' Cup finals. When he returned in 1982, it was as manager, charged with renewing the club's reputation as an exciting, attacking side. He did so to good effect before falling victim to a run of inconsistent results late in 1985, when Arie Haan replaced him.

WILFRED VAN MOER

It was an apt comment on the standard of the 1980 European Championship finals that one of the few stars should be a balding little 35-year-old who had made his international debut 14 years earlier. Wilfred Van Moer was first capped in 1966 while with Antwerp. By the 1970 World Cup, now playmaker for Belgian champions Standard Liège, he was a vital cog in his country's midfield and in Mexico was one of the few Belgians to distinguish himself.

A broken leg in 1972 might have prematurely ended his career, but he battled back with Beringen, an unfashionable provincial team generally to be found in the bottom six of the Belgian League.

Guy Thys, the national team manager, pulled a brilliant stroke in recalling him during the 1979–80 season, using him sparingly but to splendid effect in Italy, after which he reached 50 international caps and moved back to the more successful Beveren, the club with whom he had begun as a nine-year-old.

CZECHOSLOVAKIA

Even before the state of Czechoslovakia had been created, the Bohemian city of Prague was established as a football capital of central Europe.

Representative matches between Prague and Vienna began in 1896, a Bohemia F.A. was set up in 1901 and joined the fledgling F.I.F.A. five years later. But it was not until after the First World War, when the map of Europe was redrawn, that the formal history of Czechoslovak football begins.

Two great professional clubs, Sparta and Slavia, established international reputations in the Mitropa Cup. On top of that, Czechoslovakia reached the 1934 World Cup final, led hosts Italy with nine minutes to go but eventually lost 2–1 in extra time. The goalkeeper-captain, Frantisek Planicka, and the left-wing partners Oldrich Nejedly and Antonin Puc were among the greatest players of their day.

The strength of Czechoslovak football had been its ability to learn and adopt new ideas. After the Second World War, however, political demands restricted international contact and progress. Football was reorganised under state Communist auspices and the old traditions were overturned. Sparta and Slavia even suffered the temporary indignities of being forced to change their names to Spartak and Dynamo to survive.

As in all the Eastern bloc countries, the army sports section became a focus for football achievement. In Czechoslovakia that meant Dukla Prague, and it was around the nucleus of Dukla's fine side of the early 1960s that Czechoslovakia built the national team which finished runners-up to Brazil in the 1962 World Cup.

There have been occasional flourishes since then. In 1969 Slovan Bratislava won the Cup-Winners' Cup, in 1976 Czechoslovakia won the European Championship and in 1980 they collected the Olympic title in Moscow. But the great days appear to have gone forever.

Members of the Czech team, after beating the West Germans in a penalty shoot out, triumphantly lift the European Championship cup in 1976.

THE CLUBS

Dukla Prague

Dukla have been the dominant club of the post-war era in Czechoslovakia although they went through two name changes, from A.T.K. to U.D.A. before taking the present title in 1956.

Simultaneously they also acquired three of the country's greatest-ever players, left-back Ladislav Novak and wing-halves Svatopluk Pluskal and Josef Masopust. Dukla's privileged position as the army club meant they could commandeer virtually any player they wanted.

The most promising, however, never fulfilled his potential: Rudi Kucera was forced into premature retirement after being concussed in a European Cup tie against Poland's Gornik.

Political changes later stripped Dukla of much of their influence. Their best performance in the European Cup – reaching the semi-finals in 1967 – marked the end of an era. Dukla produced more fine players such as defender Jan Fiala, centre-forward Zdenek Nehoda (a record 90 caps) and winger Ladislav Vizek, but by then power had swung back to the traditional old clubs, Sparta and Bohemians. They did, however, win the League for the 11th time in 1982 and the national Cup for a record seventh time in 1985.

Sparta Prague

Sparta are the most popular club in Czechoslovakia, the most successful and one of the two oldest (after Slavia). Founded as King's Vineyard in 1893, they took the Sparta title a year later. In the 1920s Sparta led the professional revolution and were one of the giants of the Mitropa Cup. Sparta won the inaugural event in 1927, beating Rapid Vienna in the final. They won again in 1935, beating Ferencvaros of Hungary, and were runners-up in 1936.

After the war and the reorganisation of Czech sport, attempts were made to destroy Sparta's identity. But though the club were forced to change their name to Spartak Sokolovo, the supporters never cheered for anyone but Sparta. Their loyalty was rewarded when Sparta were allowed to reclaim their old name in 1965; that same year they won their first League title in more than a decade. In the 1980s, under veteran coach Vaclav Jezek, Sparta were once again the country's top club.

Dukla Prague's Novak clears on the line from Benfica's Coluna, in a European Cup quarter final. Masopust is wearing the No. 6 shirt.

PLAYER PROFILES

JOZEF CHOVANEC

Few players have made their international debuts in such inauspicious circumstances as Jozef Chovanec – for Czechoslovakia as a substitute in a 5–1 thrashing by West Germany in Prague in April 1985. Chovanec has played all his senior career with Sparta, where his career has flourished under the guidance of veteran coach Vaclav Jezek. Chovanec was a key figure in Sparta's 1984 league-and-cup-double season and was voted Footballer of the Year in 1986. Formerly an under-21 international, Chovanec was unlucky to emerge at a time when Czechoslovak football was going through a bad time – the national team failing to qualify for the finals of the 1984 and 1988 European Championships as well as missing out on the 1986 World Cup in Mexico. A forceful player, able to undertake an intelligent covering role as sweeper, or push forward out of midfield – Chovanec was at his best in Sparta's 1983–84 U.E.F.A. Cup campaign, when they beat Real Madrid, Widzew Lodz and Watford before losing to Hajduk Split in the quarter-finals.

An international career out of adversity – Josef Chovanec pictured against Wales in 1987.

Above: *Antonin Panenka, whose penalty-kick made Czechoslovakia European champions in 1976.*

Left: *Josef Masopust, the only Czech to be voted European Footballer of the Year.*

JOSEF MASOPUST

Josef Masopust, who played 63 times for Czechoslovakia in the 1950s and 1960s, was one of central European football's all-time greats. Born in the provincial town of Most on 9 February 1931, Masopust began with Union Teplice as a centre-forward and was conscripted for newly-organised Dukla in the mid-1950s by the famous coach Karel Kolsky. Masopust made his debut for Czechoslovakia in 1954 and was crowned European Footballer of the Year in 1962. He earned the award thanks to his superb form in the World Cup that year in Chile, when Masopust not only inspired the Czechs' progress to the final but scored the opening goal against Brazil (one of 11 he scored for his country). Masopust was nominally a left-half but took such a roving commission that he was more of a throwback to the old-fashioned attacking centre-halves. He played for the Rest of the World against England at Wembley in 1963 and, after retiring, became manager of the Czechoslovak national team from 1984 until after the European Championship qualifiers in 1987.

ANTONIN PANENKA

Antonin Panenka will always be remembered for one moment's action: the decisive spot-kick in the penalty shoot-out at the end of the 1976 European Championship final against West Germany in Belgrade. Uli Hoeness had just missed for the Germans and Panenka placed his penalty coolly beyond Sepp Maier to turn Czechoslovakia into European champions. Apart from his deadly ability with penalties and free kicks, Panenka was also an outstanding midfield general.

He played all his 'home' football with Bohemians of Prague then joined Rapid Vienna in the spring of 1981, shortly after having been voted Czechoslovak Footballer of the Year. At 33 Panenka was recalled for the Czechs' World Cup effort in Spain. He played 62 times for his country.

FRANTISEK PLANICKA

The 1934 World Cup final remains unique because both captains were goalkeepers: Giampiero Combi for Italy, Frantisek Planicka for Czechoslovakia. Planicka, born in Prague on 2 June 1904, began with local clubs Slovan and Bubenec. The family home was a stone's throw from the Sparta stadium and Planicka went on trial there. Sparta never gave him a chance and so he offered his services to their great rivals, Slavia. That was in 1923. Three years later he was making his international debut against Italy in Turin.

The Czechs were beaten 2–1 by Italy in the 1934 World Cup final, but Planicka was still first-choice keeper in 1938 in France. In the quarter-finals against Brazil Planicka broke an arm three minutes from the end of his 76th international. Somehow he held out until extra-time finished with the score at 1–1. But without him in the replay, the Czechs lost 2–1.

FRANCE

For four years between 1982 and 1986, France once again had a football team to match its rugby XV for both style and success. But depressingly quickly, stars like Michel Platini, Alain Giresse and Jean Tigana turned their backs on international football and France were only a moderate side once again.

There had been one golden period in earlier years. That began in the mid-Fifties when Albert Batteux coached Reims to two European Cup finals, including the thrilling first one against Real Madrid. Raymond Kopa, the star of the team, linked superbly with Just Fontaine to inspire third place in the 1958 World Cup, but decline was also swift. Four years later France did not even qualify for the finals, losing a play-off to Bulgaria.

And although Batteux, again, prompted St Etienne's brief flourish in the mid-Seventies, the record of French clubs in Europe is appalling considering the outstanding record of its administrators, so prominent in the introduction of F.I.F.A., U.E.F.A., the World Cup, European Championship and European Cup.

Disappointment in the 1966 World Cup finals, when France were unexpectedly eliminated instead of going through with England, was followed by failure to qualify at all in the next two competitions. Not until 1978 was there any real encouragement, in unlucky defeats by Italy and Argentina.

Platini was now established in midfield, playing behind Bernard Lacombe (who scored after barely 30 seconds against Italy) Dominique Rocheteau and Didier Six (later and briefly to join Aston Villa).

The 1982 team lost its opening game to England in the heat of Bilbao but, unlike Ron Greenwood's team, improved thereafter with every game, strolling through the rest of the group and the second stage to confront West Germany in a memorable semi-final which was lost on penalties.

Four years later, as European champions, they eliminated holders Italy, then Brazil on penalties in the best match of the tournament, only to fall to the Germans at the penultimate stage again. The squad quickly disintegrated and in subsequent European Championship qualifiers, France won just one of eight group matches.

The style of a master. Michel Platini bends in a cross with the outside of his right foot as France attack in the 1986 World Cup semi-final.

THE CLUBS

Jean Tigana of Bordeaux and France slips deftly away from two Spaniards in the 1984 European Championship final.

Bordeaux

A lack of outstanding club sides, above all in the capital Paris, has not helped popularise domestic football down the years in France.

Long-overdue success for Bordeaux was therefore all the more welcome in the 1980s, especially since it sprung from a bold policy of buying exciting players.

The 'Girondins' celebrated their centenary in 1981 with only one Championship win (1950) and only one Cup win (1941) to their name. But bringing in players like Dieter Müller and Caspar Memering from Germany, then Fernando Chalana from Portugal (for £1.5 million) plus Patrick Battiston, Bernard Lacombe and Jean Tigana paid off.

They took the title in 1984, retained it in 1985, won the French Cup in 1986 and did the double in 1987. Only European success remained elusive.

St. Etienne

Not even the great Reims side of the Fifties dominated French football as comprehensively as St. Etienne ten years later. Champions eight times between 1964 and 1976, they also received the acclaim of the whole Continent for their results in the European Cup.

Both teams were coached by the same extraordinary man – Albert Batteux, whose departure from Reims in 1963 led to their sad decline. He took St. Etienne to four of their titles in a row (1967–70) before making way for the club's former international centre-forward Robert Herbin, whose team narrowly lost a European Cup semi-final in 1975 and the final in 1976, both to Bayern Munich.

Dominique Rocheteau and the Revelli brothers, Hervé and Patrick, are names from that side remembered with particular affection. Like Reims, however, the fall was swift and painful, encompassing an illegal payments scandal as well as relegation to the Second Division.

St Etienne, 'the Greens', attack against Bayern in their 1976 European Cup final in Glasgow.

A.S. Monaco

Previously better known for its hedonistic pleasures and its motor racing grand prix, the independent state of Monaco finally made an impression on football when its principal club followed their French League title in 1988 with a good run to the European Cup quarter-final.

The club, which was still amateur until 1948, had won previous Championships in 1961, 1963, 1978 and 1982 without achieving anything on a wider stage. But manager Arsène Wenger, given the backing of Prince Rainier III to buy players like Glenn Hoddle, Mark Hateley and Patrick Battiston, was able to regain the title in his first season with what was clearly Monaco's most formidable team yet.

Royal patronage makes up for a lack of income from spectators. Although European ties fill the magnificent Stade Louis II, average gates were for many years the lowest in the French League.

A.S. Monaco surrendered their French championship to Marseille in 1988–9.

PLAYER PROFILES

JUST FONTAINE

Born in 1933 in Morocco of a Spanish mother and French father, Just Fontaine became France's leading international goalscorer, his total of 30 in only 21 games unsurpassed until Michel Platini reached his peak in 1984. Fontaine's other record, of 13 goals in the 1958 World Cup finals, has been approached only by Gerd Müller's ten in 1970 and could stand for ever.

What qualities brought all these goals? Pace, control and power, principally. He once said of himself: 'I can hit the ball hard with both legs and my head,' adding ruefully, 'but I wish I had more class, like Kopa.'

'I can hit the ball hard, with both legs.' Just Fontaine (left) in action for Reims against Lens in 1958.

Fontaine and Raymond Kopa became club-mates at Reims in 1960, though both were past their best and prone to injury. First capped in 1956 when with Nice, then dropped for a year, Fontaine went to the 1958 finals only as a reserve. An ankle injury to the Reims forward René Bliard proved a fortuitous one for Fontaine and French football.

RAYMOND KOPA

Raymond Kopa was a contemporary, colleague and friend of Just Fontaine, for whom he made many of the goals which took France to third place in 1958. Although playing as a deep-lying centre-forward in the finals, he also scored three himself, out of a total of 18 in his 45 international appearances from 1952–63.

Two years older than Fontaine, he was born Raymond Kopazewski, son of a Polish miner who worked in northern France. After two years with Angers, Kopa became the leading light of a bright Reims side which almost turned the first European Cup final in Paris into a 'home' victory: Real Madrid scraped home 4–3 but had already agreed to sign Kopa, who played outside-right for them over the next three seasons.

Returning to Reims in 1959, he inspired them to two more Championships. Later he took up the cause of freedom of contract for players with the ringing declaration 'Les joueurs professionels sont les ésclaves' (professional footballers are slaves).

MICHEL PLATINI

Michel Platini was the world's most outstanding player until eclipsed by Diego Maradona at the 1986 World Cup, where a detailed comparison should have been possible between them in the final. Sadly, France went out, once again, to West Germany in the semi-final, and at the end of the following season Platini retired, having played his last international against Iceland in April, aged 32.

For all his enormous range of skills, Platini's trademark was the direct free-kick from anything up to 30 yards out, swerved, curled or dipped past a helpless wall of defenders and a despairing goalkeeper. Such shots helped him to a staggering total of goals for a midfielder.

Beginning as a centre-forward, he totalled more than 150 in 262 French League games for little-known Nancy (1972–78) and St. Etienne (1978–82), then top-scored regularly for Juventus in the ruthless Italian League, helping them to the national Cup, European Cup-Winners' Cup and the 1985 European Cup. At the 1984 European Championships he was more than a cut above the rest, scoring in every match before holding up the trophy as French captain.

Michel Platini, one of the great European soccer players of recent years.

HOLLAND

The sudden emergence of an outstandingly talented crop of youngsters in the early 1970s turned Holland into Europe's most exciting team of the decade. It was nevertheless a decade which finished without that team winning a major trophy, something which had to be left to their two dominant club sides, Ajax (Amsterdam) and Feyenoord (Rotterdam).

The youngsters first made an impression on the outside world as Ajax reached the 1969 European Cup final, although English supporters had had a foretaste two years earlier when they had dumped Bill Shankly's Liverpool out of the European Cup, winning 5–1 in Amsterdam after leading 4–0 at half-time.

Piet Keizer, their outside-left, dates the rise of Dutch football from a match in the 1969 European Cup campaign, when 40,000 Ajax fans travelled to Paris and willed their team to victory in a play-off against Benfica.

That emphasised the growing enthusiasm for the Dutch game, which had only just embraced professionalism. The subsequent successes in the competition of Feyenoord (1970) and Ajax (1971, 1972 and 1973) underlined its abilities, which were passed on to the national team. They started to benefit in the 1971–72 season, beginning a run of only two defeats in 24 games – the second of which came in the World Cup final.

In both 1974 and 1978 Holland, playing their 'total' football, were unquestionably the most gifted team at the finals. It was their misfortune to come up against the host country on each occasion, though they might easily have won both competitions, and the 1976 European Championship as well.

Failure to qualify for the finals of 1982 and 1986 (both caused by defeats against eternal rivals Belgium) meant a barren period, from which the new team of Ruud Gullit and Marco Van Basten emerged to revive Dutch spirits and expectations.

Cruyff in control as usual, this time against a bemused Uruguay defence in 1974.

THE CLUBS

Ajax
Englishmen did at least some of the groundwork which led to Ajax Amsterdam becoming established as one of Europe's foremost clubs.

Jack Reynolds, one of many British coaches working in Holland, led them to five Dutch Championships between 1931 and 1939; later Vic Buckingham got a promising batch of young players, including Johan Cruyff, on to the staff before making way for the iron disciplinarian Rinus Michels.

That was in 1964 and by 1968 Michels' team had a hat-trick of championships and a growing European reputation. Cruyff, Piet Keizer, Wim Suurbier and Barry Hulshoff all played in four European finals, following the 1969 defeat by A.C. Milan with three successive wins from 1971–73.

Statistically at least a peak was reached in 1972 when, with Johan Neeskens and Rudi Krol now equally valuable contributors, the team added the World Clubs' Cup and the first European Super Cup, as well as another Dutch League title. By that time, Rumanian Stefan Kovacs had replaced Michels, who left for Barcelona. When Cruyff and Neeskens followed him, Ajax were reduced to mere mortals again.

Feyenoord
Until the comparatively recent success of P.S.V. Dutch football was dominated by Ajax and the leading Rotterdam club Feyenoord.

While naturally envious of their rivals' European Cup hat-trick in the Seventies, Feyenoord could at least claim to have got their hands on the trophy first, thanks to Ove Kindvall's extra-time goal in the 1970 final against Celtic. For good measure they beat Estudiantes of Argentina to become unofficial World Club champions.

Like Ajax, they had a coach of international renown in Ernst Happel (who would later succeed Michels as Dutch team manager). Wim Van Hanegem was the leading light of his side in 1974 which overcame Spurs and their rioting supporters to win the U.E.F.A. Cup, but the Dutch Championship that season was their last until the sensational signing of Cruyff, who led them to a League and Cup double in 1984.

Marco Van Basten's header wins Ajax the 1987 European Cup-Winners' Cup against Loko Leipzig.

P.S.V. Eindhoven

The Philips electrical company's enormous financial muscle has helped to establish P.S.V. at the highest levels of the game.

In the early seventies, when both Ajax and Feyenoord won the World Clubs' Cup, P.S.V. were just another Dutch provincial team: coach Kees Rijvers began to change that as his side, including the twins Rene and Willy Van der Kerkhof, won the Championship in 1975, 1976 and 1978 as well as the U.E.F.A. Cup.

Shrewd signings, as much as Philips' money, laid the foundations for a stunning run of success in the Eighties. Ruud Gullit and Ronald Koeman, snatched cheaply from Feyenoord and Ajax (and later sold for millions to Milan and Barcelona), stood at the heart of the team which won the League again in 1986 and 1987 and then, with Gullit gone to Milan, completed a hat-trick adding the 1988 European Cup, albeit on penalties against Benfica.

Ruud Gullit: a modern romance with football.

PLAYER PROFILES

JOHAN CRUYFF

Johan Cruyff, managed Barcelona when they won the 1988–9 European Cup-Winners Cup.

For all Franz Beckenbauer's technique, for all Gerd Müller's lethal finishing, it was surely Johan Cruyff who took over from Pele as the world's greatest player.

Lean, long-striding and magnificently athletic, he could play as principal striker, drop deep to confuse his markers or move to either wing with devastating effect: a favourite trick out on the left wing was to drag the ball behind him with his right foot, turn through 180 degrees and accelerate away outside a bemused defender.

An outspoken nature often led him into trouble, like the sending off in only his second international, which, together with a premature retirement from the national team before the 1978 World Cup restricted him to 48 caps (producing 33 goals).

European Footballer of the Year in 1971, 1973, and 1974, he became the world's most expensive player when Barcelona paid Ajax £922,000 for him. In 1979 he came out of a brief retirement to play in north America, returning to inspire Ajax and then, astonishingly, their enemies Feyenoord, to further championships. He took over as Ajax coach in 1985, resigning in a huff two years later.

RUUD GULLIT

Ruud Gullit, voted World Footballer of the Year in 1987, was the player Ajax missed. Although born in Amsterdam, he elected to begin his career with Haarlem, serving them for four years before joining Feyenoord as a fully-fledged international in 1982. In 1983–84 he was inspired, like everyone else, by the presence of Johan Cruyff and won a championship medal, adding two more in successive seasons after moving to P.S.V. Eindhoven.

His performances there, and with the re-emerging Dutch side, attracted the attention of the world's biggest clubs and in the summer of 1987 A.C. Milan paid an amazing £5.5 million for him.

They got not just an outstanding all-round footballer, now settled in midfield, though he can play as sweeper, but a colourful personality of the kind that Italian fans love: a disco-dancing anti-apartheid campaigner complete with Rastafarian hairstyle, the most modern of football's moderns.

JOHAN NEESKENS

Midfield foil to Cruyff with Ajax, Barcelona and Holland for many years, Johan Neeskens had to compensate for the master's absence from the 1978 World Cup, where he himself became the team's main inspiration.

More powerful than Cruyff, for whom he would so often win the ball, Neeskens was an even better example of the dynamic modern footballer – a more gifted Bryan Robson, perhaps.

It was in fact at right-back that he played the first of his three successive European Cup finals, though he had been in his more normal midfield position for the quarter-final demolition of Celtic that season, and would be so again as Arsenal were beaten at Highbury 12 months later en route to victory in the final over Inter.

After going so close to a World Cup winners medal in 1974, when he coolly despatched a first-minute penalty, Neeskens followed Cruyff to Barcelona and, later, to the U.S.A.

Johan Neeskens – often the ball-winner for Cruyff.

HUNGARY

Hungary will always be first and foremost the home of the Magical Magyars of Ferenc Puskas in the early 1950s – one of the greatest teams of all time.

Yet that team was the product of the firmest of foundations. Football had been brought to Hungary by English students in the 1870s and before the turn of the century three of the most powerful domestic clubs – then and now – had been formed in M.T.K., Ferencvaros and Ujpest. In 1916 the legendary coach Jimmy Hogan arrived at M.T.K., discovered the first great Hungarian individual footballer in Gyorgy Orth, and prepared Hungarian football for the advance of professionalism in the 1920s and 1930s.

It was an era climaxed in 1938 by Hungary's appearance in the World Cup final in Paris with a team inspired by the academic centre-forward or centre-half Gyorgy Sarosi. Hungary lost 4–2 to Italy – but that was as nothing compared with the upset in 1954 when Hungary lost the World Cup final again, this time by 3–2 to West Germany in Berne, Switzerland.

For four years the team built around goalkeeper Gyula Grosics, right-half Jozsef Bozsik and the inside-forward trio of Sandor Kocsis, Nandor Hidegkuti and Ferenc Puskas had reigned supreme in Europe. They had won the 1952 Olympic title and ended England's record of invincibility against Continental opposition with a stunning 6–3 triumph at Wembley.

But tragedy was close at hand. Defeat in the World Cup, in the one match they had to win, was shortly followed by the break-up of the team in the wake of the Hungarian Revolution of 1956. That peak has not been equalled since. Goalkeeping blunders halted Hungary at the quarter-finals stage of the 1966 World Cup after a famous victory over Brazil at Goodison. Consolation has been a double Olympic success and the emergence of a steady stream of skilled forwards, from Florian Albert via Tibor Nyilasi to Lajos Detari.

The Hungarians at Wembley, 1953. Left to right: Puskas, Grosics, Lorant, Hidegkuti, Buzansky, Lantos, Zakarias, Czibor, Bozsik, Budai, Kocsis.

No problem. Nandor Hidegkuti rounds the goalkeeper to score again for Hungary.

THE CLUBS

Honved

Honved were far and away the most successful of the army clubs set up throughout Eastern Europe in the post-war political upheaval.

The club was created on the back of the traditional old Kispest club, taking over their players – who happened to include one Ferenc Puskas – and using the National Service excuse to take a string of young talents (such as Ferencvaros' Sandor Kocsis and Zoltan Czibor) from elsewhere. Honved formed the nucleus of the great Hungarian national team of the early 1950s. But they were in western Europe for a European Cup tie against Bilbao when the Hungarian Revolution broke out. Puskas, Kocsis, Czibor and several other players stayed in the west and it was almost a quarter of a century before Honved regained their leadership of the Hungarian game. Honved have appeared a dozen times in Europe, but without ever threatening a return to the glory days when they were Europe's premier club and much in demand for exhibition games – such as the famous Molineux friendly which they lost 3–2 against Wolves.

Ferencvaros

Ferencvaros, or Fradi, or simply the 'green-and-whites', remain Hungary's leading club despite all the fame achieved by Honved and even though they have not won either Championship or Cup since 1981. Founded in 1899, the Ferencvarosi Torna Club have outlasted and outrun all their original contemporaries. They have always attracted the best players: from Imre Schlosser in the early days to the great Gyorgy Sarosi in the 1930s and Florian Albert in the 1960s.

In the 1920s and 1930s Ferencvaros twice won the prestigious Mitropa Cup and supplied four members of the Hungarian national team beaten by Italy in the 1938 World Cup final. Ferencvaros also provided the backbone for the Hungarian team which reached the quarter-finals of the 1962 and 1966 World Cups. It was their outside left, Mate Fenyvesi, who scored the goal with which Ferencvaros beat Juventus in the 1965 Fairs' Cup final – thus becoming the only Hungarian club to lift a European trophy.

Sandor Kocsis of Honved, leading scorer with 11 in the 1954 World Cup finals.

The Honved team lines up for their 1954 friendly against Wolves at Molineux. The Hungarian national side had defeated England in the famous match at Wembley the previous year, but Wolves narrowly won a thriller 3–2 between the countries' champions of the 1953–4 seasons.

PLAYER PROFILES

FLORIAN ALBERT

Florian Albert is the only Hungarian to have been voted European Footballer of the Year. Albert, born on 15 September 1941, was the first star to emerge in the post-Puskas generation when Hungary were rebuilding after the upheavals of the revolution. He made his international debut when still only 17, in a 3–2 win over Sweden in Budapest in June 1959 – a few days after taking his last school examinations.

Albert was three times top league scorer, was Hungary's centre-forward in the 1962 and 1966 World Cups and played his most memorable match in the 3–1 victory over Brazil at Goodison Park in the 1966 finals. Albert played all his club career for Ferencvaros, with whom he won four championship medals. He was so clearly head and shoulders above the other players of his era that he attracted criticism for his influence off the pitch with club and country. In 1969 he suffered a serious knee injury in an international against Denmark and was never the same player again. Altogether, he played 74 games for Hungary.

LAJOS DETARI

Lajos Detari made his debut for Hungary against Switzerland in August, 1984 at the age of 21. He cost an East European record fee of £1.2 million when Eintract Frankfurt of West Germany signed him from Honved in the summer of 1987. Detari had convinced Frankfurt he was the player to revive their fortunes when he scored the first goal and created the other two in a 3–0 win over Brazil in Budapest in March 1986. He credits wife Andrea with his success; she was the daughter of Honved coach Imre Komora and it was to impress his prospective father-in-law that Detari cut out the high living and concentrated on making the most of his footballing ability.

He was the top league scorer in Hungary in both 1985, with 18 goals, and in 1986, with 27, which included a penalty hat-trick in a 5–5 draw between Honved and M.T.K. Budapest. Detari was voted Hungarian Footballer of the Year in 1985 and played for the Rest of the World in the Football League centenary in 1987.

Best of the new breed of Hungarians – Lajos Detari.

LADISLAV KUBALA

Ladislav Kubala is the only man to have played acknowledged full internationals for three countries – three for Hungary, seven for Czechoslovakia and 19 for Spain.

Kubala was born in Budapest of Czech parents on 10 June 1927. He made his First Division debut in Hungary with Ganz, progressed to Ferencvaros and was then lured to play in Czechoslovakia for Bratislava. He returned in 1947 to Vasas on the understanding that after a year they would help him to a club in Italy. The promise was forgotten and so Kubala smuggled his family out of Hungary. Italian clubs were afraid of signing him because of possible sanctions through F.I.F.A., and so he joined Barcelona and inspired them to one triumph after another in the early 1950s. Kubala scored twice for the Rest of Europe against England at Wembley in 1953 and did not retire until after Barcelona's 1961 European Cup final defeat by Benfica. Later he was manager of Spain for 11 years.

Well past his peak, but still a threat, Puskas at the 1962 World Cup, when he played for Spain.

Ladislav Kubala, capped by three countries. Plenty of others would have liked him too.

FERENC PUSKAS

Ferenc Puskas was one of the very greatest footballers of all time. Born on 2 April 1927 Puskas was a boy wonder when his Budapest club, Kispest, were converted into the army team, Honved. As captain of Honved and Hungary, Puskas toured the world – scoring hundreds of goals with his thunderbolt left foot and winning every match . . . except the one which mattered most, the 1954 World Cup final. Puskas was abroad with Honved when the Hungarian Revolution broke out. Puskas wanted to sign for an Italian club but they thought him too old. Real Madrid did not. They paid the Galloping Major a £10,000 signing-on fee in 1958 and were rewarded when his partnership with Alfredo Di Stefano reached a grand climax in the 7–3 European Cup final beating of Eintract Frankfurt in 1960. Puskas scored a hat-trick against Benfica in the 1962 final as well – though Madrid lost – and played for Spain a few weeks later at the World Cup finals in Chile. He won 84 caps for Hungary and three for Spain. Puskas retired in 1966 and in 1971 took Greek champions Panathinaikos to the European Cup final.

ITALY

Victory in the 1982 World Cup final enabled Italy to match Brazil's record of three wins in football's principal competition. Yet despite the countries' common passion for the game, their approach to it could hardly be more different.

While Brazil, though occasionally flirting with European power-football, remain in love with flair, Italy have only recently looked like throwing off the shackles of the ultra-defensive 'catenaccio' which became the rage in the 1960s.

Long before that they had established themselves as perhaps the most formidable European nation – with much more positive methods. During the 1930s, for instance, under Vittorio Pozzo, they won the World Cup twice, the Olympic football tournament once and beat the Austrian 'Wunderteam' more times than they lost.

A less successful period after the Second World War led to prolonged agonising over whether expensive foreign players should be encouraged or banned. Humiliating defeat by North Korea in the 1966 World Cup was a low point which did nothing to weaken the hold of the defensive bias that Helenio Herrera had first introduced at Inter, deadly dull winners of the 1964 and 1965 European Cups.

Enzo Bearzot, national team manager from the mid-Seventies, also found it difficult to move his country's football on to a more positive plane, though he was able to win the World Cup on the back of Paolo Rossi's goals after the team had begun, typically, with three low-scoring draws.

The tradition of success in European club competition started by Fiorentina and A.C. Milan has continued, however, with Inter, Juventus and Roma all having won at least one competition, and all prepared to pay huge fees to secure the best players in the world.

Champions again. Italy celebrate after beating West Germany in the 1982 World Cup final.

THE CLUBS

Inter and A.C. Milan

One of the great big-city rivalries in world football is that between A.C. Milan and Inter. It is all the keener because Inter began in 1908 as a breakaway group from the heavily-anglicised Milan, originally known as the 'Milan Cricket and Football Club'.

Left: *The great Milan rivals, Inter and AC., meet in October 1984. Liam Brady is on the ball for Inter.*

Below: *Michael Laudrup of Juventus takes evasive action as Barcelona's José Alexanco challenges in the 1986 European Cup quarter-final. Holders Juventus lost on aggregate.*

It was A.C. Milan who led the way into Europe, winning three Italian titles in the 1950s, pushing Real Madrid hard in the 1959 European Cup final and winning it in 1963. That same year Inter took the national Championship and followed up by relieving Milan of the European Cup, then retaining it in 1965.

Inter's inspiration was the controversial coach Helenio Herrera whose 'catenaccio' was eventually cracked by Celtic and Ajax in later European finals. From 1971 Inter won only one title in 17 seasons despite investing heavily in players like Liam Brady, Karl-Heinz Rummenigge, Daniel Passarella and Enzo Scifo.

After Napoli had paid a world record fee for Diego Maradona and won the 1987 Championship, Milan spent even more on Ruud Gullit to take the 1988 title.

Juventus

For many years the Turin clubs, Juventus and Torino, dominated Italian football. While Torino have never recovered from the air disaster of 1949 which wiped out their whole squad of 13 internationals, 'Juve' have remained the most regular Championship winners.

The club's most tantalising objective was the European Cup. They failed to win it until 1985, when the triumph over Liverpool was of course ruined by the death of more than 30 of their supporters. It was understandably overlooked at the time that the team of Michel Platini and Paolo Rossi had completed a notable double, having won the Cup-Winners' Cup the previous season: they added the World Clubs' Cup by beating Argentinos Juniors on penalties.

As well as spending millions over the years (much of it provided by the Fiat motor company) on players like John Charles, Omar Sivori, Michel Platini, Michael Laudrup and the unsuccessful Ian Rush, Juventus have always been well represented in the best Italian national teams: they had half-a-dozen representatives in the World Cup winning sides of the 1930s and 1982, including goalkeeper-captains Giampiero Combi and Dino Zoff.

PLAYER PROFILES

VALENTINO MAZZOLA

Those who remember the Munich air disaster of 1958 which devastated Manchester United can well imagine the effect of the Superga crash nine years earlier. Torino were the team of the moment in Italy, winners of the last three League championships and well set for a fourth; they had eight current Italian internationals, due to defend the World Cup in a year's time. Unlike Munich, there was not a single survivor.

Valentino Mazzola was captain of club and country, a strong inside-forward of enormous influence in both teams. Born in Venice, he was still only 30 at the time of his death, his international appearances restricted by the War to a modest 12.

That makes comparison difficult with his son Sandro, backbone of Inter on and then off the field for some 20 years. Six years old when his father died, he won the first of 70 caps in 1963 and after retirement served as executive director for five years.

ALESSANDRO ALTOBELLI

A fixture in the Inter and Italian teams for some ten years, 'Sandro' Altobelli's 60 internationals brought him 25 goals – the fifth highest total by any Italian striker.

The best remembered of them was in the 1982 World Cup final when he put his country 3–1 up against West Germany, effectively deciding the game.

Inter plucked him from Brescia in the Serie B (Second Division) in 1977 and he served club and country well for the next decade before moving on, as a 32-year-old, to Juventus. Tall, curly-haired, usually bearded and immensely popular, his final tally with Inter was 128 League goals in 317 appearances.

PAOLO ROSSI

Paolo Rossi's career was dogged by controversy and later by injury, and is fondly remembered by all Italians for his goals in just three games.

After four matches at the 1982 World Cup finals, he had failed to score, but a devastating hat-trick against Brazil in Barcelona then ensured a place in the semi-final.

Two more Rossi goals despatched Poland and in the final he put his country on the way to victory over West Germany with the first goal, meeting a cross from Gentile at the near post. Doubts had been expressed before the tournament

Paolo Rossi triumphant at the 1982 World Cup final, where he scored Italy's first goal.

about his fitness, since he had only just completed a two-year suspension for his part in a betting scandal while with Perugia – in which he strenuously denied any involvement.

Although the happy outcome was his nomination as European Footballer of the Year, Rossi's star was never so bright again. Sold after Juventus had won the European Cup against Liverpool, he lasted only one season at Milan and after making the Italian squad for the 1986 World Cup was not called upon to play.

GIANNI RIVERA

An idol of A.C. Milan supporters from 1960 until 1979, when he moved 'upstairs' to continue an extraordinary, long-running rivalry with Inter's Sandro Mazzola, Gianni Rivera was the classic inside-forward stylist.

Milan had grabbed him in 1960 from Alessandria, where he was a first-teamer at 15. Small but enormously skilful, he helped them win the European Cup and Cup-Winners' Cup (twice each), and the World Clubs' Cup in 1969, the year he was elected European Footballer of the Year.

First capped aged 19, he lasted for four World Cups, though only in 1970 did Italy achieve much. In that tournament he scored the winning goal in the epic 4–3 semi-final win over West Germany, only to be given just six minutes in the final as a substitute for Mazzola.

DINO ZOFF

Playing in the World Cup finals at the age of 40 should be considered an achievement in itself: captaining the winning team sounds like boys' comic stuff. Dino Zoff managed it in 1982 at what was, nevertheless, only his third World Cup.

Despite playing in the successful Italian 1968 European Championship team, he missed out on the 1970 World Cup to Enrico Albertosi. He had to wait until four years later when nobody could argue with his record – Zoff went into the finals without having conceded a goal in 12 successive internationals. Of all sides, it was little Haiti who broke the spell.

In 1978 questions were asked when he was beaten by long-range shots by Arie Haan and Ernie Brandts which gave Holland a crucial victory. He answered them in Spain.

Remarkably Zoff had been rejected by a number of clubs before joining Udinese in 1961, progressing to Mantova (1963), Napoli (1967) and then Juventus (for £400,000) in 1972.

A World Cup winning captain at 40: Dino Zoff.

POLAND

For years Polish football was ranked in Europe's third division. Apart from one brief moment of glory in the 1938 World Cup – when Ernest Wilimowski scored four times in a 6–5 defeat by Brazil – little was heard of Poland until the 1970s.

Much of the problem lay in the political upheavals in central and Eastern Europe in the first half of the century. Thus while Krakow remains the traditional old home of football in Poland it was not until after the First World War that the resurrection of national identity could be reflected in the formation of a federation. A first international, two years later, ended in a very respectable single-goal defeat by Hungary in Budapest.

A national Championship was set up in 1927 and Poland surprised everyone by reaching the semi-finals of the infamous Berlin Olympics of 1936 – even though they were without the ineligible Ernest Wilimowski. His moment of glory came two years later in the 1938 World Cup held in France.

But one more year and Hitler's armies occupied Poland. Wilimowski agreed to play for the Greater German national team and his name and achievements have been shunned by Poles ever since. Yet it was not until the late 1950s that Polish football produced a player of similar stature, in Ernest Pol, from the Silesian miners' club of Gornik Zabrze.

Gornik became, in 1970, the first Polish club to reach a European final when they went down 2–1 to Manchester City in the rain in the Cup-Winners' Cup in Vienna. It was a defeat, however, which heralded great things to come. In 1972 Poland won the Olympic title in Munich. A year later the nucleus of that team – Kazimierz Deyna, Robert Gadocha and Jerzy Gorgon – came to Wembley to tip England out of the World Cup qualifiers and then went on to finish third in West Germany.

Poland finished third again in Spain in 1982 when the conveyor belt which had suddenly produced so many outstanding players in such a comparatively short time came up with perhaps the best of all, in Zbigniew Boniek.

Kazimierz Deyna is one of very few Poles to play in English football. He joined Manchester City from Legia for a short spell in the mid-Seventies.

THE CLUBS

Gornik
Gornik are the miners' club from Roosevelt Street in the Silesian coal city of Zabrze. Founded in 1948, they were fortunate to benefit from the successive discoveries of two of Poland's greatest players – Ernest Pol, who is still the league's record scorer with 186 goals, and then Wlodzimierz Lubanski.

Between 1959 and 1972 Gornik won the league on nine occasions and the cup six times and their appearance in the 1970 Cup-Winners' Cup final (the only Polish club yet to get so far) opened up a remarkable decade for Polish football. Gornik's first European experience had been a humiliating 4–2, 1–8 defeat at the hands of Tottenham. But players such as goalkeeper Hubert Kostka and centre-back Stanislas Oslizlo were among the best in their roles in Eastern Europe.

In the mid-1970s Gornik suffered a crisis and were relegated. But they returned, reorganized and refreshed in 1979 and stars such as Jan Palasz, Jan Urban and Andrzej Iwan inspired a Polish League title four-timer from 1985 to 1988.

C.W.K.S. Legia
Legia's achievements over the years do not bear adequate testimony to the central role the Warsaw club has held in the Polish game. They were founder members of the league in 1916 yet had to wait until after they had been concerted into the army club in the early 1950s before they first won any prizes. Then Legia collected the league-and-cup double for two successive seasons and made their debut in the European Cup – in which they reached the semi-finals in 1970 before going down 0–0, 0–2 to eventual winners Feyenoord of Holland. Legia were now managed by Kazimierz Gorski. He would guide Poland to the 1972 Olympic title and then on to third place in the 1974 World Cup, thanks to a large extent to the midfield promptings of Legia's Kazimierz Deyna and to the goals of club-mate Robert Gadocha. As reward, Deyna and Gadocha were allowed to leave for England and France respectively. But their replacements lacked the personality on which Legia could maintain a challenge to Gornik and Widzew Lodz.

Manchester City's Neil Young (extreme right) is about to score the goal which beat Gornik in the 1970 Cup-Winners' Cup final.

PLAYER PROFILES

ZBIGNIEW BONIEK

Zbigniew Boniek became the first £1 million Eastern European player when Italy's Juventus signed him from Widzew Lodz after the 1982 World Cup finals. Boniek had scored a brilliant hat-trick against Belgium but suspension cost him a place in the semi-final which Poland lost 2–0 to Italy. Boniek was born on 3 March 1956 in Bydgoszcz where his father had played for Polonia. He joined another local club, Zawisa, at 12 and then Widzew in 1975. It was from here that he went on to Juventus and then Roma. Boniek had a reputation for rising to the occasion. It was his penalty goal for Widzew which once knocked Juventus out of Europe; it was his goal which proved the winner against F.C. Porto in the final of the 1984 Cup-Winners' Cup; and it was Boniek's pace, again, which provoked the controversial penalty from which Michel Platini scored the winner in the tragic 1985 Champions' Cup final in Brussels. He played 78 times in attack for Poland until his switching back to sweeper after the 1986 World Cup.

GRZEGORZ LATO

One of the most durable of Polish internationals, Grzegorz Lato earned his fame as a striker at the 1974 World Cup finals where he was competition top scorer with seven goals. One of those goals took Poland to their 1–0 victory over Brazil in the third place match in Munich. Lato played his football for Stal Mielec until after the World Cup finals of 1978, when he was rewarded for his loyal service with a permit to transfer to the Belgian club, Lokeren, at the suggestion of international team-mate Wlodzimierz Lubanski. Lato expected to be ignored by Poland but he was recalled in a midfield role for the 1982 World Cup finals in Spain where he played his 100th international. His first was a 2–0 win over Spain in 1971 and his 104th, and last, was a 1–0 defeat against Belgium in Warsaw in April 1984. By this time he was 34 years old and had left Belgium to try his luck in Mexico, where he proved as popular as ever with Atlante.

Eastern Europe's first £1 million footballer, Siggy Boniek.

Grzegorz Lato, a veteran of 104 internationals.

ERNEST POL

Ernest Pol was the first great player of post-War Polish football. Pol scored what was then a record 40 goals in his 49 internationals, including one particularly spectacular effort against Scotland at Hampden Park in 1960 and five in one match against Tunisia the same year. His international career lasted for ten years between 1955 and 1965. Pol was born in the mining city of Zabrze on 3 November 1932 but it was not until 1957 that he joined his home-town club after making his reputation during three years with the army club, Legia. Pol was the key player in Gornik's rise to domestic and European success in the early 1960s. Their first appearance was a disaster, ending with an 8–1 defeat by Tottenham at White Hart Lane. Even then, Pol emerged with personal credit for a superbly-struck goal against the line of flight and against the run of play. Pol totalled 186 league goals in his career for Legia and Gornik.

JAN TOMASZEWSKI

Jan Tomaszewski was the goalkeeper described, in one of Brian Clough's most memorable comments, as 'a clown' on the night Poland held out for a 1–1 Wembley draw with England in the 1974 World Cup qualifiers. Tomaszewski's goal certainly bore a charmed life that night but he earned his luck with bravery and a self-confidence which spread through the team. Tomaszewski was a star in the finals, when Poland finished third, and also played in 1978 in Argentina. After brief spells with home-town clubs Gwardia and Slask of Wroclaw, as well as with Legia, Tomaszewski settled with unfashionable L.K.S. Lodz. In September 1978 he moved to Belgium to join Beerschot, made headlines with three penalty saves in his first few matches and collected a cup medal. The next season his eccentricity saw him charging upfield in the last seconds of a league match against R.W.D. to deflect a corner for a team-mate to equalise. 'Toma', by then 33, returned to L.K.S. for one last season in 1981. He played 59 times for Poland.

Cloughy's Clown: Jan Tomaszewski.

PORTUGAL

The revival of Portuguese football in the 1980s was immensely welcome to a country which feared that its days of glory might have disappeared with the colonies which once produced so many stars. Even so, the achievements of the national team still amount to no more than one splendid World Cup (1966) and one brave European Championship (1984), the first preceded by Benfica's success and the second followed by F.C. Porto's.

Portugal did not start playing international football until 1921 and even in the 1950s were still catching up. England, 10–0 winners in Lisbon in 1947, were beaten 3–1 in 1955 but that was one of only half a dozen Portuguese victories in eight seasons. And so English supporters were as surprised as anyone when in 1961 Benfica succeeded Real Madrid as champions of Europe.

Eusebio and Mario Coluna, both from Mozambique, would become particularly good friends of Wembley's, despite their unfortunate record of defeats there – for Portugal in 1961 (0–2) and in the 1966 World Cup semi-final (1–2); for Benfica in the European Cup finals of 1963 (1–2 v. Milan) and 1968 (1–4 v. Manchester United).

The 1966 team had thrilled north-west England, winning their group against Hungary, Brazil and Bulgaria with a 100 per cent record, then beating North Korea 5–3 in an astonishing quarter-final after trailing 3–0. Benfica supplied the four-man attack of José Augusto, Eusebio, José Torres and Antonio Simoes, plus Coluna in midfield and Pereira in goal.

The remnants of that side failed even to qualify four years later and Portugal were not seen at the finals again until 1986. There, after a bitter financial dispute, they shocked England 1–0 in Monterrey and still managed to finish bottom of the group.

At club level Porto did at least achieve something more substantial, landing the European Cup and then the World Clubs' Cup in 1987.

Eusebio on the ball against Hungary as Portugal thrill English spectators at the 1966 World Cup.

THE CLUBS

Jubilation after Porto's thrilling European Cup final victory in 1987.

Benfica

Portuguese football has always been dominated by three clubs – Benfica and Sporting Lisbon from the capital, and Porto. Only one other team, Belenenses in 1946, has ever won the national Championship!

Although Sporting once took the title seven times in eight years (1947–54) and later won the European Cup Winners' Cup (1964), they could do little to stop neighbours Benfica establishing themselves as Europe's finest team in the early 1960s.

Bela Guttmann, the Hungarian coach who believed that 4-2-4 was too negative a system, was the force behind the side which won the 1961 European Cup final against Barcelona in 1961, retained it in spectacular fashion (5–3) against Real Madrid and then unexpectedly failed to complete the hat-trick against Milan after Eusebio had put them in front.

Much the same team, gradually growing older, lost the finals of 1965 and 1968 but still continued to dominate domestic football until 1977.

Since then there has been little continuity under a bewildering chain of managers, including John Mortimore, who resigned immediately after winning the double in 1987.

Porto

After winning their first Portuguese Championship in 1935, then spending years playing third fiddle to the Lisbon clubs, Porto succeeded in 1987 where even Beifica's greatest team had failed, by adding the unofficial World Club Championship to the European Cup.

They did so in farcical conditions, a rare snowstorm having covered the pitch in Tokyo on which they defeated South American champions Penarol after extra-time, but their adaptability won the day. Other qualities, surprising many observers, had been in evidence seven months earlier when Porto won a thrilling European Cup final against Bayern Munich with second-half goals by Rabah Madjer and Brazilian substitute Juary.

Remarkably, leading players Fernando Gomez Lima Pereira, Pacheco and Casagrande had all been unable to play.

That success might have been the second rather than the first in Europe: in 1984 they narrowly lost the European Cup-Winners' Cup final to Juventus after defeating holders Aberdeen in the semi-final. Their coach during those golden years was Artur Jorge, who left for one unsuccessful season with Matra Racing in Paris, only to return in autumn 1988.

PLAYER PROFILES

Eusebio is about to score in the 1963 European Cup final at Wembley against A.C. Milan, but he finished on the losing side.

EUSEBIO

Portugal's best-ever player was not born in the country at all, but, like Coluna, in Mozambique. Too young to play in the 1961 European Cup final, he made his debut a week later, impressing Santos's Pele in an international tournament, and played his part in all of Benfica and Portugal's triumphs over the next decade.

Six times leading scorer in the Portuguese League, as late as 1973 he was scoring 40 of Benfica's 101 League goals they dropped just two points out of a possible 60!

While English crowds have fond memories of him as the sporting loser of 1966 and 1968, his performance at Goodison Park against North Korea summed him up best: taking hold of the game single-handed as his team-mates blinked in disbelief at going three-nil down, he scored four and made the fifth in a stunning individual display.

MARIO COLUNA

Born in Mozambique in 1935, Mario Coluna was the captain and general of the superb Benfica and Portuguese teams of the Sixties. Originally a centre-forward when taken to Lisbon, he switched to inside-forward to accommodate Jose Aguas, the prolific Angolan goalscorer, and became the dominant midfield influence.

A noted high-jumper in his home country, he was well-built but capable of the most delicate feints and passes as well as powerful shots. His goal against Barcelona in the 1961 European Cup final eventually proved the winner, while a 30-yard equaliser against Real Madrid the following year set Benfica up to kill off the ageing opposition.

He was 33 by the time of his fifth final against Manchester United in 1968 but still a force in a game which, it is easily forgotten, Benfica could well have won in normal time.

PAULO FUTRÉ

The highlight of Porto's European Cup victory over Bayern was Paulo Futré's run through the German defence which finished with a shot just wide of the far post. It deserved a goal but was notice enough there here was a genuine talent.

Glimpses of similar skills had been in evidence at the 1986 World Cup, when he seemed to be under-used;

but foreign clubs richer than Porto were already aware of his ability. Atletico Madrid had tried to buy him in 1985 and two years later succeeded, though it cost them more than £2 million.

All of which was particularly vexing for Sporting Lisbon, the club he joined at the age of 12 and was still with when he became Portugal's youngest-ever international at 17. In 1984, still only 18, he opted to join Porto, sharing in their greatest days.

Paulo Futré, Portugal's youngest international.

FERNANDO GOMES

Portugal's fleeting hopes of recapturing former glories were fired by the goals of Fernando Gomes da Silva. A tall, gangling striker, who confesses to be interested only in scoring, he took a while to adapt to the pace of senior football when introduced to it at 18 but within two years was leading goalscorer in the Portuguese League.

He achieved that six times in the seven seasons between 1977 and 1985 in which he was available, spending the other two playing – or, rather, not playing – in Spain with Gijon. A series of injuries made that sojourn a disastrous one and it was an ideal solution all round when he returned to Porto, twice winning the European Golden Boot as he hit another 96 goals in three seasons.

Only at the big international tournaments have goals eluded him. In 1984 he started only one match and in Mexico two years later failed to score in Portugal's three group games.

Fernando Gomes playing against West Germany in 1985.

SOVIET UNION

Glasnost, the new freedom of expression, made itself felt in Soviet football long before the term came to be recognised as a political concept.

Centralised control of every aspect of Soviet life had for years inhibited progress in Soviet football. Authority was exercised from Moscow, most national team managers were Russians and it was not until 1961 that a club from beyond Moscow won the championship. Significantly, that team was Kiev Dynamo from the Ukraine who, along with Tbilisi, have combined the traditional strength and stamina of the Russian game with the Latin touch and technique of Ukraine and Georgia.

Ever since the Soviets entered the international competitive community at the 1952 Helsinki Olympics, they have been successful. The Soviet Union won the 1956 Olympics and then the first-ever European Nations Championship four years later. They were also European runners-up in 1964 and 1972 as well as World Cup quarter-finalists in 1958, in 1962 and 1979 and fourth in 1966. But, it has only been since the advent of Kiev as a force in the European club game in the mid-1970s, that the national team has been admired for skill, flair and style.

The English Charnock brothers who introduced football to workers in their cotton mills in the 1880s would have been astonished to know where their recreational brainwave led. In the 1960s, for example, political disapproval of the 'cult of personality' made itself felt in Soviet football to the game's detriment.

By the time of the 1988 European Championship, when the Soviets made an excellent impression in finishing runners-up, professionalism was being embraced, and leading players were allowed to move abroad. Veteran Oleg Blokhin, transferred to Austrian club Steyr, was the first; followed by stars like Alexander Zavarov (Kiev to Juventus), Renat Dassayev (Spartak to Seville) and Sergei Baltacha (Kiev to Ipswich Town).

THE CLUBS

Moscow Dynamo

Moscow Dynamo remain an international legend because of their remarkable tour of Britain in the winter of 1945–46. At a time before the Soviet Union had entered F.I.F.A. and before they had even played a full international, Dynamo proved a wonderful advertisement for Soviet soccer.

Goalkeeper Alexei 'Tiger' Khomich set a high standard which would be maintained by successors such as the great Lev Yashin, while star inside-forward Konstantin Beskov went on to become the national team's World Cup manager. Dynamo were originally set up as the sports club of the electrical trades union in 1923 and were later taken over by the police authority. The pattern was copied throughout Eastern Europe in the Communist-led upheavals after the Second World War.

It was appropriate that in 1972 Dynamo should become the first Soviet side to reach a European club final. By half-time in the Cup-Winners' Cup final in Barcelona they were 3–0 down to Glasgow Rangers, but recovered two goals with four minutes to go . . . just too late.

Dynamo Kiev

Kiev have led the way for Soviet football. It was Kiev who were the first Soviet provincial club to break the Moscow domestic title domination (winning the championship in 1961); it was Kiev who were first to win a European trophy (the Cup-Winners' Cup in 1975); it was Kiev who were first to bring sophisticated computer science to their training programme (thanks to coach Valeri Lobanovsky); and it was Kiev who were first to sign a shirt sponsorship deal for European ties (with computer company, Commodore).

Kiev have also been in the lead, along with Dnepr Dnepropetrovsk, in pushing towards professionalism. Their skill and technique thrilled Europe when they won the Cup-Winners' Cup both in 1975 and in 1986. But the Kiev players were worked so hard (all were in the national squad) that, each time, fatigue prevented them following through and winning the Champions' Cup. Individual consolation was provided by European Footballer of the Year awards to Oleg Blokhin (in 1975) and Igor Belanov (1986).

Moscow Dynamo defend against Glasgow Rangers in the 1972 European Cup-Winners' Cup final. Their brave rally came too late to prevent a 3–2 defeat.

Left: *Sergei Baltacha became the first player from the Soviet Union to play in the Football League when he signed for Ipswich during the 1988–9 season. His presence was not quite enough to lift Ipswich into the Second Division Playoffs, but as he settles down in his new environment, the team are likely to be strong contenders for promotion in 1989–90.*

PLAYER PROFILES

IGOR BELANOV

Igor Belanov made his debut for the Soviet Union as a 79th-minute substitute in a 4–0 win over Switzerland in the World Cup qualifiers in May 1985. When Belanov was voted European Footballer of the Year in 1986, the Kiev forward became the third Soviet player to achieve the honour after Yashin and Blokhin. Yet Belanov had been a late choice for the Soviet squad at the World Cup finals in Mexico a few months earlier – owing his place to a late managerial change which saw Kiev coach Valeri Lobanovsky replace Eduard Malofeyev at the head of the national team. Belanov proved the outstanding Soviet player in the finals, scoring a hat-trick in the thrilling extra-time defeat by Belgium in the second round. Belanov was then selected for the World All-Stars in a fund-raising match for Unicef as well as for the Rest of the World in the Football League centenary match at Wembley in August 1987. He was still only 26.

OLEG BLOKHIN

Oleg Blokhin scored a record 44 goals in a record 108 internationals for the Soviet Union in the 1970s and 1980s. Blokhin, the 1975 European Footballer of the Year and all-time Soviet top scorer with 302 career goals, might have been a star sprinter if he had not favoured football. One of his friends is Valeri Borzov, the former Olympic double sprint gold medallist. Outside-left Blokhin was in inspired form and contributed a goal in both Kiev's Cup-Winners' Cup triumphs: in 1975 against Ferencvaros of Hungary, and in 1986 against Atletico Madrid. He became the first Soviet player to reach 100 internationals in a 2–1 defeat by Rumania in April 1986. Blokhin played in the World Cup finals of both 1982 in Spain and 1986 in Mexico. In the spring of 1988 at the age of 35, he became the first 'name' Soviet player to be allowed a transfer abroad when he joined the Austrian club Vorwärts Steyr.

RENAT DASSAYEV

Renat Dassayev's selection for the Rest of the World in the Football League centenary match at Wembley in 1987 underlined his ranking as a worthy successor to such great Soviet goalkeepers as Khomich and Yashin. Dassayev was born at Astrakhan on 13 June 1957, made his debut for the Soviet Union in a 1–0 win

Above: *Oleg Blokhin, highest scorer in Soviet history.*

Left: *Known as 'Igor the Terrible', Belanov was a tormentor of defences at the 1986 World Cup.*

over East Germany in 1979, and first drew to international attention when he kept goal for the Soviet team which finished third in the 1980 Olympics in Moscow. Dassayev enhanced his reputation in the World Cup finals tournaments for both 1982 in Spain and 1986 in Mexico. He began his career as a centre-forward but switched to keeper with such success that he made his international debut just four months after his first league appearance for Moscow Spartak. After winning his 85th cap in the 1988 European Championship final against Holland, he joined the exodus of Soviet players by moving to Seville in Spain for a reported £1.3 million.

LEV YASHIN

When a South American magazine recently polled sports journalists around the world on their all-time ideal team, the legendary Soviet goalkeeper Lev Yashin was almost as indisputable a choice as Pele.

Yet Yashin, when a Moscow Dynamo reserve in 1953, was about to turn his back on soccer in favour of ice hockey when regular keeper, the great 'Tiger' Khomich, was injured. Yashin took over and a year later, in September 1954, a month short of his 25th birthday, made his international debut in a 3–2 win over Sweden. He missed only two matches in the next seven years, playing 78 times for his country, and became a worldwide celebrity not only for saves which bordered on the miraculous but for his sportsmanship. He was a worthy European Footballer of the Year in 1963 and ended his career with winner's medals from the 1956 Olympics and the 1960 European Championship as well as the Order of Lenin. He also played in the World Cup finals in 1958, 1962 and 1966 – when the Soviets finished a best-ever fourth.

Right: *Lev Yashin, ice hockey's loss . . .*

SPAIN

It is surprising and, to Spaniards, hugely disappointing, that their country has not made more of an impact in World Cups. Clubs like Real Madrid and Barcelona draw huge crowds (Barcelona once averaged more than 100,000 over a full season), pay correspondingly large transfer fees for some of the world's best players and have become regular contenders in the major European competitions; but, unlike Italy, who also import expensive foreigners after once having banned them, Spain have rarely been able to produce an outstanding national team.

Such successes as have been achieved tend to have been laboured ones. For the second European Championship, from 1962–64, Spain had to dispose only of Rumania, Northern Ireland (who gave them a fright by drawing the away leg) and the Republic of Ireland to reach the last four on home ground. In the semi-final they edged past Hungary and then beat the U.S.S.R. thanks only to Marcelino's late goal.

The best World Cup performance, statistically, was to finish fourth in 1950. Having won the group in which England managed to lose to the U.S.A., Spain then drew with eventual winners Uruguay, but lost emphatically to Brazil and Sweden. After a poor 1982 performance as host country, 1986 represented an improvement with the dramatic 5–1 win over Denmark and a quarter-final defeat by Belgium on penalties.

Not even 'naturalising' players like Ferenc Puskas and Alfredo Di Stefano helped. Both might have played for Spain in the 1962 finals, alongside Luis Del Sol, Luis Suarez and Francisco Gento. But Di Stefano was injured and the other four could not prevent the Spaniards finishing bottom of a difficult group.

Throughout the post-war period it has been the clubs who have caught the public's imagination: and not only the big two. Atlético Madrid, Bilbao, Valencia and Zaragoza have all reached European finals as well.

Spain's performance in the 1982 World Cup finals was among the worst by any host country.

THE CLUBS

Barcelona

To Barcelona, like Juventus in Italy, football's Holy Grail is the European Cup. They have found it even more difficult to attain.

Twice it seemed well within reach. In 1961, having inflicted a first-ever defeat in the competition on their age-old rivals Real, their magnificent forward line of Ladislav Kubala, Sandor Kocsis, Evaristo, Luis Suarez and Zoltan Czibor was strongly fancied to defeat Benfica. But after taking the lead, they went down 3–2, goalkeeper Antonio Ramallets taking much of the blame.

Exactly 25 years later, under English manager Terry Venables, they were again expected to win the final. This time they could not score against Steaua Bucharest either in normal play or from the penalties which decided the match.

Venables, having sold Diego Maradona to Napoli, had at least won the Spanish Championship in 1985 – Barcelona's first for 11 years. Johan Cruyff, star of the 1974 team, took over as manager in 1988 following a disastrous season in which Venables was sacked, Cruyff winning the Cup-Winners' Cup within 12 months.

Real Madrid

The rise of Real Madrid coincided perfectly with the birth of the European Cup and their team which dominated it for five years was surely the greatest club side ever seen.

The 1954 Spanish Championship won on the back of new signing Alfredo Di Stefano's goals was Real's first in a period of 21 years during which provincial clubs and even neighbours Atletico had overshadowed them. Santiago Bernabeu's vision (and money) helped construct a magnificent new stadium and a team to grace it: the finishing touch was added in 1958 when an overweight Ferenc Puskas, drifting aimlessly around Europe in the wake of the Hungarian Revolution, was united with Di Stefano.

Later Real teams were still capable of dominating Spain's football if not Europe's, winning six out of seven national titles from 1975 to 1980 and following two successive U.E.F.A. Cup victories (1984 and 1985) with further Championships from 1986 to 1989, when Welshman John Toshack took over as manager.

Below: *Laurie Cunningham, a great talent but not one of Real's more successful imports.*

Below left: *Clash of giants – Real Madrid's Hugo Sanchez fails to stop Barcelona's Gary Lineker getting a cross in.*

PLAYER PROFILES

AMANCIO AMARO

Amancio was born, like Luis Suarez, in La Coruna, moving not to Barcelona but to Real, who paid £35,000 for him in 1962. Two years later, converted from inside-forward to winger, he was an important influence as Real reached the European Cup final and Spain won the European Championship, Suarez opposing him in the first competition and playing behind him in the second.

After the defeat by Inter, he had to wait until 1966 before joining the greats who had won a European Cup winners' medal for Real, scoring the equaliser against Partizan Belgrade. In all, he spent 14 years with the club as a player, later returning from the nursery team Castilla to succeed Alfredo Di Stefano as manager.

It was not a happy tenure. Despite overcoming Spurs in an exciting U.E.F.A. Cup quarter-final, he was dismissed even before the semi-final was played.

EMILIO BUTRAGUENO

'El Buitre' (the vulture) was the appropriate nickname foisted on the newest goalscoring hero of Real Madrid and Spain, who made his international reputation with a single match.

That was the 1986 World Cup second round tie in which Spain were underdogs against the free-wheeling Danes. Emilio Butragueno put no fewer than four spokes in the Danish wheels with the greatest individual scoring feat in a World Cup tournament since Eusebio's four

Butragueno (red shirt): The Vulture.

against North Korea 20 years earlier. He even won the penalty which brought Spain's other goal and could have scored five had he taken it himself.

'Sharp' is perhaps the best word to describe his striking skills. That sharpness is as likely to result in goals for team-mates as for himself and has contributed substantially to Real's latest run of success.

Left: *Gento, the flying winger.*

FRANCISCO GENTO

Born in northern Spain in 1933, Francisco 'Paco' Gento was the most durable of all Real's 1950s stars, playing on until the 1971 European Cup-Winners' Cup final against Chelsea. Amazingly, he appeared in eight European Cup finals, winning six.

Once regarded as the world's fastest winger, he added even greater craft and subtlety as his legs grew older, retaining his ability to hit perfect crosses and powerful shots. It was his goal which won the 1958 European Cup final against Milan.

Like such talented club-mates as Luis Del Sol and José Santamaria, his principal disappointment lay in never being able to inspire the Spanish national team to anything like the same heights.

LUIS SUAREZ

Luis Suarez, dapper, slim and elegant, was the most potent force in Barcelona's largely vain attempts to match Real's exploits. Personal recognition was at least granted in 1960 when he followed Stanley Matthews, Alfredo Di Stefano and Raymond Kopa as European Footballer of the Year.

The dreadful disappointment of failing to succeed Real as European champions in 1961 was partly assuaged by a world record transfer (the first of £200,000) to Inter. If anything, his role there was even more important as his former Barcelona manager Helenio Herrera abandoned his attacking principles for the cat-and-mouse game of counter-attack.

It was sweet revenge to win the European Cup at last against first Real (1964) and then Benfica (1965). Ending his playing career with Sampdoria, Suarez later coached Genoa and then Inter themselves.

Below: *Luis Suarez, sweet revenge with Inter Milan.*

WEST GERMANY

In terms both of international results and overall strength at club level, West German football compares favourably with any in the world. Their record is all the more remarkable given the inevitable problems football faced after the Second World War and the fact that no national league existed until the 1963–64 season.

Before the war Germany had been outshone by numerous other European nations, to the disgust of the Nazi leaders, who were particularly infuriated by defeats in Berlin against England (3–6 in 1938) and even Norway in the 1936 Olympics. Nor did grabbing Austria's best players produce any success in the 1938 World Cup.

They did not resume international football until 1950 yet despite having lost many clubs and players to East Germany progress was swift. By the 1954 World Cup finals the national team, under Sepp Herberger, had lost only two out of 24 carefully chosen fixtures. Eventual victory was an outstanding achievement, even if Hungary were the best team of the era.

The Germans have been contenders at just about every World Cup since as their record illustrates: 1958 – 4th; 1962 – quarter-finalists; 1966 – runners-up; 1970 – 3rd; 1974 – winners; 1978 – second stage; 1982 – runners-up; 1986 – runners-up. In the European Championship they were winners in 1972 and 1980 and runners-up on penalties in between times.

A national First Division, the 'Bundesliga' improved the club teams, who became finalists in all three European club competitions, with Bayern Munich and Borussia Moenchengladbach outstanding in the 1970s. That any country should reach the World Cup final twice running with teams which by their own standards were only moderate is as great a tribute as any.

Rudi Völler (green shirt, centre) stoops to conquer against Argentina, who nevertheless went on to win 3-2 in the 1986 World Cup final.

THE CLUBS

Hamburg's Hans Bastrup bravely goes for the same ball as Gentile in the 1983 European Cup final victory against Juventus.

Bayern Munich

The club now recognised as West Germany's greatest did not merit a place in the first Bundesliga in 1963. At that time Bayern had recorded only one Championship (1932) and one German Cup win (1957) and played in the shadow of neighbours 1860.

Once promoted, however, they immediately took the German Cup (1966 and 1967), the European Cup Winners' Cup (1967) and in 1969 the Championship itself. Sepp Maier in goal, Franz Beckenbauer in midfield and Gerd Müller in attack were already established. When others as capable as Paul Breitner and Uli Hoeness (later general manager) joined them, a hat-trick of Championships (1972–74) and European Cups (1974–76) was achieved by what at that time was clearly Europe's premier club side.

Karl-Heinz Rummenigge and his younger brother Michael were key figures as the team was later rebuilt, winning five more German titles between 1980 and 1987.

Hamburg

Unlike comparative upstarts Bayern and Borussia Moenchengladbach, Hamburg have long been one of Germany's biggest clubs and were automatic members of the first Bundesliga, in which they finished sixth. Prior to that they had dominated German football in the north, winning the Oberliga Nord 25 times in 29 seasons.

They were within 60 seconds of the 1961 European Cup final before losing a play-off to Barcelona, and unluckily lost the 1980 final to Nottingham Forest, with Kevin Keegan in the side, but eventually claimed the premier trophy three years later against Juventus, when Felix Magath scored the only goal.

Uwe Seeler and Gerd Dörfel were the stars of the early Sixties and Keegan became immensely popular after a difficult settling-in period. He stayed three seasons before returning to England with Southampton, after which Hamburg won two more German titles (1982 and 1983) and missed a hat-trick only on goal difference.

Bayern won their first European Cup in 1974. Uli Hoeness scores the second goal in a 4-0 replay win over Atletico Madrid.

PLAYER PROFILES

FRANZ BECKENBAUER

Franz Beckenbauer was unquestionably one of Bayern's youthful thoroughbreds. Born just two months earlier, the exceptionally elegant Beckenbauer broke into the national team before Gerd Müller and stayed later, recording 103 caps between 1965 and 1977, when he accepted the New York Cosmos offer of a 2.5 million dollar contract.

His international debut, as a midfielder, was in 1965 and led to a regular place in the following summer's World Cup at the age of 20. Even at such a tender age and despite his creative ability, manager Helmut Schön was happy to give him a man-marking job on Bobby Charlton in the final.

Beckenbauer's revenge for that defeat was prolonged as he scored the goal which beat England in 1968 (Germany's first-ever victory over them), scored again in the 1970 World Cup victory and captained the team which beat them on the way to winning the 1972 European Championship.

By then he personified the modern, positive sweeper, free not just to mop up in defence but to stride downfield, often scoring himself. He became West Germany's team manager and carefully played down the team's chances in the 1986 World Cup before leading them all the way to the final.

'Kaiser' Franz Beckenbauer, scourge of England.

UWE SEELER

Uwe Seeler's international career spanned 16 years and took him to the final stages of four World Cups, two of them (1966 and 1970) as his country's captain.

Something of a childhood prodigy, he was scoring goals for Hamburg well before his 18th birthday and was still only 17 when first picked for West Germany, just after they had won the 1954 World Cup.

Seeler had a particularly good right foot, he played with immense determination and did especially well in the air considering his stocky build. He was Germany's Footballer of the Year three times, including his retirement year of 1970. He inspired the 3–2 victory over England in the World Cup quarter-final that year, scoring the equalising goal and making the winner.

GERD MÜLLER

The successor in the German team to Seeler, often playing happily alongside him between 1966 and 1970, Gerd Müller soon surpassed even Uwe's goalscoring feats, establishing records and scoring ratios which may never by bettered.

Müller was, simply, a natural goalscorer; a poacher who did all his best work within 15 yards of goal. Short, like Seeler, and equally thickset and powerful, with a low centre of gravity, he was particularly adept at the sort of swivel which produced the winning goal in the 1974 World Cup final.

That was the peak of a career which produced well over 600 goals, a record 365 in the Bundesliga and a staggering 68 in 62 internationals. Not bad for a player scornfully described by Bayern's coach as 'an elephant among thoroughbreds' when he joined the club from T.S.V. Nordlingen in 1963.

Karl-Heinz Rummenigge, following in a fine tradition.

Uwe Seeler has got in front of Bobby Moore during the 1970 World Cup quarter final.

KARL-HEINZ RUMMENIGGE

Ten years younger than Franz Beckenbauer and Gerd Müller, Karl-Heinz Rummenigge succeeded the former as captain and the latter as principal goalscorer for Bayern and West Germany – while emulating both by becoming European Footballer of the Year.

When Bayern began their hat-trick of European Cup wins in 1974, 'Rummi' was still a teenager. He appeared in the 1976 final against St. Etienne and made his international debut against Wales the following October.

When Müller left for Florida in 1979, Rummenigge was moved from the wing to a more central role and increased his scoring rate accordingly, to top the Bundesliga list in 1980 (26), 1981 (29) and 1984 (26). He then joined Inter Milan to test himself in the harsher confines of Italian football, leaving for Servette after a period of nagging injuries which handicapped him in the World Cups of 1982 and 1986.

YUGOSLAVIA

Yugoslavia has been Europe's greatest modern exporter of coaching and playing talent. Hundreds of fine players have taken advantage of the game's exit permits to earn hard currency throughout western Europe.

Even in 1930, when Yugoslavia were one of only four European nations to attend the inaugural World Cup in Uruguay, goal-scoring inside forward Ivan Bek was simultaneously on his way to play for the French club, Sete. Indeed, not only that, but he finished up playing for the French national team as well.

Yugoslavia's wealth of talent should have been reflected in a string of international prizes. Instead, they have made a habit of being second best. Yugoslavia did win the Olympic title in 1960, but they have been runners-up three times. In the World Cup they were fourth in 1962 and quarter-finalists in 1954 and in 1958; in the European Championship they were runners-up in 1960 and 1968 and then finished fourth as hosts in 1976.

Partizan Belgrade became in 1966 the first Eastern European club to reach the final of the Champions' Cup when they went down 2–1 to Real Madrid in Brussels. A year later Dinamo Zagreb won the Fairs Cup. But that was all.

Among the great personalities, Miljan Miljanic coached Real Madrid and Valencia in Spain, while Branko Zebec took Hamburg to the 1980 European Cup final and 'Tschik' Cajkovski built the Bayern Munich team in which West Germany's youthful Franz Beckenbauer and Gerd Müller made their names.

This abundance of talent would surely have reaped more success, were it not for the twin administrative problems posed by Yugoslavia's domestic provincial and ethnic rivalries, and by the rigid insistence on national service which takes players out of the game for a year at a crucial stage in their careers. This is why the Yugoslav team which won the World Youth Cup in Chile in 1987 is unlikely to fulfil its potential.

Yugoslavia line up for the 1974 World Cup tie against Scotland.

THE CLUBS

Partizan

Partizan are the only Yugoslav team to have reached the final of the European Champions' Cup.

Their defeat by Real Madrid in Brussels in 1966 was the end of an era since goalkeeper Milutin Soskic, full-back Fahrudin Jusufi, half-back Velibor Vasovic and forwards Kovacevic and Milan Galic were all, controversially, about to take up offers in western Europe.

That was nothing compared with the controversy sparked in 1986. Partizan won the League on the last day of the season – but then lost it to Red Star Belgrade when the federation ordered the entire round to be replayed because of match-fixing suspicions. Partizan were among several clubs penalised six points for the 1986–87 campaign. Defying F.I.F.A. rules, they went to court and were eventually vindicated when the federation agreed to stand by the original 1986 table and scrap the points penalties. That meant Partizan not only 'regained' the 1986 title but collected the 1987 crown too because, even despite the points penalty, they had finished only just behind Vardar Skopje at the top of the table.

Red Star

Red Star Belgrade are the most famous of Yugoslav clubs – quite an achievement considering the variety of names by which they are known. Crvena Zvezda in Yugoslavia; Red Star in Britain; Stella Rossa in Italy; Estrella Roja in Spain and Latin America; Roter Stern in Germany and Austria; Etoile Rouge in France. All the translations spell one thing: quality football.

Red Star hold a special place in English football history because they were Manchester United's opponents before the Munich air crash – and highly respected opponents too, with great players such as the fierce-shooting Bora Kostic and schemer Dragoslav Sekularac.

Kostic was first in a long line of brilliant left-wingers who included Dragan Dzajic and Vladimir Petrovic. It was during the Petrovic era – with Milan Miljanic as coach – that Red Star remarkably won a European Cup tie, both home and away, against Liverpool in 1973–74. They remain the only Slav club to have reached the semi-finals in all three European tournaments.

Petar Krnokuca heads clear for Red Star at Tottenham, November 1972.

PLAYER PROFILES

DRAGAN DZAJIC

Dragan Dzajic played a record 85 times for Yugoslavia in the 1960s and 1970s. He was appropriately nicknamed 'The Magic Dragan' by the English Press before helping Yugoslavia beat England and go on to finish runners-up at the 1968 European Championships in Italy. Dzajic, who had made his international debut at 18 in a 2–1 defeat by Rumania in 1964, boasted smart acceleration and crossed the ball with pinpoint accuracy. He was the key figure at Red Star Belgrade from 1963 to 1975 and returned to a position in the club management after winding up his playing career in the French League with the Corsican club, Bastia, in 1979 when he was 33.

It was a measure of the extent to which Dzajic 'became' Yugoslav football that he was invited to play for Rest of the World teams in celebration matches against Brazil in 1968, in the Lev Yashin Farewell match in 1971 and for Europe against South America a year later in a charity match organised by F.I.F.A. in Basle.

DRAGOSLAV SEKULARAC

Dragoslav Sekularac was the flawed genius of Yugoslav football in the late 1950s and early 1960s.

Born on 8 November 1937, Sekularac was discovered by Red Star

Dzajic, 'the Magic Dragan'.

Belgrade as an outside-left. But such was his vision that he was switched to inside-right to lay on goals for the record-breaking Bora Kostic. Sekularac made his international debut in September, 1956, when he was only 18. The occasion was a 2–1 defeat by Czechoslovakia but Sekularac did enough to earn a place in the team beaten in the Melbourne Olympic final by the Soviet Union that December. He played in the World Cup finals of 1958 and 1962 – when Yugoslavia finished a best-ever fourth. Always temperamental, Sekularac fell out with the federation after striking a referee in a league game. He was banned for a year then transferred to Karlsruhe in West Germany. In 1967 Sekularac returned briefly to O.F.K. Belgrade but ended his career in Colombia with Santa Fe and Millionarios.

Stojkovic, Rest of the World team member.

DRAGAN STOJKOVIC

Born on 3 March 1965, Dragan Stojkovic made his debut for Yugoslavia as a substitute in a goalless draw against France in Zagreb in November 1983 when he was 18. His arrival on the international scene caused initial confusion because of the presence in the Yugoslav side of Nenad Stojkovic (no relation) of Partizan. Dragan played in the 1984 European Championship finals and was then lost to football for a year while he undertook his National Service. In his absence his club, Radnicki Nis, were relegated. Stojkovic came back, Radnicki returned to the First Division – and were then persuaded to 'sell' him to Red Star Belgrade in exchange for five players and a new set of floodlights! Red Star believe Stojkovic will prove the club's fifth major star, after Rajko Mitic, Dragoslav Sekularac, Dragan Dzajic and Vladimir Petrovic. Stojkovic was the 'mystery' substitute who appeared without an identifying number on his shirt for the Rest of the World in the Football League Centenary match at Wembley in August 1987.

BRANCO ZEBEC

One of European football's most versatile players, Branko Zebec played 65 times for his country. When the Rest of Europe met England at Wembley in 1953 the other four members of the five-man forward line were playing centre-forward for their clubs; but Zebec, outside-left at Wembley, was centre-back with Partizan. Yet Zebec had made his Yugoslavia debut as a 22-year-old centre-forward in a 7–3 win over Switzerland in June 1951. He scored twice that day and a year later scored four in a 10–1 thrashing of India in the Helsinki Olympics. Zebec scored 111 goals in 263 matches for Partizan before surprisingly transferring to Red Star in 1958. He ended his playing career with Alemannia Aachen in West Germany then returned home to coach Dynamo Zagreb to victory in the 1967 Fairs Cup. Later Zebec coached Bayern Munich, Stuttgart and Hajduk Split before guiding Hamburg to the 1980 European Cup Final, where they lost to Nottingham Forest.

BULGARIA

Bulgaria have been among the most successful of nations when it comes to qualifying competitions at World Cup, Olympic Games and European Championship level. Where they have singularly failed has been in producing teams which can then win important matches.

Football was introduced to Bulgaria in 1894 by a Swiss sports instructor whose initial work was developed by students returning from university in Constantinople. A federation was formed in 1923 and F.I.F.A. membership obtained in 1924 – the year which saw a Championship launched.

Bulgaria twice took the Balkan Cup in the mid-1930s, but apart from isolated victories in the European Youth Championships (1959 and 1969) they have won nothing since. Despite qualifying for the World Cup finals on no fewer than five occasions in the past 30 years, they have only once got beyond the first stage, when losing to hosts Mexico in 1986.

Failure to qualify for the 1988 European Championships was a particular disappointment. Needing only one point from the final group match, at home to Scotland, they lost to an 87th minute goal which put the Republic of Ireland through instead.

Two clubs have dominated Bulgarian soccer, though both now appear under different names. The army team C.S.K.A. Sredets (formerly C.D.N.A.) won nine successive League titles between 1954 and 1962 (a European record at that time); Levsky, now known as Vitosha, have won the Cup most times. The clubs were effectively disbanded and then reformed after a mass brawl in the 1985 Cup final.

For years Bulgaria were known for only a couple of players, Ivan Kolev (born 1 November 1930) and the man he created many chances for, centre-forward Georgi Asparukhov. The latter was killed in a car crash in 1971.

In the 1970s, midfielder Hristo Bonev achieved a record 96 caps. He was among the coaching staff at the 1986 World Cup, when the best player was goalkeeper Borislav Mikhailov. Newest star is Nasko Sirakov, whose 28 goals in 30 games won Vitosha the 1988 League title and earned him a transfer to Spain with Real Zaragoza, whereupon C.S.K.A. again became the strongest team.

The army side have a reputation as tough opponents in European ties and claimed a remarkable hat-trick in the European Cup by eliminating Ajax (1973–74), Nottingham Forest (1980–81) and Liverpool (1981–82) when all three were the defending champions.

In the last of those seasons, they reached the semi-final, before losing 7–4 on aggregate to Bayern Munich.

The other clubs forming Sofia's 'big four' are Lokomotiv and Slavia, while Plovdiv clubs Lotomotiv and Trakia are the other seasoned European competitors.

Bulgarian goalkeeper Mikhailov holds a cross against Argentina at the 1986 World Cup.

DENMARK

While Denmark is still unable to stop most of its best players moving abroad, it has been able, in recent years, to put together a fine team when they have all been available.

That team began to emerge in the late Seventies: Morten Olsen, Soren Lerby, Frank Arnesen, Henning Jensen, Preben Elkjaer and European Footballer of the Year Allan Simonsen all tested England in the 1978–79 European Championship qualifiers and four years later helped defeat them at Wembley.

With Michael Laudrup, one of Europe's most exciting young players, partnering Elkjaer in attack, they deserved better than to lose a semi-final on penalties to Spain.

Two years later in the World Cup finals, now including Jesper Olsen (Manchester United) and Jan Molby (Liverpool) in their squad, they were again confounded by Spain, who won an extraordinary second round match 5–1 after Olsen's penalty had put the Danes ahead.

The country's emergence as a football power dates from the introduction of semi-professionalism in 1978. Before that, they had achieved success only in the Olympic Games, reaching the final in 1908 and 1912 and rarely losing an international against fellow-amateurs until the 1920s.

The Olympic sides of 1948 (placed third) and 1960 (runners-up) also made a good impression, the outstanding players immediately turning professional. Most went to Italian clubs, though full-back Viggo Jensen joined Hull City, where he was a popular and valuable stalwart between 1948 and 1956.

Not surprisingly, Danish clubs have enjoyed little success in European competition, though Ferenc Puskas once summed up their whole-hearted approach after playing for Real Madrid against Odense: 'If I were an amateur, I wouldn't run around as much as these Danes.'

Michael Laudrup is for once dispossessed in Denmark's 6-1 win over Uruguay, World Cup 1986. Spain then beat them 5-1.

Allan Simonsen, a former European Footballer of the Year, takes on France's defence at the 1984 European Championship

EAST GERMANY

East Germany have never matched, in the world's premier team game, the results achieved by their athletes and swimmers. Only on one occasion, in 1974, have they reached the World Cup finals – though they did cause a tremendous stir then by defeating neighbours and hosts West Germany 1–0. East Germany's one success to date remains the 1976 Olympic title. To be fair, political problems after the war prevented the D.D.R. playing a full international in western Europe until they faced Wales in the 1958 World Cup qualifiers.

Clubs are linked to various state and social institutions. Vorwärts, for instance, are the army team who dominated in the 1950s and 1960s and therefore made the first impact on European competition; Magdeburg won the Cup-Winners' Cup in 1974; Carl-Zeiss Jena (1981) and Lokomotiv Leipzig (1987) have both been runners-up.

But no club in East Germany or anywhere else has matched the record of Dynamo Berlin, who took ten successive League titles between 1979 and 1988, all under coach Jürgen Bogs. Astonishingly, they had never won one before that run began, and only once in the ten seasons did they win the Cup as well.

Stars of the side were strikers Andreas Thom and Rainer Ernst, worthy successors of the most famous East Germans of an earlier period, Joachim Streich and Jürgen Sparwasser.

Streich, born in 1951, and his contemporary 'Dixie' Dörner both reached 100 caps. Magdeburg's Sparwasser, three years older, and scorer of the historic goal which beat West Germany in the 1974 World Cup, defected to the West in January 1987.

As with other leading eastern European teams, Dynamo have achieved only spasmodic success against western clubs. In the 1988–89 European Cup they seemed poised to eliminate Werder Bremen after winning their home leg 3–0, but succumbed 5–0 in the return, conceding four second-half goals.

That loss was followed by a traumatic period for the national team, who were expected to qualify for the World Cup finals, at least as runners-up to the USSR. A 3–1 defeat in Turkey cost manager Bernd Stange his job, but his successor Manfred Zapf fared even worse, losing to the Turks in Magdeburg and then, more predictably, to the Soviets.

Joachim Streich, the Magdeburg forward capped more than 100 times.

GREECE

Although football was played in Greece before the turn of the century, a 9–0 defeat by Sweden in their first-ever international (at the 1920 Olympics) rather discouraged the country's administrators – who did not arrange another game for nine years.

In fact the Greek F.A. was not officially founded until 1926, whereafter regular matches were played against Bulgaria, Rumania and Yugoslavia.

In their own country, they have often been difficult to beat, partly because of the volatile and intimidating crowds. Ferenc Puskas, taking charge of the Athens club Panathinaikos, was able to build on that in a startling run to the 1971 European Cup final. Howard Kendall, wing-half for one of their victims, Everton, has recalled: 'It was a frightening experience. Even our international players were surprised how hostile it was.'

Red Star Belgrade lost the semi-final second leg 3–0 in Athens after winning 4–1 at home, and although never looking likely to win the final at Wembley against Ajax, Panathinaikos were not effectively beaten until the last few minutes.

The greatest achievement in international competition has been to reach the 1980 European Championship finals. Significantly, Greece won all their home games in the qualifying group and snatched just one away point, which was enough to put them on top of the U.S.S.R., Hungary and Finland. In Italy they lost only 1–0 to Holland and 3–1 to holders Czechoslovakia.

A goalless draw at Wembley in the 1984 qualifying group helped ruin England's chances of qualifying and four years later they led a difficult group until the last two months, finishing runners-up to Holland. Striker Nikos Anastopoulous was top scorer in that group as well as helping his club Olympiakos, from Piraeus, to a record 25th national championship. Panathinaikos and A.E.K. Athens remain their greatest rivals.

Panathinaikos, in the dark strip, against Ajax at Wembley in the 1971 European Cup final.

NORWAY

With a smaller population than Denmark, but more than twice as many registered clubs, Norway waits and hopes for a similar breakthrough. So far they have had to be content with occasional dramatic victories rather than sustained success.

Such a victory, perhaps the most sensational of all, was recorded at home to Ron Greenwood's England team in September 1981. No minor friendly either – it was a crucial World Cup tie in which a 2–1 defeat might have eliminated England. Albertsen and Thoresen were the heroes whose goals won the game in front of an ecstatic 28,000 crowd after Bryan Robson had put England ahead.

A fine 3–1 win in the next European Championship over eventual group winners Yugoslavia was followed by an unusually good year in 1984 (only two defeats in nine games) and a stunning 2–1 victory away to Italy.

But taking three points from France in the 1988 European Championship qualifiers was offset by losing twice to Iceland and again finishing bottom of the group.

In earlier eras, the only comparable highlight was at the 1936 Olympics, when a Berlin crowd, including Adolf Hitler, was shocked by Norway's 2–0 victory over the host country: they lost the semi-final to Italy but won the third-place match.

Age Hareide, who featured in several of the Seventies and Eighties triumphs, is one of the few Norwegians to be given a chance in English football. He played in defence for Manchester City and Norwich from 1981 to 1983.

Many British coaches have worked in Norway, though, and speak highly of the commitment, enthusiasm and organisation among the many different teams to be found at each club.

Einar Ass (4) and Trevor Francis battle it out in Norway's sensational 1981 victory over England.

REPUBLIC OF IRELAND

Qualification for the 1988 European Championship finals was a huge step forward for a country whose achievements had not previously matched the range of talent available.

While Northern Ireland reached three World Cup finals, the Southerners repeatedly failed: then Jack Charlton and Maurice Setters took charge, narrowly and unexpectedly winning their qualifying group with a more direct style of play based on getting the ball behind opposition defences.

It was appropriate that two Englishmen should be running the team, which because of the liberal qualification rules included players born in Preston, Liverpool, Huddersfield and West Ham, as well as Glasgow and Dublin. The whole side though was drawn from Football League clubs, who regularly pick up the best players from such prolific nurseries as Home Farm and more established clubs like Shamrock Rovers.

Shamrock's dominance has been one of the few continuous features of soccer history since the split with Northern Ireland in 1921, after which the country's first internationals were played under the name 'Irish Free State'. Those were in the 1924 Olympics. The Irish also showed considerably greater enthusiasm for international competition, entering all the early World Cups except the very first.

Perhaps this wider experience helped towards their historic victory against England at Goodison Park in 1948 – the first game England had lost at home to a non-British country. At that time players like Johnny Carey, the majestic Manchester United captain, still appeared for Northern Ireland as well, finishing his international career with 29 caps for the South and 11 for the North!

One of the most gifted of all Irish players, Liam Brady, who spent seven seasons in Italy between his time with Arsenal and West Ham.

RUMANIA

Rumania earned their place in football history when King Carol agreed to pay the wages of the country's top players, in their absence, while they travelled to Uruguay for the inaugural World Cup finals in 1930. They were eliminated in the first round group by their hosts and have been struggling ever since to assert themselves in the shadow of their more illustrious Eastern European neighbours.

British engineers in the Ploesti oilfields took the game to Rumania at the turn of the century. King Carol founded the first Rumania F.A. in 1910 and the national team attended the World Cup finals not only in 1930, but in 1934 and 1938. It was not then until 1970 that they returned.

Captain and star forward was Mircea Lucescu, who later became national manager and was unlucky not to steer his team through to the 1986 World Cup back in Mexico. However, Rumania's progress was confirmed that year by Steaua Bucharest's victory over Barcelona in a European Cup final penalty shoot-out.

No-one had paid much attention to Rumanian clubs before then. Dinamo Bucharest had once reached the last four of the European Cup and Craiova had lost on away goals to Benfica at the same stage of the U.E.F.A. Cup. Then along came Steaua, founded in 1948 as the army team C.C.A., to change all that. Brilliant tactics, expertly carried out, and strong nerves in the penalty shoot-out brought the victory over Barcelona.

Steaua were the first Eastern European winners and went on to defeat Dynamo Kiev in the Supercup too. In 1986–87 and 1987–88 they did the domestic double without losing a single game and along with Dinamo had become embarrassingly superior to the rest.

Not surprisingly, they achieved some prodigious scoring feats. Dinamo's Georgescu twice won the Golden Boot as Europe's top League scorer, totalling a record 47 in 1977. In 1987 club-mate Rodion Camataru emulated him in more controversial circumstances, 21 of his 44 coming in the last seven games, amidst suspicions that Dinamo had exchanged points for goals to help him win.

Steaua's Victor Piturca and Gheorghe Hagi (signed in 1987 from S.S.B.) needed no such help in averaging almost a goal per game as their club went on to become established European Cup contenders. Although Anderlecht had their revenge in 1987, winning a second round tie, the Rumanians reached the semi-final in 1988 (beating Glasgow Rangers before losing to Benfica) and then the final again, where they found the Dutch-inspired A.C. Milan too good for them.

Steaua's Helmut Ducadam never played again after celebrating victory in the 1986 European Cup with his penalty saves.

SWEDEN

The Swedes were by far Scandinavia's leading football nation until Denmark suddenly produced such a fine team in the late 1970s. Like their neighbours, they have one of Europe's oldest League Championships, dating back in their case to 1896: Örgryte of Gothenburg, who won it for the first four years, remain a First Division club but have been overshadowed by Malmö and I.F.K. Gothenburg.

Malmö, under English coach Bob Houghton (later to join Bristol City), were the surprise team of the 1979 European Cup, their weakened team losing a poor final 1–0 to Nottingham Forest. I.F.K., 'the Angels', shocked Hamburg by beating them home and away in the 1982 U.E.F.A. Cup final and won it again five years later against Dundee United.

But as an illustration of the greater resources available to Swedish clubs than Danish ones, I.F.K. were able to spend some £150,000 on Lennart Nilsson as a replacement for another export, Johnny Ekström.

Internationally, their outstanding achievement was finishing runners-up to Brazil when hosting the enjoyable 1968 World Cup finals. But despite qualifying for the World Cup finals of 1974 and 1978, the Swedes have subsequently tended to miss out, albeit narrowly, on the major international competitions.

Malmö's defence in depth caused a poor European Cup final against Nottingham Forest, who won it 1-0.

SWITZERLAND

The outstanding Swiss player of modern times, Claudio Sulser, causing Ipswich problems at Portman Road in 1979.

Although failing to qualify for the World Cup finals since 1966, Switzerland generally have an international team capable of making life difficult for larger countries, while sponsorship has made it possible to attract foreign players and ensure a reasonable standard in the national league.

England were victims, by two goals to one, in May 1981, a result which decided manager Ron Greenwood on retirement (he subsequently changed his mind). The winning goal was scored by Claudio Sulser, the outstanding Swiss player of modern times. A law student, he led the European Cup goalscorers of 1979, when the Grasshoppers reached the quarter-final before losing to Nottingham Forest.

F.C. Zurich and Young Boys Berne have both reached European Cup semi-finals and are now, like the majority of leading Swiss clubs, approaching their centenary.

A famous victory over England – by 2–1 in 1938 – was masterminded by coach Karl Rappan, an Austrian who devised the 'Verrou' (bolt) system of defence. Like any other tactical device, it worked better-some days than others: in the 1954 World Cup, Switzerland defeated Italy twice, only to lose to Austria 7–5 in one of the competition's most amazing games ever.

FINLAND

Football in Finland has to compete for popularity with track and field and with winter sports. Thus the game remains part-time and amateur and players with ability move to clubs in West Germany, Holland and Belgium. Central defender Arto Tolsa and winger Juhani Peltonen led the way, followed more recently by Aki Lahtinen (who had a spell at Notts County), Jari Rantanen (Leicester) and Petri Tiainen (Ajax).

English businessmen took football to Helsinki in the 1890s, a federation was formed in 1907 and the national team entered the 1912 Olympics in Stockholm. Finland beat Italy and Tsarist Russia but then crashed 4–0 to England amateurs and 9–0 to Holland. The national team has hardly enjoyed much more success since, despite the work in recent years of former national manager Martti Kuusela.

Finland's top club are H.J.K. Helsinki, who have won the Championship on a record 16 occasions since it was launched in 1908.

Right: *Asegir Sigurvinsson, the most successful of Iceland's football exports.*

Below: *Finland's Jari Rantanen tangles with John Barnes.*

ICELAND

Iceland claim to be Europe's last true amateurs. Yet they have achieved some remarkable results over the years, despite their perpetual role as World Cup and European Championship minnows. Their greatest success was under English manager Tony Knapp in the 1976 European qualifiers against East Germany, who had reached the World Cup finals two years earlier. Iceland drew 1–1 away, then won 2–1 at home.

Iceland have exported some fine players over the years, starting with Albert Gudmundsson (later F.A. president), who played in France in the 1950s, as well as Jo Edvaldsson (Celtic), Siggi Jonsson (Sheffield Wednesday) and Arnor Gudjohsen (Anderlecht). Their best player has been midfielder Asgeir Sigurvinsson, a great success with Standard Liège, Bayern Munich and Stuttgart.

Icelandic clubs have made little impression on European competition. Akranes (founded 1911) have dominated the domestic game lately. K.R. Reykjavik hold the record of 20 league titles but the last of those was back in 1968.

TURKEY

Rulers of the Ottoman Empire were highly suspicious of students' attempts to introduce football in the 1890s. They feared football clubs were mere 'fronts' for revolutionary political organisations. But Turkish football has threatened no-one. On the one occasion they qualified for the World Cup finals, in 1954, they owed it all to a blind boy drawing lots after a play-off against Spain.

Both at national and club level the Turks have tended to suffer from a failure of temperament. When Galatasary reached the European Cup semi-final in 1989, their quarter-final home leg had to be played on neutral ground because of crowd trouble in a previous round – which made the achievement all the more remarkable. Their star was Tanju Colak, whose 39 League goals the previous season made him Europe's leading goalscorer.

The domestic game is dominated by the three-way Istanbul rivalry between Galatasaray, Besiktas and Fenerbahce, who hold the record of ten league titles since a national championship was established only in 1958–59.

Erdal Keser, one of the few Turkish stars to have played abroad.

Every one of F.I.F.A.'s six worldwide confederations has its minnow nations – the cannon-fodder expected to feed the major teams' goal difference column.

CYPRUS and **MALTA** are obvious qualifiers as islands in a European ocean. The Cypriots' one claim to fame was the year Sotiris Kaiafas won the Golden Boot award by scoring 36 league goals in a season. But a better example of the minnows' worth was the recent transfer to Italy last year of Malta's star forward, Carmelo Busuttil. He was sold to Verbania . . . in the Italian regional league.

LUXEMBOURG once beat Portugal – Eusebio and all – in a World Cup qualifier. But a measure of their success since was the delight shown by their players after forcing a goalless draw against Scotland in the last European Championship. **ALBANIA** has talent but also temper. Four players, including captain and goalkeeper Perlat Musta, were banned by their own federation after being sent off playing for Partizan Tirana against Benfica in the European Cup.

Left: *Albania's Perlat Musta, a temperamental talent.*

ARGENTINA

Argentina is football's greatest melting pot. Into its clubs are poured the ingenuity and enthusiasm of a host of immigrant nationalities. River Plate, with their British middle-class image; Boca Juniors, the 'Italian' club from the port; Racing, obviously French. Then there are the railway clubs: Quilmes, Ferrocarril Oeste and Rosario Central.

Argentina has produced more of the world's great players than most other countries – from Bernabe Ferreyra in the 1920s, via Jose Manuel Moreno, Alfredo Di Stefano, Adolfo Pedernera, Angel Labruna and Omar Sivori through to Mario Kempes and Diego Maradona. It has also exported most, which explains why Argentina took so long to win the World Cup. The triumphant host manager in 1978 was Cesar Menotti, who had been succeeded by Carlos Bilardo when Maradonna's magic conjured up a repeat in Mexico in 1986.

Argentina's charismatic manager, César Menotti, who led the team to success in the 1978 World Cup.

Bilardo had been an abrasive midfielder with Estudiantes de La Plata, one of five Argentine clubs who dominated the South American Cup over the years.

Argentina pose before playing, and beating 2–0, Bulgaria in the 1986 World Cup.

THE CLUBS

Boca Juniors

Boca Juniors are traditionally the 'other' club in Argentina alongside River Plate. The clubs are such bitter rivals that only a handful of men have played for both. Whereas River Plate are seen as the middle-class set-up, Boca are the port club – founded in 1913 by an Irishman, Patrick MacCarthy, and a group of newly-arrived Italian immigrants. Boca won the last Argentine amateur championship in 1930 and the first professional title the following year. They also adopted professionalism quickly enough to make some startling signings in the 1930s, including the great Brazilian full-back Domingos da Guia. In 1963 Boca became the first Argentine club to reach the South American Club Cup final. They lost to Pele's Santos but returned eventually to take the title in 1977 and 1978 under the controversial coach Juan Carlos Lorenzo. For much of the 1980s Boca have been weighed down with financial problems, which meant selling star players instead of buying them.

River Plate

No review of the world's great clubs dare overlook Club Atletico River Plate. Since being founded on 25 May 1901, River have been in the forefront of Argentine

Above: *Hugo Gatti, goalkeeper of Boca Juniors.*

Another goal for the incomparable Di Stefano, the inspiration behind Real Madrid's five successive European Cup wins.

soccer – from the 1920s battle over professionalism through the 1930s when River's big-spending transfer policy earned the nickname 'Millionarios'.

In the 1940s River put together a legendary forward line of Munoz, Jose Manuel Moreno, Pedernera, Angel Labruna and Loustau which carved up so many opposing defences it was called La Maquina (The Machine). Alfredo Di Stefano and Omar Sivori built their original reputations with River Plate – indeed it was thanks to the world record sale of Sivori for £91,000 to Juventus in 1957 which enabled River to complete construction of the stadium which was principal host venue for the 1978 World Cup. The club's one outstanding ambition was achieved in 1986 when River beat America of Colombia to win the South American Club Cup and went on to overcome Steaua of Rumania for the world crown.

Independiente

Independiente completed one of the game's greatest transfer scoops in the 1930s when they signed Paraguayan centre-forward Arsenio Erico in exchange for the equivalent of £1 plus a £1 donation to the Red Cross! Erico, the boyhood idol of Alfredo Di Stefano, inspired the club from the industrial city of Avellaneda to two league titles in the late 1930s – their most successful era until the arrival of manager Manuel Giudice in the early 1960s.

Independiente realised, far quicker than many of the more famous South American clubs, the importance of the Copa Libertadores. Their successes in 1964 and 1965 brought them worldwide attention and record gate receipts. Independiente invested sensibly and, in the 1970s, won the South American club title a record four years in a row. They landed the World Club title in 1973, beating Juventus 1–0 in Rome, and again in 1984 against Liverpool, also 1–0, in Tokyo. Midfielder Ricardo Bochini has been their most famous modern player.

Percudani jostles for the ball with Gary Gillespie as Independiente become World Club champions for the second time by beating Liverpool in 1984.

PLAYER PROFILES

Ossie Ardiles, whose close-dribbling skills delighted Tottenham supporters after his signing in 1978.

OSVALDO ARDILES

An inventive, hard-working midfield star of Argentina's 1978 World Cup triumph, Osvaldo Ardiles then transferred from Huracan to Tottenham for £325,000. His arrival at White Hart Lane, along with compatriot Ricky Villa, was a brave but highly-successful gamble – even though Ardiles spent one season in exile with Paris Saint-Germain in 1982–83 because of uncertainties created by the Falklands war. His success in the Football League persuaded many more clubs to dip into the foreign transfer market, though few met with similar success. Ardiles's career with Tottenham probably reached its peak with the 1981 F.A. Cup final victory over Manchester City, though it took a replay before 'Ossie's Dream' came true. Ardiles was born in the provincial city of Cordoba on 3 August 1952, began with a boys' team called Red Star, signed for first division Instituto, then moved to Huracan in 1975 – the year he earned the first of his 56 caps.

ALFREDO DI STEFANO

Alfredo Di Stefano was the most complete footballer of all time: a goal-scorer, goal-maker and director of play all rolled into one thanks to remarkable stamina built up running the streets of Buenos Aires as a boy. Di Stefano, born on 4 July 1926, began with River Plate, exploded during a brief spell on loan to Huracan, then became the brightest star of the pirate league in Colombia in the early 1950s, with Millonarios of Bogota. Real Madrid signed him after he starred against them in a tournament in 1952. He inspired Madrid's trend-setting run of five successive victories in the European Cup, culminating in the great 7–3 victory over Eintract Frankfurt in Glasgow in 1960. Di Stefano, still the European Cup's record marksman with a career total of 49 goals, missed out only on the World Cup. He was a member of Spain's squad in Chile in 1962 but was unable to play because of injury. In all, he played seven times for Argentina in the 1940s and 31 times for Spain in the 1950s and 1960s.

MARIO KEMPES

Mario Kempes was Argentina's hero of heroes after the 1978 World Cup triumph. He scored six goals in the finals, including two in the 3–1 victory over Holland which earned Argentina the Cup. By then Kempes had already moved to Valencia of Spain, having earned his transfer from Rosario Central with the potential displayed in the 1974 World Cup finals in West Germany. In his first season with Valencia he was top scorer in the Spanish League. Then came the World Cup success. However he later fell out with coach Alfredo Di Stefano, lost form, suffered a series of injuries and was virtually unrecognizable when Valencia beat Arsenal on penalties in the 1980 Cup-Winners' Cup final. The old Kempes re-emerged after a transfer home to River Plate in 1980 when he was still only 26. He regained his international place in time for the 1982 World Cup then wound down his career in Austria. He played 51 games for Argentina.

Mario Kempes, most heroic of Argentina's World Cup-winning heroes of 1978.

ANGEL AMADEO LABRUNA

Angel Amadeo Labruna was born on 28 September 1918 and enrolled in the River Plate club when he was only six because he spent so much time playing football in the streets his father was afraid he would be run down by a car.

He graduated through the youth sections and made his first-team debut at 18 in 1937, becoming an outstanding member of the great Maquina attack which won four championships in the 1940s. After turning down all offers from Europe, Labruna masterminded another five titles in the early 1960s. He played until he was 40, appearing 36 times for his country, then turned to coaching with equal success – with smaller clubs Platense, Rosario Central and Talleres of Cordoba as well as River Plate. He steered them to six Argentine titles but could not bring his beloved club the one honour coveted above all others, the South American Club Cup. River got there in the end – but three years after Labruna had died in September 1983.

DIEGO MARADONA

Diego Maradona is unrivalled as the current world No. 1, whatever feelings may persist in England about his 'hand of God' goal in the 1986 World Cup.

Maradona was born on 30 October 1960 and made his league debut at 15 and first played for Argentina as a 17-year-old substitute in a 5–1 win over Hungary in 1977. But he was judged too inexperienced by Argentine manager Cesar Menotti for the 1978 World Cup and was dropped from the squad on the eve of the finals.

He captained Argentina to victory in the 1979 World Youth Cup before figuring in three multi-million transfers. The first was from Argentinos Juniors to Boca Juniors in 1981; his second to Barcelona after the 1982 World Cup; and his third for a then world record £5 million to Napoli in 1984.

Maradona had a disappointing World Cup in 1982 but more than made up with his Cup-winning inspiration and great goals in Mexico four years later. He followed up by leading Napoli to their first-ever Italian League title.

BIBIANI RAIMUNDO ORSI

Bibiani Raimundo Orsi, nicknamed 'Mumo' and born on 2 December 1901, played 37 times for Argentina in the 1920s and 16 times for Italy in the 1930s. Orsi began with Independiente and was a championship-winner in Argentina in 1922 and 1926. With the national team he won a silver medal at the 1928 Olympics in Amsterdam and then signed for Juventus. The fee was £50 to Independiente and a Fiat 509 car for Orsi. The transfer provoked a scandal and Orsi was suspended for a year. He then emerged as a member of the legendary Juventus team which won the Italian League five years in a row and, in 1934, was a World Cup winner with Italy. Immigrant Argentians of Italian stock were eligible for National Service in Italy so manager Vittorio Pozzo decreed: 'If they can die for Italy, they can play for Italy.' Orsi returned home in 1935, playing successively for Independiente and San Lorenzo in Argentina, Penarol (Uruguay) and Flamengo (Brazil), where he ended his career as Rio state champion in 1939. He died in April 1986.

Maradona: a talent worth millions.

England versus Argentina in the 1966 World Cup. Rattin, the Argentine captain, argues with the referee before being ordered off the pitch.

ANTONIO UBALDO RATTIN

Antonio Ubaldo Rattin is as much a legend in England as he is in Argentina, though for somewhat different reasons. In Argentina Rattin is remembered as a pillar of Boca Juniors from 1956, when he made his debut, until his retirement, prematurely enforced by injury, in 1970. He is also remembered as the last of the big, powerful, old-fashioned attacking centre-halves in a line which extended from Luisito Monti in the 1920s via Nestor Rossi in the 1940s and 1950s.

Rattin played for Argentina at the 1962 World Cup finals in Chile but it was in the 1966 tournament that he earned notoriety with his expulsion by West German referee Kreitlein in the quarter-final against England at Wembley. Rattin, born on 16 May 1937, learned his football in the town of Tigre on the River Plate delta and cost Boca just the price of a second-class rail ticket. He played a then club record 357 league games for Boca, won five championship medals and appeared 37 times for his country.

OMAR SIVORI

Born on 2 October 1935, playing 18 times for Argentina in the 1950s and nine times for Italy in the 1960s, Omar Sivori was part of a great succession at River Plate, learning from Angel Labruna, just as Labruna had learned from the great Jose Manuel Moreno in the 1940s. Sivori thrilled all the Italian spies when Argentina won the 1957 South American championship and was signed for a world record £91,000 by Juventus. With Welshman John Charles, Sivori made up one of the most successful attacking partnerships in Italian football history. He loved teasing defenders with a 'tunnel' or 'nutmeg' but his temper earned him a record number of suspensions. Sivori was voted European Footballer of the Year in 1961 and justified his award when, in the spring of 1962, he scored the goal which brought Real Madrid's first home defeat in the European Cup. Sivori ended his career with Napoli and was later, briefly, manager of Argentina before becoming a TV soccer analyst.

BRAZIL

Give anyone, anywhere a magic spell to turn them into a star player in the style of any country they choose and the odds are they will choose Brazil.

Even though Brazil have won nothing at senior international level since the 1970 World Cup in Mexico, their pulling power remains second to none. When Brazil go on tour, the rest of the world comes along to watch.

All that is owed to the great players of Brazil: starting with the first, Arthur Friedenreich. A mulatto, he broke through the racial barriers and opened up a shanty-town dream. The poorest boy, if he had the talent, could become rich and famous if he were discovered by one of the big clubs.

It happened to so many: to Pele, to Didi, to Garrincha. And it is their genius which built a football image so imposing it survives even the domestic game's administrative chaos.

Brazil were the first nation to win the World Cup three times and to win on the 'wrong' continent; they also gave the game Pele. What more can anyone ask?

THE CLUBS

Flamengo

Controversy continues to this day over whether Flamengo are the oldest football club in Brazil. The truth is that the Clube de Regatas do Flamengo was set up as a sailing club in 1895 but did not organise a football section until 1911. The middle-class sailing image has long since disappeared; Flamengo are now the football

Brazil on their way to victory in the 1970 World Cup final as Pele opens the scoring.

club of the masses with more than 70,000 members – second only in Brazil to Corinthians of Sao Paulo. Flamengo and their great rivals Fluminense are the two great sporting institutions of Rio. A string of great players have graced the red-and-black hoops of Flamengo over the years, from Domingos da Guia and Leonidas in the 1930s and 1940s to Zico and Socrates in the 1970s and 1980s.

But Flamengo, for all their traditional skill and artistry, have also been able to stand up for themselves – as in the rugged victory over Cobreloa of Chile in the 1981 South American Club Cup final. Zico and Flamengo then showed a more enchanting style in beating Liverpool 3–0 for the world crown in Tokyo.

Fluminense

If Flamengo are the club of the masses, great rivals Fluminense retain an upper-class image. Their nickname is 'white powder', referring to the face powder used by the aristocracy at the turn of the century. Fluminense is more of a private club than Flamengo when it comes to membership and members' facilities.

Founded by English immigrants organized by Oscar Cox in 1902, Fluminense were prime movers behind the organization of the Rio de Janeiro (or Carioca) championship, the creation of a national federation and a national team. Great players to have worn the red and green stripes include Brazil's 1950 World Cup centre-forward Ademir de Menezes, the great midfield general Didi, the 1970 World Cup hero Roberto Rivelino, and most recently, the Paraguayan Julio Cesar Romero.

He inspired Fluminense's 1980s hat-trick in the Rio championships when he was generally considered the finest player in Brazilian football – quite a compliment! However, 'Flu' have yet to make a mark on the South American Club Cup.

Santos

The rise and fall of Santos from nowhere to worldwide celebrity and back again was linked inevitably with Pele. His 'discovery' in the mid-1950s encouraged the club to build a team worthy of his talents.

That was easy while money flowed in from the worldwide exhibition tours Santos undertook in the 1960s and early 1970s. At their peak Santos were competitive as well as entertaining and the manner of their victory over Benfica in the 1962 World Club Cup final entered into football legend. The constant touring, however, burnt out many of their promising youngsters. Santos' defeat by Independiente in the 1964 South American Cup coincided with a dispute which led to temporary boycott of the competition by Brazilian clubs. By the time they returned Santos were past their best. More time and effort went into taking the 'circus' round the world than went into domestic competition. Since Pele's last season in 1973, Santos have won the Paulista title – once.

Defeat by Italy in a thrilling game ended Brazil's hopes in 1982. Socrates on the ball.

PLAYER PROFILES

CARECA

New generation striker Careca made his debut in a 1–1 draw against Czechoslovakia in March 1982. Born on 5 October 1960, he began his career with Benfica, a minor club in Campinas state. He was signed by Guarani and helped them win the Brazilian championship, under future national team boss Carlos Alberto Silva, when still only 17.

Careca missed the 1982 World Cup after being injured in training in Spain on the eve of the finals.

Careca was then sold to Sao Paulo and made World Cup amends in superb style with his leadership of the Brazilian attack in Mexico in the 1986 finals.

He scored five goals, including two against Northern Ireland. Careca was the 25-goal top scorer when Sao Paulo won the 1986–87 Brazilian national championship. One of those goals arrived in the final against . . . his old club, Guarani.

He was then sold to Diego Maradona's Napoli for £3 million in the summer of 1987.

DIDI

Didi was the midfield master for Brazil's World Cup victories of 1958 and 1962. Born Waldir Pereira on 8 October 1928 in the provincial town of Campos, 130 miles from Rio de Janeiro, he began with local club Americano before being brought to top football by Madureira in 1949.

Fluminense signed Didi a year later when he scored the first goal in the new Maracana stadium. Didi's World Cup baptism came in 1954, then it was his typical, swerving free kick which beat Peru and took Brazil to the 1958 finals in Sweden. By now Didi had joined Botafogo and his understanding with club-mate and outside right Garrincha was one of the crucial factors in Brazil's World Cup 'double'.

In between the 1958 and 1962 finals he spent a brief unhappy spell with Real Madrid before returning to Botafogo, then turning to coaching. Didi's biggest managerial success was guiding Peru to the 1970 World Cup quarter-finals. He won 70 caps for Brazil.

Careca left dangerously unattended by Spain at the 1986 World Cup finals.

A characteristic swerving free-kick from Didi troubles Czechoslovakia in the 1962 World Cup final. Brazil won 3-1.

GARRINCHA

Garrincha's was a classic soccer tragedy. Born on 21 March 1933, and raised in poverty, the 'Little Bird' was half-crippled as a child by polio.

He knew little of school, starting work in childhood in a textiles factory, where he was discovered playing football by Botafogo in 1952. His mischievous approach endeared him to his team-mates, if not to his coaches. Vicente Feola took Garrincha to the 1958 World Cup finals but was advised not to play him by the team psychologist.

After Brazil's second game, a goalless draw against England, Garrincha's Botafogo club-mates urged Feola to think again. The rest is history.

He ran rings round his full-backs in those finals of 1958 and of 1962, when his brilliance made up for the absence of the injured Pele. He played 51 times for Brazil but injuries and domestic problems caught up with him in the mid-1960s. Garrincha could not cope. He died of alcoholic poisoning at 49 in January 1983. His real name was Manuel Francisco dos Santos.

Garrincha leaves another defender standing at the 1962 World Cup finals in Chile.

GERSON

Born on 11 January 1941, Gerson de Oliveira Nunes played 78 times for Brazil in the 1960s and 1970s. He was the midfield controller in the great Brazil team which won their third World Cup in Mexico in 1970.

Gerson has since brought the good sense he showed on the pitch to his work as a television and radio commentator. He began with Flamengo, played for Brazil in the Rome Olympics of 1960, then joined Botafogo in 1963. He stepped straight into the midfield role left vacant by Didi with both club and country.

If Gerson was a disappointment at the 1966 World Cup, he learned from the experience. In 1967 and 1968 he was the fulcrum around which Botafogo won the Rio league title. A year later they surprisingly accepted a £100,000 offer from Sao Paulo, but their belief that he was finished was shattered by his form at the 1970 World Cup.

Gerson spent his time laying on goals for team-mates – until the final against Italy when he cracked home a glorious left-foot shot of his own.

JAIRZINHO

Brazil have a tradition for great outside rights. Julinho in the early 1950s was followed by Garrincha and then along came Jairzinho – developed in Garrincha's shadow at Botafogo.

Jairzinho, born Jair Ventura Filho on Christmas Day, 1944, was a far more orthodox winger than Garrincha but his pace and explosive shooting were similarly devastating. In the 1970 World Cup Jairzinho

Jairzinho, scorer in every game Brazil played at the 1970 World Cup.

became the only player to score in every match at every stage of a finals tournament.

Jairzinho twice broke his right leg and though he recovered full fitness his acceleration had been impaired by the time the 1974 World Cup came around.

His reputation earned a transfer to Marseille but he could not adjust to life or football in France. In 1976 he returned to Brazil to join Cruzeiro, with whom he won the South American Club Cup in 1976, before trying his luck in Venezuela with Portuguesa of Caracas. He was capped 85 times by Brazil.

LEONIDAS

Leonidas da Silva, the 'Black Diamond', was Brazil's greatest footballer in the 1930s, appearing with enormous success at the World Cups of 1934 and 1938. Leonidas began with Bonsucesso of Rio de Janeiro and made a dramatic debut for Brazil in December 1932, scoring both goals in a 2–1 win over Uruguay, when still only 19. Nacional of Montevideo immediately signed him but Leonidas returned to Brazil in 1934 after injuring a knee and led Vasco da Gama to the Rio state championship. He repeated the trick for Botafogo in 1935 and Flamengo in 1938 and then won five Paulista titles with Sao Paulo. In between he starred in the 1938 World Cup finals where he scored four goals in Brazil's first round match against Poland. The Brazilians grew so confident they rested Leonidas from the semi-final against Italy, so that he would be fresh for the final. But without him, Brazil lost 2–1. He played 19 times for his country.

PELE

The most famous footballer of all time exploded on the game as a 17-year-old when he scored twice for Brazil in the 5–2 victory over Sweden in the 1958 World Cup final in Stockholm.

Pele missed the 1962 defeat of Czechoslovakia because of injury and was literally kicked out of the finals in England in 1966.

In 1970 he returned in all his glory to inspire Brazil's triumph in Mexico – a tournament in which Pele produced classics such as the 'wrong-way' dummy round the Uruguay goalkeeper and the shot at goal against Czechoslovakia from just inside his own half.

Pele, born Edson Arantes do Nascimento on 21 October 1940, had played his club football only for Santos when he retired in 1973. Then he was persuaded into a comeback in the North American Soccer League as part of the New York Cosmos attempt to 'sell' soccer to the U.S. Pele, the game's greatest ambassador, triumphed; Cosmos were not so lucky. Pele played 93 times for Brazil between 1957 and 1971.

Pele: the most famous footballer of them all.

Zico – holder of 78 caps.

ZICO

Zico had three elder brothers who were First Division footballers, but when he joined Flamengo as a teenager he was so waif-like they put him on special vitamin and weight-training courses.

In 1976 Zico scored a dramatic winner from a free kick on his international debut against Uruguay and went on to appear in the World Cup finals tournaments of 1978, 1982 (his best) and 1986, after which he retired from the national team at the age of 33. He had played 78 times for Brazil. Zico missed a decisive penalty in the 1986 quarter-final against France. But savage treatment from opposing defenders and a string of knee operations made it a miracle that he was out on the pitch in Guadalajara at all.

Zico played all his club career with Flamengo, apart from a short, unhappy spell with Udinese in Italy. In 1981 his brilliance inspired Flamengo's World Club Cup victory over Liverpool in Tokyo. His real name is Artur Antunes Coimbra.

URUGUAY

'Other countries,' said Ondino Viera, Uruguay's 1966 World Cup manager, 'have their history. Uruguay has its football.'

Uruguay, a tiny nation perched on the north bank of the River Plate and squashed by Brazil to the north, east and west, boasts a remarkable record. In 1924 they amazed Europe with the quality and skill as they became the first non-European Olympic champions. They also won four years later in Amsterdam then, two further years forward, staged the inaugural World Cup and won that as well.

In 1950 Uruguay sprung one of the game's sensations when they beat runaway favourites Brazil in Rio de Janeiro to regain the World Cup. And, four years later in Berne, Switzerland, their vain attempt to defend their crown against Hungary produced a semi-final often regarded as the greatest match of all time – though Uruguay lost 4–2 in extra-time.

With such a history, it's no surprise that the Peñarol and Nacional clubs should have been in the forefront of launching the South American Club Cup.

THE CLUBS

Nacional

Nacional took their name from their first match, when a mixture of players from the Montevideo Football Club and the Uruguay Athletic Club were chosen to represent Uruguay against an Argentine Select in Buenos Aires in 1899.

Nacional/Uruguay won 3–2 and never looked back. Their rivalry with Peñarol over the years has been bitter and intense; Nacional fans still enjoy stories of the club's Quinquenio de Oro (Golden Five Years) at the turn of the 1940s when Nacional beat Peñarol 8–0.

Since 1960 the clubs have been bitter

Uruguay briefly in trouble in the decisive match of the 1950 World Cup finals against hot favourites Brazil. They recovered to win 2-1.

competitors at international level, too, in the South American Club Cup. Nacional beat Estudiantes of Argentina in 1971, Sao Paulo of Brazil in 1980 and Newell's Old Boys (Argentina) in 1988.

Each time they went on to win the World Club's Cup – against Panathinaikos of Greece, Nottingham Forest and then, on penalties, against P.S.V. Eindhoven.

That was the first world club showdown in Tokyo and Nacional won with a single goal from their man of the match, centre-forward Waldemar Victorino.

Peñarol

Arthur Davenport, Frank Henderson, Frank Hudson and Roland Moor could have had no idea what they were starting when, in 1891, they founded the Central Uruguay Railway Cricket Club.

One year later they also tried their hand at football, beat the British School of Montevideo 2–0 and would become instrumental in organizing a first Uruguayan championship.

When the British sold their railway company interests at the start of the First World War the Italians moved into the sports club and named it after the suburb where they played – Pignarolo in Italian, Peñarol in Spanish.

Peñarol became the dominant club in Uruguay, and one of the greatest in South America. They provided the backbone of Uruguay's 1950 World Cup-winning side, were first winners of the South American Club Cup (in 1960) and, a year later, became first South American winners of the World Club Cup.

Great names over the years have included Obdulio Varela, Rodriguez Andrade, Juan Schiaffino, Nestor Goncalves, Pedro Rocha and Fernando Morena.

PLAYER PROFILES

ENZO FRANCESCOLI

Born on 12 November 1961, Enzo Francescoli made his debut for Uruguay in their victorious 1982 Nehru Cup campaign in India. Francescoli was one of the few positive contributions of a rugged Uruguayan team at the 1986 World Cup finals and was sold immediately afterwards, by his Argentine club River Plate, to the Frenchmen from Racing of Paris for £1.7 million.

Racing struggled in his first season, provoking speculation that sooner or later Francescoli would be sold to one of the big Italian clubs.

The 1984 South American Foot-

Enzo Francescoli, one of Uruguay's few successes in 1986.

baller of the Year, Francescoli attended the same school as an earlier Uruguayan 'great', Fernando Morena. He joined Wanderers, a minor Montevideo club, at 15 and two years later made his First Division debut.

Francescoli was sold to River Plate of Buenos Aires in 1983 and inspired Uruguay's South American championship triumphs both that year and in 1987. In 1985 he was the Argentine league's 25-goal top scorer as River won the title.

FERNANDO MORENA

As a teenager Fernando Morena could not decide whether to concentrate on football or become a Roman Catholic priest. In the end he opted for football and, totalling 667 goals, developed into Uruguay's most prolific marksman. He also played 46 times for Uruguay. Morena did start young – making his first division debut with minor club River Plate (nothing to do with the Argentine outfit) when only 14 in 1966. In two-and-a-half years he scored 51 goals before joining Peñarol.

Morena stayed seven years, playing in the 1974 World Cup finals, before moving to Spain to play for Rayo Vallecano and Valencia. He averaged 20 goals a season – brilliant work in the tough Spanish League – before returning to Peñarol in time to score the decisive goal in their victory over Cobreloa of Chile in the final of the 1982 South American Club Cup.

Morena then had a short spell with Boca Juniors in Argentina before returning to Peñarol and later becoming their coach.

OBDULIO VARELA

Obdulio Varela's career was a classic rags-to-riches story. Having left school at 13 to work on a building site, he was 'rescued' by first division Wanderers.

Fernando Morena in action against Holland at the 1974 World Cup.

Varela had already made his Uruguay debut when he was transferred to Peñarol in 1942. He was 33 when he captained underdogs Uruguay against Brazil in the 1950 World Cup final in Rio. His experience proved vital after Brazil went ahead two minutes into the second half. Varela picked the ball out of the net and hung on to it while Brazilian euphoria died down.

It was then centre-half Varela who helped set up Juan Alberto Schiaffino's equaliser and Varela, at the end, who carried off the World Cup. Varela also captained Uruguay in the 1954 finals even though he was 37. He scored one goal and made another in a 4–2 win over England in the quarter-finals, but a pulled muscle kept him out of the semi-final defeat by Hungary and on returning home he retired. He had played 52 times for his country.

Pedro Rocha, Uruguay's best player in the 1966 World Cup.

PEDRO ROCHA

Born 3 December 1942, in the provincial town of Salto, Pedro Rocha played for a local club called Peñarol before joining the 'real' Peñarol at 17. Rocha was a star of the Uruguayan team which reached the 1966 World Cup quarter-finals in England but was underrated in Europe. One reason was bad luck in the 1970 finals when he was injured in the first match and could only watch as his team-mates reached the last four.

Then, when Peñarol could no longer afford to keep him, it was Sao Paulo of Brazil rather than a European club who snapped him up. At the time, both Spain and Italy had banned player imports.

Rocha won seven Uruguayan League titles with Peñarol as well as the World Club Cup in 1966. He was an instant success in Brazil: Sao Paulo won the state championship in his first full season and then finished runners-up in the national championship. After retiring he stayed on in Brazil as a coach. He had been capped 62 times.

JUAN ALBERTO SCHIAFFINO

Juan Alberto Schiaffino was a thin, classic inside-forward who could both make and take goals. At 20 he was the Uruguayan League's joint top scorer with 19 goals in Peñarol's title campaign. That earned him selection for Uruguay's South American championship bid that year.

They finished fourth but five years later, in 1950, Schiaffino was on top of the world after scoring Uruguay's equaliser in their shock 2–1 World Cup final victory over Brazil in Rio.

Schiaffino starred in the World Cup finals in Switzerland in 1954, and was then at 29 transferred to Milan for a world record £72,000. He was on the wrong end of a World Cup upset himself in 1957–58, as a member of the Italy team beaten by Northern Ireland in the qualifiers. The same season he narrowly missed European club honours when Milan lost 3–2 in extra-time – despite a Schiaffino goal – to Real Madrid in the Champions' Cup final. Schiaffino ended his career with Roma. He played 22 times for Uruguay and four times for Italy.

CHILE

Where can you find Everton and Rangers in the same First Division? The answer is Chile, where football was introduced in the last century by British sailors.

Though one of Chile's host of fledgling federations joined F.I.F.A. in 1912, it was not until five years later that agreement was reached over unified administration. In 1926 Chile won the South American Championship and four years later were present in Uruguay for the first World Cup.

In 1962 Chile were hosts themselves, making a remarkable success of the job considering the havoc wrought some months earlier by a major earthquake. Eladio Rojas, Leonel Sanchez and Alberto Fouilloux, stars of the Chilean team which finished third that year, still rank among the country's all-time greats, despite the later emergence of the Colo-Colo sharpshooter Carlos Caszely and several fine goalkeepers. One of them, Roberto Rojas, became a national hero when Chile finished runners-up to Uruguay in the 1987 South American Championship.

PERU

Peru was the centre of international football concern at the start of 1988, when the first-team squad of Alianza of Lima was wiped out in an air crash.

Among the dead was Marcos Calderon, who had managed Peru at the 1978 World Cup finals. And it was one of his old stars, Teofilo Cubillas, perhaps Peru's greatest-ever player, who came out of retirement to line up alongside the reserves and borrowed players as Alianza patched up a side to continue their fixture schedule. Alianza have won the championship a record 16 times and are one of Peru's three top clubs, along with Universitario and Sporting Cristal.

Peruvian football history is unusual in that the championship was set up in 1912, some ten years before the federation. Professionalism was introduced in 1941 but it was not until 1970 that Peru reached the World Cup finals for the first time. An entertaining, attractive team coached by former Brazil star, Didi, reached the quarter-finals before losing to . . . Brazil.

Peru's greatest? Teofilo Cubillas.

PARAGUAY

It was not the British, but a Dutchman, William Praat, who introduced football to Paraguay. He had been appointed in 1890 as physical training instructor at a school in Asuncion. The first game was not a success: one of the other teachers broke a leg.

The first official club were Olimpia, founded in 1902, and who rank today as one of the leading clubs in South America. Olimpia were beaten finalists in the first Copa Libertadores final but returned in 1979 not only to win the South American title but go on to take the World Club Cup as well.

Paraguay have also played their part in World Cup history. They competed in Uruguay in 1930, surprisingly ousted Uruguay in the 1958 qualifiers then went to Mexico in 1986 boasting two of South America's finest players in midfielder Julio Cesar Romero and striker Roberto Cabanas. Romero had been Paraguay's two-goal hero in their 1979 South American title triumph against Chile.

Former South American Footballer of the Year, Romero.

COLOMBIA have long been the biggest threat to the South American soccer 'hierarchy'. In the early 1950s it was thanks to the infamous pirate league which lured away star players without paying a transfer fee.

Now Colombian clubs can afford to pay top rates and cream off the stars of Argentina, Uruguay and Brazil legitimately. They have their own heroes too, such as South America's 1987 Footballer of the Year, Carlos Valderrama.

BOLIVIA have to rely on the problems posed by playing at altitude in La Paz to upset their fellow South Americans in competition. But at least they appeared in the World Cup finals in 1930 and 1950 – **VENEZUELA** and **ECUADOR** are the two South American nations who have never got that far. In Venezuela, football is second in popularity behind baseball. But Ecuador have exported some outstanding players over the years, the most famous being Alberto Spencer, who scored many important goals for the Uruguayan club, Peñarol, in the 1960s.

Left: *Colombia's new hero Carlos Valderrama.*

MEXICO

Mexico has dominated central America ever since international football has been played there. The country's size in terms of area, population and economy has always placed it head and shoulders above its smaller neighbours.

Mexico became, in 1986, the first country to host the World Cup twice. However, the absence of serious regional opposition has been more of a hindrance than a help. In nine World Cup finals appearances the Mexicans' best effort has been to reach the quarter finals twice – both occasions when they were hosts.

Television money plays an important role in the Mexican game. The giant Azteca stadium is owned by TV interests and the Mexican federation made a handsome profit with a TV deal under which the national team played their 1986 World Cup warm-up matches north of the United States border, in Los Angeles.

The Mexican Championship was launched in 1903 and professionalism introduced, after a football 'civil war' in 1931.

THE CLUBS

America, who play their home games in Mexico City's awesome Azteca stadium, and Guadalajara (nine titles) have been overtaken in recent years by the U.N.A.M. (Universidad Nacional Autonoma de Mexico) as the country's top team. U.N.A.M., nicknamed the Pumas, owed their success over the past decade to a string of expert goalscorers – Brazilian exile Cabinho, Mexico's Hugo Sanchez and then Luis Flores. But it was America who became the first C.O.N.C.A.C.A.F. club to win the Interamerican Cup when they beat South American champions Boca Juniors in 1978.

THE PLAYERS

A goalkeeper and a goalscorer have proved Mexico's most famous and most popular players. The goalkeeper was Antonio Carbajal (born June 7, 1929) who holds the record of appearances in five World Cup finals tournaments – the last in England in 1966. It was not until the end of the 1970s that Mexico found, in Hugo Sanchez (born 11 July 1958) a star of equal fame. Hugo, a qualified dentist, led Mexico at the Montreal Olympics then took his scoring talents to Spain's Atletico and Real Madrid to become league top scorer four years in a row.

Host country Mexico reached the quarter-final of the 1986 World Cup before losing on penalties to West Germany. Hugo Sanchez (white strip) was the Mexican hero.

In real terms it is a nonsense that *El Salvador*, *Haiti* and *Honduras* boast more World Cup finals appearances between them than the *United States* and *Canada*.

But football passions run far higher in the cluster of small central American nations than in their giant neighbours. That was clear from the 'football war' which broke out after El Salvador beat Honduras in the 1969 World Cup qualifiers. It was clear too from the enthusiasm both countries brought to the 1982 finals in Spain, when they qualified together.

El Salvador lost their three games but left behind in Spanish football an exciting forward named 'Magico' Gonzalez. Honduras, however, forced draws with both Spain and Northern Ireland. Their giant-killing bid revived memories of how Emmanuel Sanon of unrated Haiti had, in 1974, punctured Italy's famous 'catenacio' defence.

The Americans have qualified twice for the World Cup finals, though their first appearance has been overshadowed by the shock waves sent out by their 1–0 victory over England in Brazil on their second appearance in 1950. Previously the Americans had reached the 1930 semi-finals with a team managed by Jack Coll of Brooklyn Wanderers and including five former Scottish professionals.

But no effort was made to build on that success. Soccer flourished only in the ethnic leagues. Not until the 1960s were serious attempts made to establish soccer nationally, culminating in the brash experiment of the North American Soccer League. Huge interest was generated as New York Cosmos brought Pele out of retirement to partner Rick Davis, the best American player of the era.

For all the bluster of the N.A.S.L., the regional reality was best expressed by the fact that the U.S. national team never once qualified for the World Cup finals. Instead it was Canada, junior partners in the N.A.S.L., who broke through to the finals.

The U.S.A. now need to capitalize on interest generated by hosting the 1994 World Cup.

AFRICA

ALGERIA have made rapid soccer strides since obtaining independence in 1962. In 1976 Mouloudia Chalia won the African Champions' Cup at first attempt and then, in 1982 and 1986, Algeria became the first African nation to qualify for the finals of two successive World Cups.

In 1982 it took a controversial 'non-aggression pact' between West Germany and Austria to prevent them reaching the quarter-finals. Algeria's top player is Rabah Madjer, voted the 1987 African Footballer of the Year for his decisive role in helping his Portuguese club, F.C. Porto, win the European Cup.

CAMEROON were the first Black African nation to make an international impact. But long before they forced draws with Italy, Poland and Peru at the 1982 World Cup, they were established among Africa's best.

Oryx and Union of Douala as well as Canon of Yaounde had all won the African Champions' Cup and Union, Canon and Tonnerre had won the Cup-Winners' Cup. Goalkeeper Thomas Nkono, an African Footballer of the Year, has starred in Spain with Español, while centre-forward Roger

Rabah Madjer was the 1987 African Footballer of the Year.

Milla has scored freely for various clubs in France. Cameroon have won the last two African championships after losing to Egypt (on Penalties) in 1986.

MOROCCO's bid to host the 1994 World Cup underlined the progress and ambition evident ever since 1970, when they became the first African nation to appear in the finals.

Morocco returned to Mexico in 1986 with an outstanding goalkeeper in Zaki and midfielder in Mohammed Timoumi and gave eventual runners-up West Germany a second-round scare before losing to a last-minute free kick. It had been a great 12 months for Morocco and their Brazilian manager, Jose Faria. The previous December F.A.R., the armed forces club also managed by Faria, had become the first Moroccan team to win the African Champions Cup.

Morocco's outstanding goalkeeper Zaki.

EGYPT were for many years Africa's major force so it is ironic that they have never competed in the World Cup finals. However the success of top clubs Al Ahly, Zamalek and Arab Contractors in the African club competitions has provided consolation.

Egypt have also won the African Nations' Cup on three occasions, most recently in 1986 in front of President Mubarak and a 100,000 crowd in Cairo – a fitting climax to the career of one of Egypt's greatest forwards, Mahmoud Al Khatib. Appropriately, the African confederation has its headquarters in Cairo.

African influence in world football has been more significant than is obvious. Many European countries benefited over the years from the colonies – *Mozambique*'s Eusebio and Mario Coluna, for example, were key members of Benfica's European Cup-winning teams of the 1960s.

Even after colonial independence, African players still headed for Europe. Now, however, they take their talents home when it comes to World Cup time. Long gone are the mid-1970s when *Zaire* went naively to the World Cup in West Germany to be thrashed out of sight because they lacked big-occasion experience.

Only a handful of African nations have been granted worldwide TV exposure through the World Cup. That is misleading. There is an awful lot of talent in the wings in *Ivory Coast*, *Nigeria*, *Senegal* and *Ghana* – to name but a few more.

Waiting in France alone for an international breakthrough are players such as Ivory Coast's Yousouf Fofana (Monaco) and Ghana's Ayew Pele (Marseille). They are the tip of an exciting iceberg.

World football cannot ignore political pressures.

The Gulf War between *Iraq* and *Iran* has meant both countries playing home internationals on neutral sand. Iranian football has remained locked in uncertainty since the ayatollahs took over.

Political isolation meant that *North Korea* arrived as mystery men in England for the 1966 World Cup. All was impressively revealed as they beat Italy before losing to Portugal in a quarter-final thriller. At least that was further than *South Korea* got on their two appearances in 1954 and 1986.

Israel have it toughest of all. Expelled from the Asian confederation, they must take a pacific trek to *Australia* and *New Zealand* for World Cup and Olympic qualifiers. Since stars such as Avi Cohen, Eli Ohana and Ronnie Rosenthal cannot regularly gain release from their European clubs it's no wonder Israel have made little progress since their one World Cup finals outing in 1970.

THE HISTORY OF TACTICS

The great watershed in the history of football tactics was the change in the offside law of 1925; itself preceded by the tactical innovation of 'the offside game'.

When, in 1925, the number of defenders required to place a man in an onside position when the ball was played was reduced from three to two, in feverish haste, the floodgates opened. Goals galore were initially scored, in the English League, but the reaction was severe.

In no time at all, Arsenal had invented the third back game, and the era of counter-attacking, essentially defensive, football had begun. It is with us still, whether in the form of 'catenacchio' (sweeper-defence), 4-4-2, or even 4-5-1.

Indeed, with the shining exception of Total Football, which was deployed for a while, especially by the West Germans and the Dutch, and perhaps the 4-2-4 scheme initiated by the Brazilians in the 1958 World Cup, counter-attack has dominated the game for over 60 years.

When modern football began, in the mid-1860s, tactics were inevitably rudimentary, and the emphasis was strongly on attack. Indeed, of the 11 men in any team, no fewer than eight were designated forwards. In the early 1870s, however, the number of attackers had been cut down to seven, with two on each flank, and another three in the middle. In the late 1870s, one forward was turned into an extra back. It should be noted that only in 1870 was the goalkeeper permitted to use his hands!

1883 was an important year. By now, submerged professionalism was rife in England, and a less carefree tactical approach followed. Still another forward was withdrawn, to become the centre-half, the pivotal player in the formation, usually as much an attacker as a defender, though the balance would gradually shift, to make him more cautious.

Broadly speaking, this formation endured in Britain till the mid-1920s, and a great deal longer on the Continent of Europe and in South America. Indeed, the 'stopper' centre-half introduced by Arsenal did not make his appearance in Italy until just before the Second World War, and well after it in Austria.

The 1883 formation had both full-backs playing in the middle of defence, the wing-halves playing, as their name would suggest, on the flanks; they were expected not only to counter the opposing wingers, but to join in attacks. This tradition was eventually revived in Britain in the 1960s, when full-backs became attackers almost as much as defenders, and it never really died in South America, even when the stopper centre-half made his appearance in the 1950s.

Shortly before the First World War, offside tactics began to creep into English League football, particularly as practised by the celebrated Notts County full-backs Morley and Montgomery. The scheme was simple enough. The full-backs awaited their moment, then moved quickly if surreptitiously upfield, so that when the ball was played by the opposition, one or more forwards found themselves offside, with fewer than three men between themselves and the goal line; or, in general terms, with fewer than two between themselves and the Notts County goalkeeper.

Charlie Buchan pictured in his last season, 1927–28.

It is perhaps surprising that no such methods had been used before, since they were always quite feasible. The answer must be that they were contrary to the less 'professional' spirit of the times, that as football became more competitive, with more and more at stake, and became less and less of a sport, so such forms of 'gamesmanship', legal but negative, became a possibility.

It was after the Great War, however, that offside tactics threatened to ruin the game. Now the two most expert practitioners were the Newcastle United full-backs, Frank Hudspeth and Billy McCracken. The latter, a wily strategist capped many times for Ireland (and later to become a noted manager and scout), was at the root of such stratagems. So demoralised did Newcastle's opponents become that there is a story of a team which arrived at Newcastle station, and heard a guard blow his whistle 'Blimey', said one of the players, 'offside already'.

By a strange irony, it was at Newcastle that Arsenal were thrashed 7–0, in 1925, shortly after the offside law had been changed, and moved to implement the 'third back' game with its W formation. It is almost incredible, at this distance, to think that the momentous change in the law took place after such scant deliberation and experiment.

At that time, and for over 60 years to come, the four British associations dominated the law-making International Board, with a majority of four to two over the other members of F.I.F.A., the international body. In effect, it was the English Football Association which called the shots. They it was who organised the perfunctory trials which eventually decided the issue. In particular, there was a match at Highbury, the Arsenal Stadium, where the 'new' dispensation of having only two men rather than three between player and goal-line was tried out for only 45 minutes.

But with so many First Division matches being confined, by offside tactics, to an area only 20 yards long on either side of the half-way line, something had to be done. The new rule was introduced, and led immediately to a flood of goals. Indeed, despite Arsenal's invention of the 'third back' game, the goals continued to flow for several seasons to come. It was in 1927–28 that Bill 'Dixie' Dean, the Everton centre-forward, scored 60 goals in a season, finishing with a hat-trick against Arsenal themselves at Goodison Park.

Herbert Chapman, who took the credit for inventing the 'third back' game in the late Twenties.

Captain of Arsenal that day, and playing his last match, was Charlie Buchan, the virtual inventor of the 'third back' game. Buchan had joined Arsenal in 1925 from Sunderland. After the 0–7 game against Newcastle, he insisted to Herbert Chapman, the recently appointed manager of the London club, that he should stick an extra defender between the full-backs, to mark the opposing centre-forward, as he had been suggesting for some time. To compensate for the absence of the centre-half from midfield, Buchan proposed that an inside-forward, preferably himself, be pulled back from the front line into that area.

To Buchan's surprise, Chapman, who was later generally credited for the tactical innovation, accepted his plan, but used in the vacant space in midfield an inside-forward called Andy Neil. Arsenal played a midweek game at West Ham in East London and won; the third back game was born.

What it entailed was to push the full-backs out on the flanks to mark the wingers, filling the empty spaces by using the wandering centre-half as a central marker, and pulling the wing-halves in from the flanks to mark the opposing inside-forwards. These in turn were in due course both obliged to do a great deal more work, linking defence with attack, the wing-halves' role now becoming defensive.

The pivotal system obliged the two full-backs to cover their centre-half, so that when the ball was not on their wing, they were expected to move across and keep an eye on the middle. Marking was thus generally zonal, a policing of a given area rather than a given man, except in the case of the third back stopper centre-half, whose concern was always chiefly the opposing centre-forward; though he was himself expected to come across to cover, if a winger beat one of his full-backs and cut in on goal.

'Raiding' wingers now became the order of the day, ready to use their pace not just to go down the touchlines, but to go directly for goal, rather than crossing the ball into the middle. The centre-forward became more of a battler than ever, though such storming leaders as Jack Lambert, Ted Drake and Tommy Lawton had had many predecessors in the likes of Sunny Jim Quinn, of Glasgow Celtic, before the First World War.

Not every English club blindly and immediately followed Arsenal. West Bromwich Albion, notable Cup fighters for decades, were one which long held out. Nor were the tactics generally popular.

Herbert Chapman once told his players that whenever they went on to the field, it was 0–0 and they therefore had one point. Should they not concede a goal, then they came off with at least a point.

Arsenal were the specialists in breakaway tactics. Cliff Bastin, a famous left-winger, once told me that if they had a lot of the play, they began to grow worried. There was something almost parasitic, cynical even, about such an approach, and the fact that it worked so well, that Arsenal won so many matches by a single goal or so when they had largely been under pressure, did not endear them to the country at large.

Tommy Lawton's strength in the air and on the ground suited Arsenal's breakaway style.

The odd thing was that while Arsenal pursued their policy of 'realpolitik' with increasing success, the romantics still ruled on the Continent. Hugo Meisl, in the 1920s, built the brilliant Austrian 'Wunderteam', helped by the gifted little Lancastrian coach, Jimmy Hogan. In Italy, Vittorio Pozzo, in a somewhat more muscular way, stayed loyal to the tactics of the Manchester United teams he had watched and admired from the terraces as a poor student some time before the Great War.

Both Meisl and Pozzo stayed faithful to the attacking centre-half, kept their full backs in the middle of the defence, their wing-halves on the flanks. Pozzo had greatly admired the old Manchester United methods and had made a point of speaking to the famous 'roving' centre-half, Charlie Roberts, a founder-member of the Players' Union.

From Roberts, he came to admire the long, raking passes which he encouraged his own centre-halves to deploy in the inter-war Italian teams which twice won the World Cup.

Meisl's Vienna school of football placed heavy emphasis on polished technique and swift, accurate short passing. Again, a pivotal, attacking centre-half, usually Smistik, played an important part. The very embodiment, the 'ne plus ultra' of the Vienna school was Mathias Sindelar, the Man of Paper, a lanky centre-forward who could dribble his way right through a defence, before pushing the ball over the line.

At Chelsea in 1932, in a memorable match, the cruder English methods prevailed over Austria, to the tune of 4–3, but it was generally believed that Austria had given England a footballing lesson.

The W formation was so named because a letter W, or an M, could be traced by linking up the positions of wingers, inside-forwards and centre-forward. Despite the success of the Italian World Cup teams and the immense prestige of the 'Wunderteam', European football inexorably moved towards the 'third back' game after the Second World War.

Meanwhile, in Switzerland in the late 1940s, another method of defence – 'verrou', 'catenaccio' or bolt defence – was being perfected curiously enough by an Austrian, Karl Rappan.

Manager of the Swiss international team at that time, Rappan developed a strategy which features an extra defender, playing behind the rest, known as a 'verroulleur', a 'battitore libero', or a sweeper-up (*libero*, for short). The task of this player, as his name would suggest, was to 'clean up' behind the other defenders, picking off any pass or opponent to elude the rest. Two large full-backs played in the middle of the field, as stoppers. The tendency was towards man-for-man, rather than zonal, marking.

Brazil's 1950 World Cup team.

In the early 1950s, Internazionale of Milan brought 'catenaccio' methods into the Italian First Division, though it was the Padova team managed by Nereo Rocco, later manager of A.C. Milan, who were probably the first to employ them. Inter used a sweeper behind the defence, in a strictly destructive role, and withdrew their outside-right, Armano, into a deep position.

The tactics proved extremely successful, and by the end of the 1960s were in general use, employed not only in the Championship but by the Italian national team, which had previously adopted the 'third back' game, instead of the old attacking centre-half formation.

'Catenaccio' took defensive, breakaway football to its limits. It is a far more negative, defensive system than the 'third back' game, which came to seem almost permissive by comparison. But in 1958, at the World Cup in Sweden, Brazil unveiled yet another new strategy, which – Italy apart – would sweep the game.

Vicente Feola, the corpulent, rumbling

Franz Beckenbauer, a 'thinker' from his earliest days in the West German team who later became national manager.

manager of that Brazilian team, had not in fact invented 4-2-4. It is usually attributed to Fleitas Solich, a Paraguayan who was managing the Flamengo club of Rio when he introduced, or at least implemented, the method.

It was especially welcome to Brazil, who had gone over to the 'third back' game after their disaster against Uruguay in the decisive World Cup match of 1950 in Rio. Their 'diagonal system' of defence was badly exposed by Uruguay's attack.

For the 1954 World Cup, Brazil went over to a stopper centre-half, but the style wasn't suited to Brazilian defenders, who never really mastered the diagonal covering; as was shown by their displays on their European tour of 1956.

So in Sweden, Brazil fielded four rather than three men across the back, two in the centre, an attacking wing half (Dino, then Zito) a brilliant creative inside-forward in Didi, two wingers and two central strikers, one of them the astonishingly precocious Pele.

Danny Blanchflower, clever captain of the Northern Ireland team which played in those finals, was among those who praised the shrewd simplicity of a four-man back line, which neutralised the pivotal covering. It also, however, led to a kind of identity crisis for centre-halves, no longer master of their fates and captains of their souls. Henceforth there would be two of them, though in the original Brazilian scheme, a classical stopper was abetted by a defensive wing-half; a feature of the brilliantly successful Hungarian teams of the earlier 1950s.

Where Brazil led, the world at large, though not Italy, followed suit; Britain included. For some years to come the tactical battle now would be between the four in line defences – modulated to 4-3-3 by the Brazilian team which retained the World Cup in 1962 in Chile – and 'catenaccio'.

The trouble was, as with the 'third back' game, that most of the teams which adopted the new tactics hadn't the men to make them work. Just as Arsenal's imitators often lacked a marvellous midfield general and hitter of long balls such as Alex James, raiding wingers in Cliff Bastin and Joe Hulme, so very few teams of the 1960s could boast a Didi, or attacking full-backs of the quality of the two Santoses; to say nothing of the superb fast right winger Garrincha, and the wholly incomparable Pele.

In Europe, 'catenaccio' dominated club football in the early 1960s, in the shape of Helenio Herrera's severely pragmatic Internazionale teams. Where the European Cup, initiated in 1955–56, had long been dominated by the ebullient, adventurous Real Madrid teams, inspired by Alfredo Di Stefano, now four man-to-man marking, a cautious sweeper and lancing breakaways were the order of the day. West German football adopted 'catenaccio', too.

But Inter's dour tactics had their come-uppance in the European Cup final of 1967, when Glasgow Celtic bravely beat them in Lisbon, and in the early 1970s, a thrilling new revolution took place.

Once again, as in Charlie Buchan's time, a player rather than a manager was at the root of it. The highly gifted young Franz Beckenbauer had, almost from his first appearances with Bayern Munich, operated in the newly conceived role of attacking sweepers.

Beckenbauer had watched and admired the attacking surges of the tall Inter left-back, Giacinto Facchetti, and wondered why such methods should not be possible from a central defender.

The role of sweeper appeared a perfect launching pad, since the sweeper himself was never marked, lurked deep at the back, and could pick his moment to surge upfield. It would be many years before the cautious West German team manager, Helmut Schoen, at last allowed Beckenbauer to operate in such a way in the West German national team.

The 1972 European Nations Cup finals was the first time he did so in a major tournament; and he had already been playing for West Germany for six years.

With Beckenbauer as the springboard, first Bayern Munich, his club, and eventually the West German team espoused tactics which came to be known as 'total football', and which were used to equal effect by Ajax Amsterdam and the Dutch national team. Indeed, while Ajax won the European Cup for three years in a row between 1971 and 1973, Bayern won it for the next three years, and the respective international teams met in Munich in the World Cup final of 1974.

At Ajax, the moving spirit was Johan Cruyff, the superbly versatile centre-forward. Under the strong regime of Rinus Michels, Ajax's tactics were more orthodox than leading members of the side would wish. Under the new manager, the little Rumanian, Stefan Kovacs, 'total football' flourished.

Its philosophy was very much that of The Whirl, propounded in 1955 by Willy Meisl, journalist younger brother of Hugo. In essence, it was assumed that anybody could, and should, do anything; defenders attack. The overlapping full-back had been a constant, since 4-2-4 swept most of western Europe, but such examples of the genres as Rudi Krol of Ajax and Paul Breitner of Bayern Munich were spectacular. Ajax, in fact, had a West German

attacking sweeper in Horst Blankenburg. Later, Krol himself would become a sweeper, Breitner a virtual inside-forward who played and scored for West Germany in the 1982 World Cup final.

'Total football', however, demanded even more remarkable qualities from its players than the 'third back' game or 4-2-4. For a short spell, Ajax, Bayern, West Germany and Holland had such footballers, and played perhaps the most exciting soccer the game has ever seen. When the smoke cleared and the teams waned, something was left, if only a mood, an attitude, an ambition which inspired other teams.

'Total football', above all, was a wonderfully adventurous strategy, after so many years of chiefly defensive, counter-attacking football: even 4-2-4 had 'degenerated' into 4-3-3 and 4-4-2.

One looks back on it now as a brief, golden era, and perhaps we shall one day see it again. Always provided that so astonishing a crop of players emerges in the same place at the same time, and is encouraged to express its gifts.

Johan Cruyff, moving spirit as a player at Ajax, also won trophies for them as coach before leaving in 1988 for Barcelona.

THE PLAYERS

HERBERT CHAPMAN

Herbert Chapman was the most innovative of all British managers between the wars. A Yorkshireman who had a modest career as an inside-forward, notably with Tottenham Hotspur in their Southern League days, Chapman made a name as player-manager of Northampton Town, then took over Leeds City, who were dissolved for alleged payment irregularities, during the Great War.

Briefly suspended, he returned twice to win the League with Huddersfield Town. In 1925 he took over and regenerated Arsenal, deploying the new 'third back game'. He was a close friend of Hugo Meisl and Vittorio Pozzo, the exponent of many innovatory ideas, among them the use of floodlights.

His players worshipped him, seeing him as a father figure, and he was especially successful in persuading them to adopt roles they had never thought of filling before. He caught a chill and died, sadly early, in 1934, when Arsenal were on their way to their third Championship under him.

HELENIO HERRERA

Born of Argentine parents in 1916, in the backstreets of Casablanca, Helenio Herrera moved to France when he was 18, played for four French clubs, including Red Star, and, naturalised, won a couple of caps for France.

In 1945 he became a manager with Red Star, but truly established himself in Spain where he ran half-a-dozen clubs, winning the Championship twice with Atletico Madrid, but

achieving his greatest fame with a polyglot Barcelona team in the late 1950s and early 1960s. When Barcelona sacked him after they had lost the European Cup semi-final to Real Madrid in 1960, he became manager of Internazionale Milan.

His embattled 'catenaccio', breakaway style of football made Inter the strongest club in Italy and enabled them twice to win the European Cup, though there was much criticism of Herrera's flamboyant style, negative approach and the apparent favouring of Inter by European referees.

Later he would become the highly paid manager of Roma, in 1968, and he managed the Spanish World Cup team of 1962 in Chile.

Vittorio Pozzo, trainer of the Italian national soccer team that won the 1934 and 1938 World Cups.

HUGO MEISL

From a wealthy Viennese Jewish family, Meisl's early passion for football led to his 'banishment' to Trieste, where he kept in touch with a pioneering Austrian footballer, Johann Leute.

Returning to work in a Viennese bank, he gave large amounts of time and money to the Austrian Football Federation and brought Jimmy Hogan, the English coach, to instruct the players.

Hogan inculcated classical Scottish methods of play, based on ball control and short, accurate passing.

Shortly after the Great War, Austria lost 5–0 in Nuremberg to Southern Germany on a snow-covered pitch. Arguing ceaselessly on the long train journey home, Meisl and his players finally decided to stick to their Vienna School methods. These proved hugely successful in the ensuing years.

Meisl's most satisfying moment came when Austria beat England 2–1 in Vienna in May 1936. In the final minutes, he lay behind the Austrian goal, exhorting his team, his famous bowler hat lying behind the goal net.

VITTORIO POZZO

A Piedmontese, born near Turin, and a devoted Alpinist, Pozzo was 'converted' to soccer by one of the founder-players of the Juventus club, Goccione. Until then, he had been a 400 metre runner of promise.

But the game really took hold of him when, after attending the International School of Commerce in Zurich, he went to England, watched football, and became friendly with such stars as Steve Bloomer and Charlie Roberts.

His family lured him home with a return ticket to Turin for his sister's wedding; he kept the return half ever after. In 1912, at the last moment, he was asked to take an Italian team to the Stockholm Olympics, where it beat Sweden and lost 5–1 to Austria.

He became fast friends with Hugo Meisl, his Austrian equivalent. Pozzo served in the Alpine Regiment during the Great War, taking over the national team again as 'commissario tecnico' in 1924, staying in office till 1949, winning the World Cups of 1934 and 1938, a beloved disciplinarian, termed by a French journalist: 'The poor captain of a company of millionaires.'

THE EUROPEAN CUP

Bearing in mind the success of the World Cup from 1930 onwards, a competition for Europe's best clubs was a long time coming.

The Mitropa Cup, begun in 1927 by the visionary Austrian Hugo Meisl, was a forerunner of the European Cup, though as its name (a shortened form of 'Mittel Europa', or Central Europe) suggested, it had distinct geographical limitations.

Representatives of seven countries competed intermittently for it, and later French and Italian clubs joined the best of Spain and Portugal in the cumbersome Latin Cup.

British clubs stood aloof from all this, as the home nations had done from F.I.F.A. for many years, failing to capitalise even on the massive interest generated by Moscow Dynamo's fabled visit of 1946. By the early Fifties, teams like Honved and Red Banner from Hungary, A.C. Milan and Red Star Belgrade were playing friendlies in England, and it was Honved's unlucky 3–2 defeat by Wolves in December 1954 which led to claims that Stan Cullis's team were now 'champions of the world'.

Chauvinistic or not, this boast at least gave new impetus to those wanting to bring together in competition the Continent's leading clubs. The French sports newspaper *L'Equipe*, hindered rather than helped by the football authorities, did all the spade-work until the newly-formed U.E.F.A. was persuaded to sanction a European Champion Clubs' Cup tournament for the 1955–56 season.

The Football League refused Chelsea permission to compete, because of worries about overcrowding the fixture list (this was in the days before the Football League Cup, let alone all the extraneous competitions the League has introduced since!) but Hibernian represented Scotland, and reached the semi-final in the extremely distinguished company of Real Madrid, Reims and A.C. Milan. Reims knocked them out and played a magnificent inaugural final in Paris against Real, leading the Spaniards 2–0 after only ten minutes before succumbing 4–3.

The tournament was an enormous success, from a financial as well as footballing point of view. The following season, when 22 clubs took part, Manchester United emulated Hibs in reaching the last four, Matt Busby having insisted that his directors defy the League and enter.

Real beat United 3–1 in the semi-final first leg and drew 2–2 at Old Trafford, having led 5–1 on aggregate at one stage. A crowd of 124,000 watched them retain the Cup on their own ground against Fiorentina.

It is interesting to speculate how close Busby's team might have pushed Real had it not been destroyed in the Munich air disaster nine months later. United were returning from a successful quarter-final against Red Star Belgrade when their plane crashed on a third attempt at take-off, having stopped at Munich to refuel. Eight players died and two never played again.

Their patchwork team was knocked out of the semi-final by A.C. Milan, who then took Real to extra-time in the final before going down 3–2.

With the British challenge blunted, Spain itself produced the only serious challenge to Real. Atletico Madrid, their neighbours, in 1959 and Barcelona in

The 1960 European Cup final between Real Madrid and Eintracht Frankfurt was one of the greatest games seen in Britain, or anywhere else. Di Stefano scores Real's second goal in the 7-3 win.

Date	Winners	Runners-up	Score	Venue
1956	Real Madrid (Spain)	Reims (France)	4-3	Paris
1957	Real Madrid (Spain)	Fiorentina (Italy)	2-0	Madrid
1958	Real Madrid (Spain)	A.C. Milan (Italy)	3-2 aet	Brussels
1959	Real Madrid (Spain)	Reims (France)	2-0	Stuttgart
1960	Real Madrid (Spain)	Eintracht Frankfurt (W. Germany)	7-3	Glasgow
1961	Benfica (Portugal)	Barcelona (Spain)	3-2	Berne
1962	Benfica (Portugal)	Real Madrid (Spain)	5-3	Amsterdam
1963	A.C. Milan (Italy)	Benfica (Portugal)	2-1	London
1964	Internazionale (Italy)	Real Madrid (Spain)	3-1	Vienna
1965	Internazionale (Italy)	Benfica (Portugal)	1-0	Milan
1966	Real Madrid (Spain)	Partizan Belgrade (Yugoslavia)	2-1	Brussels
1967	Celtic (Scotland)	Internazionale (Italy)	2-1	Lisbon
1968	Manchester United (Eng.)	Benfica (Portugal)	4-1 aet	London
1969	A.C. Milan (Italy)	Ajax (Holland)	4-1	Madrid
1970	Feyenoord (Holland)	Celtic (Scotland)	2-1 aet	Milan
1971	Ajax (Holland)	Panathinaikos (Greece)	2-0	London
1972	Ajax (Holland)	Internazionale (Italy)	2-0	Rotterdam
1973	Ajax (Holland)	Juventus (Italy)	1-0	Belgrade
1974	Bayern Munich (W. Germany)	Atletico Madrid (Spain)	1-1 aet	Brussels
		replay	4-0	Brussels
1975	Bayern Munich (W. Ger.)	Leeds United (England)	2-0	Paris
1976	Bayern Munich (W. Ger.)	Saint-Etienne (France)	1-0	Glasgow
1977	Liverpool (England)	Borussia M-Gladbach	3-1	Rome
1978	Liverpool (England)	Bruges (Belgium)	1-0	London
1979	Nottingham Forest (Eng.)	Malmo (Sweden)	1-0	Munich
1980	Nottingham Forest (Eng.)	S.V. Hamburg (W. Germany)	1-0	Madrid
1981	Liverpool (England)	Real Madrid (Spain)	1-0	Paris
1982	Aston Villa (England)	Bayern Munich (W. Germany)	1-0	Rotterdam
1983	S.V. Hamburg (W. Ger.)	Juventus (Italy)	1-0	Athens
1984	Liverpool (England)	Roma (Italy)	1-1 aet	Rome
			decided on penalties	
1985	Juventus (Italy)	Liverpool (England)	1-0	Brussels
1986	Steaua Bucharest (Rumania)	Barcelona (Spain)	0-0 aet	Seville
			decided on penalties	
1987	F.C. Porto (Portugal)	Bayern Munich (W. Germany)	2-1	Vienna
1988	P.S.V. Eindhoven (Holland)	Benfica (Portugal)	0-0 aet	Stuttgart
			decided on penalties	
1989	A.C. Milan (Italy)	Steaua Bucharest (Rumania)	4-0	Barcelona

Above: *Celtic earned football's gratitude by defeating defensive apostles Inter in the 1967 final. Billy McNeill holds the magnificent trophy.*

Below: *Bobby Charlton looks on as Manchester United's George Best skips past a Benfica challenge in the 1968 final. United won in extra-time.*

1960 provided their most difficult games, but failed to stop them.

Reims were beaten 2–0 in the 1959 final, and in 1960 Eintract Frankfurt were demolished 7–3 in one of the greatest matches ever seen in Britain. Ferenc Puskas, whose career Real had rescued following the Hungarian Revolution, scored four, Alfredo Di Stefano claiming the other three.

Apart from the quality of the final at Hampden Park, Glasgow, the European Cup reached another peak in 1960, when the average attendance over 52 games was more than 50,500 – a figure which will never be exceeded under the competition's present format.

Real had peaked too, and in November 1960 finally lost a tie 4–3 to Barcelona. But those who assumed the Catalans would simply take over where Real had left off had reckoned without the other emerging Iberian force – Benfica of Lisbon. Shrewdly coached by the Hungarian, Bela Guttmann, they beat Barcelona 3–2 and then Real 5–3 in two more memorable

Below: *1977 and Liverpool's first European Cup win. Tommy Smith surprised even himself with this brilliant header for the second goal.*

finals, before slipping to an unexpected defeat by A.C. Milan in 1963 at Wembley.

Although Milan had always been one of the strongest clubs in Europe, it was their great rivals Inter, co-tenants of the San Siro stadium, who ushered in a new and far less glamorous era. Helenio Herrera, once coach to Barcelona, decided to perfect a system of counter-attack which frustrated opponents and spectators alike, but paid off with three Italian League titles in four years and European Cup victories in 1964 and 1965.

Real, beaten in the 1964 final, when Di Stefano, Puskas and Francisco Gento were all still playing, came back with a restructured team to win in 1966 against Eastern Europe's first finalists, Partizan Belgrade. It was 1967 before the Cup went at last to Britain, where it could easily have stayed for another three or four years.

After Celtic had earned the gratitude of the football world by beating defensive apostles Inter in 1967, and Manchester United won at Wembley against Benfica, United lost their 1969 semi-final to eventual winners A.C. Milan and the following season Celtic were beaten in extra-time by Feyenoord of Rotterdam.

The pendulum swung away from Britain to Holland and then West Germany. Ajax, inspired by Johan Cruyff, Johan Neeskens, Rudi Krol and the rest, did the hat-trick, a feat immediately repeated by Bayern Munich, comparative newcomers even in Germany.

Now it was Britain's turn again. Not even in Real's heyday had one country

taken the trophy for six successive years, as Liverpool, Nottingham Forest and Aston Villa proceeded to do between 1977 and 1982. It was, perhaps, symbolic of the era's functional football that five of those finals were won by one goal to nil, as was Hamburg's against Juventus which ended the sequence.

Remarkably, only one final (in 1974) had needed a replay, but when it was decided to do away with them, we had to endure the sight of Europe's premier competition being decided on penalty-kicks twice in three seasons. Liverpool and the unfancied Rumanians, Steaua, were the beneficiaries, Roma and Barcelona the losers.

In between, though, Brussels witnessed the most horrific day's football of modern times, probably of all time, as 39 died in rioting before the 1985 final. It was the misfortune of the European Cup to be associated with such a ghastly event.

Steaua's Viktor Piturca eludes a tackle by Barcelona's Victor in the second final in which penalties were necessary.

Above: *Aston Villa continue the run of single-goal English victories as Peter Withe (9) scores against Bayern in 1982.*

Left: *The first final decided on penalties. A relieved Graeme Souness holds the trophy in 1984.*

Right: *F.C. Porto line up before their 1987 European Cup final against Bayern Munich, winning the most entertaining final for years.*

EUROPEAN CUP-WINNERS' CUP

The dazzling success of the European Cup and the spread of the Inter Cities Fairs Cup made a competition for domestic Cup winners a logical step.

The excitement and enthusiasm generated by the F.A. Cup and Scottish Cup were not matched in other European countries, many of whom did not have a national knockout Cup at all, but there were ten entries for the inaugural European Cup-Winners' Cup of 1960–61.

For that first season, the final was played over two legs, but otherwise the format followed that of the European Cup, with ties which finished level decided by play-offs. From time to time, reverting to a home-and-away final has been proposed, but generally the finalists have been of sufficient stature to draw a decent crowd in a neutral country.

Attendances were certainly good for the first season, as the cream rose effortlessly to the top. The meetings of British giants Rangers and Wolves in the semi-final attracted huge interest: 80,000 turned up at Ibrox for Rangers' 2–0 victory in the first leg and more than 45,000 saw a 1–1 draw at Molineux three weeks later. Another full-house in Glasgow for the final was silenced as the Italians of Fiorentina inflicted a rare home defeat on Rangers, who then went down 2–1 in the second leg, despite a goal by Alex Scott.

The second goal in Tottenham's convincing 5–1 defeat of Atletico Madrid in 1963.

Represented by Leicester, Dunfermline and Swansea (the Welsh Cup holders), Britain was, not surprisingly, unable to make such an impact the following season, when Fiorentina returned to Glasgow to draw the final against Atletico Madrid. The replay did not take place until four months later, Atletico claiming a European trophy to put alongside those of Real.

The wide range of qualifiers for the Cup-Winners' Cup was vividly illustrated in 1962–63, including as it did not only Bill Nicholson's glittering Tottenham side, but Bangor City, who were halfway down the Cheshire County League. As Welsh Cup winners, they were nevertheless entitled to take their place, and did marvellously well in forcing Napoli to a play-off at Highbury, where 21,895 saw the Italians scrape home 2–1.

Spurs played to packed houses at White Hart Lane in every round, destroying Rangers (5–2), Slovan (6–0) O.F.K. Belgrade (3–1) before dishing out the same treatment to Atletico in a memorable final, which they won 5–1.

English and Scottish clubs have been fairly regular finalists ever since that first European triumph. West Ham produced a technically perfect and emotionally uplifting display against 1860 Munich in the first of three successive finals between British and German clubs. Borussia Dortmund surprised Liverpool at Hampden Park, and in 1967 Bayern, taking advantage of playing in their own country, beat Rangers, who had knocked out Borussia earlier on. It was the first that the Continent at large had heard of Bayern, who had only just reached West Germany's First Division.

Defeat for Hamburg, Germany's fourth successive finalists, was followed by a heartening success for Slovan Bratislava,

EUROPEAN CUP-WINNERS' CUP

Date	Winners	Runners-up	Score	Venue
1961	Fiorentina (Italy)	Rangers (Scotland)	2-0, 2-1	(two-legs)
1962	Atletico Madrid (Spain)	Fiorentina (Italy)	1-1 aet	Glasgow
		replay	3-0	Stuttgart
1963	Tottenham (England)	Atletico Madrid (Spain)	5-1	Rotterdam
1964	Sporting Lisbon (Portugal)	M.T.K. Budapest (Hungary)	3-3 aet	Brussels
		replay	1-0	Antwerp
1965	West Ham (England)	1860 Munich (W. Germany)	2-0	London
1966	Borussia Dortmund (W. Germany)	Liverpool (England)	2-1 aet	Glasgow
1967	Bayern Munich (W. Germany)	Rangers (Scotland)	1-0 aet	Nuremberg
1968	A.C. Milan (Italy)	Hamburg (W. Germany)	2-0	Rotterdam
1969	Slovan Bratislava (Czech)	Barcelona (Spain)	3-2	Basle
1970	Manchester City (England)	Gornik (Poland)	2-1	Vienna
1971	Chelsea (England)	Real Madrid (Spain)	1-1 aet	Athens
		replay	2-1	Athens
1972	Rangers (Scotland)	Moscow Dynamo (U.S.S.R.)	3-2	Barcelona
1973	A.C. Milan (Italy)	Leeds United (England)	1-0	Salonika
1974	Magdeburg (E. Germany)	A.C. Milan (Italy)	2-0	Rotterdam
1975	Dynamo Kiev (U.S.S.R.)	Ferencvaros (Hungary)	3-0	Basle
1976	Anderlecht (Belgium)	West Ham (England)	4-2	Brussels
1977	S.V. Hamburg (W. Ger.)	Anderlecht (Belgium)	2-0	Amsterdam
1978	Anderlecht (Belgium)	Austria/W.A.C. (Austria)	4-0	Paris
1979	Barcelona (Spain)	Fortuna Dusseldorf (W. Germany)	4-3 aet	Basle
1980	Valencia (Spain)	Arsenal (England)	0-0 aet	Brussels
				decided on penalties
1981	Dynamo Tblisi (U.S.S.R.)	Carl Zeiss Jena (E. Germany)	2-1	Dusseldorf
1982	Barcelona (Spain)	Standard Liége (Belgium)	2-1	Barcelona
1983	Aberdeen (Scotland)	Real Madrid (Spain)	2-1	Gothenburg
1984	Juventus (Italy)	F.C. Porto (Portugal)	2-1	Basle
1985	Everton (England)	Rapid Vienna (Austria)	3-1	Rotterdam
1986	Dynamo Kiev (U.S.S.R.)	Atletico Madrid (Spain)	3-0	Lyon
1987	Ajax Amsterdam (Holland)	Lokomotiv Leipzig (E. Germany)	1-0	Athens
1988	Mechelen (Belgium)	Ajax (Holland)	1-0	Strasbourg
1989	Barcelona (Spain)	Sampdoria (Italy)	2-0	Berne

whose country had been invaded by the Russians eight months earlier, causing a number of Eastern European teams to withdraw.

Dunfermline reached the semi-final of that competition, as Cardiff City had done the previous season, and for the next four years, Britain again provided a finalist.

Manchester City defeated Gornik in front of a small, rain-soaked Vienna crowd; then lost their 1971 semi-final to Chelsea, who went on to beat Real Madrid at the second attempt in Athens, Peter Osgood and John Dempsey getting the goals. Rangers' first European success, in 1972, was marred by the fighting between their supporters and the Spanish police, which cost them a one-year ban.

It was a notable competition all round for the strong British contingent as Chelsea set a new European scoring record against Hautcharage of Luxembourg, 21–0 (8–0, 13–0), and Liverpool fell to the now-established Bayern, who themselves lost to Rangers over two semi-finals.

Chelsea skipper Ron Harris is chaired off after victory over Real Madrid in the 1971 final replayed in Athens.

Above: *Aberdeen after beating Real Madrid 2-1 in the 1983 final in rain-swept Gothenburg.*

Leeds United, appearing in the competition for the first and only time, endured 90 minutes of frustration in the 1973 final against A.C. Milan, a game refereed so suspiciously by the Greek official Michas that he was promptly suspended by U.E.F.A. Two years of Eastern European success followed, though neither Magdeburg nor Dynamo Kiev caught the public imagination at their sparsely-attended finals in Rotterdam and Basle.

The competition was revived, though, by Anderlecht's vibrant mix of Belgians (like Vercauteren and Van der Elst) and Dutchmen (Arie Haan and Robbie Rensenbrink). They pulled in the crowds for three successive finals, beating West Ham (4–2) and F.K. Austria/W.A.C. (4–0) either side of a defeat by Hamburg.

After Barcelona's victory in the highest-scoring final so far, Hans Krankl scoring the winner against Fortuna, the Eighties produced more prosaic stuff. Although the European Cup was spared a final decided on penalties until 1984, the dull goalless Cup-Winners' Cup final between Arsenal and Valencia in Brussels was settled by that unsatisfactory method four years earlier, when Graham Rix went down as the unfortunate whose missed kick meant defeat.

Spain's run was extended to three wins in four seasons, when Barcelona won the 1982 competition, defeating Standard in a brutal match which raised again the question of whether a club should be allowed to play a European final on their own ground. The attendance of 100,000 – as opposed to 9,000 who saw the fine Tblisi side beat Carl Zeiss Jena the previous year – emphasised the benefits.

The leading British clubs continued to be difficult to beat. Tottenham (1982), Manchester United and Aberdeen (both 1984) all reached the semi-finals, while Aberdeen (1983) and Everton (1985) were deserved winners. But the absence of English teams and sudden poor showings of the Scottish ones thereafter made life easier, if less remunerative, for the rest.

Below: *Juventus (yellow shirts) won an unexpectedly open 1984 final against F.C. Porto.*

Above: *More British success in 1985 as Everton beat Rapid Vienna 3-1. Centre-half Derek Mountfield strides out of defence.*

Right: *Dynamo Kiev staged a brilliant exhibition in defeating Atletico Madrid to win the 1986 competition. Alexandr Zavarov scores the first goal.*

U.E.F.A. CUP

Although the concept of what is now known as the U.E.F.A. Cup is less straightforward than that of the two other main European club competitions, the method of selection tends to produce a higher-quality field than the Cup-Winners' Cup.

Countries are allotted either three, two or one of the 64 places, according to a complex system based on previous performances.

Apart from oddities like England's keeping one place for the winners of their League Cup, the entrants are the highest-placed teams in each country who don't actually win the Championship: it could almost be called the European Runners-Up Cup.

In its earliest days, starting the same year as the European Cup (1955), it was intended as little more than a sporting sideshow at trade fairs held all over the Continent. Hence the original name, the European Inter-Cities' Fairs Cup, and the fact that the first competition took three years to complete.

It was not even necessarily for clubs: London and Frankfurt fielded representative XIs. London's, although much-changed from match to match, eventually reached the final against Barcelona. After drawing the first leg 2–2 at Stamford Bridge, London were humiliated 6–0 in Spain, the brilliant Luis Suarez and Evaristo each scoring twice. Protracted or not, the competition's future was assured by some excellent attendances, an aggregate of more than 105,000 watching the final.

Some fine tuning was done before the second tournament, which still took two seasons to resolve. Chelsea represented London, as some sort of compensation for their exclusion from the inaugural European Cup, but were outshone by Birmingham City, semi-finalists on the previous occasion, who went one better, only to lose to the same team, Barcelona, in the final.

Spain's success – which, of course, paralleled that of Real in the European Cup – was interrupted briefly in 1960–61, after a dramatic quarter-final in which Edinburgh's Hibernian drew 4–4 away to Barcelona, then won their home leg 3–2. Hibs crashed 6–0 to Roma in a semi-final play-off, the Italians going on to defeat Birmingham in a final held over until September 1961.

Spanish domination was reasserted as Valencia reached the next three finals, winning the first two. They demolished Barcelona 6–2 in the first leg of the 1962 competition, won both legs against Dynamo Zagreb the following year, but then lost to fellow countrymen Zaragoza in the first final played over only one leg – in Barcelona.

During those three years, only one British team – Sheffield Wednesday – even reached the quarter-final. Manchester United made it to the last four in 1964, only to lose a play-off to Ferencvaros, who were underdogs despite the presence of the gifted Florian Albert. In the final the Hungarians also surprised a negative Juv-

Jack Charlton in full flight as Juventus, in unfamiliar blue, are beaten on away goals by Leeds in 1971.

U.E.F.A. CUP

Date	Winners	Runners-up	Score (aggregate)
1958	Barcelona (Spain)	London XI (England)	2-2, 6-0 (8-2)
1960	Barcelona (Spain)	Birmingham C. (England)	0-0, 4-1 (4-1)
1961	Roma (Italy)	Birmingham C. (England)	2-2, 2-0 (4-2)
1962	Valencia (Spain)	Barcelona (Spain)	6-2, 1-1 (7-3)
1963	Valencia (Spain)	Dynamo Zagreb (Yugoslavia)	2-1, 2-0 (4-1)
1964	Real Zaragoza (Spain)	Valencia (Spain)	2-1 (in Barcelona)
1965	Ferencvaros (Hungary)	Juventus (Italy)	1-0 (in Turin)
1966	Barcelona (Spain)	Real Zaragoza (Spain)	0-1, 4-2 aet (4-3)
1967	Dynamo Zagreb (Yugo.)	Leeds United (England)	2-0, 0-0 (2-0)
1968	Leeds United (England)	Ferencvaros (Hungary)	1-0, 0-0 (1-0)
1969	Newcastle United (England)	Ujpest Dozsa (Hungary)	3-0, 3-2 (6-2)
1970	Arsenal (England)	Anderlecht (Belgium)	1-3, 3-0 (4-3)
1971	Leeds United (England)	Juventus (Italy)	2-2, 1-1 aet (3-3) Leeds won on away goals
1972	Tottenham (England)	Wolverhampton (England)	2-1, 1-1 (3-2)
1973	Liverpool (England)	Borussia M-G (W. Germany)	3-0, 0-2 (3-2)
1974	Feyenoord (Holland)	Tottenham (England)	2-2, 2-0 (4-2)
1975	Borussia M-G (W. Ger.)	Twente Enschede (Holland)	0-0, 5-1 (5-1)
1976	Liverpool (England)	Bruges (Belgium)	3-2, 1-1 (4-3)
1977	Juventus (Italy)	Atletico Bilbao (Spain)	1-0, 1-2 (2-2) Juventus won on away goals
1978	P.S.V. Eindhoven (Holland)	Bastia (France)	0-0, 3-0 (3-0)
1979	Borussia M-G (W. Ger.)	Red Star Belgrade (Yugoslavia)	1-1, 1-0 (2-1)
1980	Eintracht Frankfurt (W. Germany)	Borussia M-G (W. Germany)	2-3, 1-0 (3-3) Eintracht won on away goals
1981	Ipswich (England)	A.Z. Alkmaar (Holland)	3-0, 2-4 (5-4)
1982	I.F.K. Gothenburg (Swe.)	S.V. Hamburg (W. Germany)	1-0, 3-0 (4-0)
1983	Anderlecht (Belgium	Benfica (Portugal)	1-0, 1-1 (2-1)
1984	Tottenham (England)	Anderlecht (Belgium)	1-1, 1-1 aet (2-2) Tottenham won on penalties
1985	Real Madrid (Spain)	Videoton (Hungary)	3-0, 0–1 (3-1)
1986	Real Madrid (Spain)	Cologne (W. Germany)	5-1, 0-2 (5-3)
1987	I.F.K. Gothenburg (Swe.)	Dundee United (Scotland)	1-0, 1-1 (2-1)
1988	Bayer Leverküsen (W. Germany)	Espanol (Spain)	0-3, 3-0 (3-3) Bayer won on penalties
1989	Napoli (Italy)	Vfb Stuttgart (W. Germany)	2-1, 3-3 (5-4)

Günter Netzer fails to stop Kevin Keegan – later to play for him at Hamburg – in the Anfield leg of the 1973 final.

entus, who were playing on their own ground, by winning 1–0.

Two-leg finals resumed in 1966, when Spanish clubs enjoyed their last success in the competition for almost two decades. Barcelona, beating Chelsea in one semi-final play-off, and Zaragoza, who knocked out Leeds in another, played two exciting games both won by the away team, Pijol's hat-trick proving decisive for the Catalans.

Now, however, it was the turn of the English. Although Leeds lost the 1967 final to Dynamo Zagreb, England took the Cup for the next six seasons – a record unlikely to be beaten. In 1968 it was Leeds, defeating Ferencvaros (who had beaten Liverpool home and away); in 1969 the unpredictable Newcastle, after an eventful semi-final against Glasgow Rangers; 1970 saw reviving Arsenal win their first trophy for 17 years, after Anderlecht had led them 3–0 in the first leg; then it was Leeds again, the conquerors of

Left: *David Fairclough, Liverpool's 'Supersub' in the Seventies heads for goal in the 1976 final against Bruges.*

Right: *Parks and goalscorer Roberts hold the cup to Tottenham supporters in 1984.*

Below: *Regular competitors Ipswich won the trophy at last in 1981. John Wark (blue shirt) threatens the Alkmaar goal in the second leg.*

Liverpool in the semi-final and Juventus in the final, on away goals.

For 1971–72, there was a new name, the U.E.F.A. Cup, and a new trophy (Barcelona beat Leeds in a challenge match to decide who should keep the old one).

This time England supplied both finalists. Spurs and Wolves, who had between them seen off the dangerous Italian challenge of A.C. Milan and Juventus, played to two full houses, who saw Martin Chivers' two goals at Molineux and Alan Mullery's header at White Hart Lane win the day.

Knocked out in the 1973 semi-final by Liverpool, who went on to win their first European trophy, Spurs were the club involved as England finally surrendered the Cup, amid scenes which were to become sadly familiar. Some of their fans were involved in serious fighting before, during and after the second leg of the final in Rotterdam, where a superior Feyenoord team capitalised on their good work in their first match.

The Germans and Dutch, dominating European football at international level, made 12 U.E.F.A. Cup final appearances between 1973 and 1982. Borussia Moenchengladbach won two and lost two, with only Juventus (1977) breaking the monopoly of northern European countries. Ipswich, regular entrants as a result of their consistently good League position, won a deserved victory in 1981, with two Dutchmen, Arnold Muhren and Frans Thijssen, in the team; and I.F.K. Gothenburg joined the ranks of those who had won the competition twice with their victories over Hamburg in 1982 and the gallant Dundee United, Scotland's first-ever finalists, five years later.

In between times, though, the bigger guns had made their mark again. Anderlecht edged out Benfica (1983), then lost on penalties to Tottenham in 1985, for whom reserve goalkeeper Tony Parks made the crucial saves.

Real became the first team to win at White Hart Lane in 43 European ties and went on to take the Cup, which they retained the following year. The highlights of Real's successes were a series of extraordinary comebacks after losing their away leg: 6–1 against Anderlecht, after losing the first match 0–3; 3–0 v. Inter, after a 0–2; 4–0 v. Borussia M-G, after losing 1–5; and 5–1 against poor Inter, after a 1–3. Real supporters knew it wasn't quite the same thing as the European Cup; but like the competition itself, it was a good second best.

Below: *Tottenham goalkeeper Tony Parks makes the first of his Cup-winning penalty saves against Anderlecht in 1984.*

Bottom: *Real Madrid won in both 1985 and 1986. Hugo Sanchez, the talented Mexican striker celebrates after the second leg in Cologne in '86.*

SOUTH AMERICAN CLUB CHAMPIONSHIP

Across a continent where European-style knock-out competitions are unknown there is only one 'Cup' – the Copa Libertadores, the South American Club Championship.

In European terms it is a cross between the Champions' Cup and the U.E.F.A. Cup with two clubs from each of the ten C.O.N.M.E.B.O.L. (South American confederation) nations taking part each year.

Uruguay were the first to understand the value of the Libertadores. Peñarol of Montevideo won the first two editions and were runners-up in the third. The Libertadores was not so much an end in itself, but a route to the lucrative World Club Cup challenge against the champions of Europe.

Pele and Santos brought brief glamour to the Libertadores before Argentine pragmatism took over. Independiente won in 1964 and 1965 by slavishly copying Italian defensive tactics. Then along came the notorious Estudiantes de La Plata, whose cynical approach made Argentina's 1966 World Cup team look like angels. Intriguingly, rugged midfielder Carlos Bilardo went on to manage Argentina's victorious 1986 World Cup campaign.

Somehow, the Cup recovered from the brink of sporting disaster. The disciplined professionalism of Boca Juniors, starring veteran goalkeeper Hugo Orlando Gatti, proved that Argentine football had turned a corner. Cruzeiro, Gremio and Flamengo revived confidence in Brazil's winning skills.

Then came the excitement of River Plate and their classic inside forward, Noberto Alonso, fulfilling their title destiny. For years River had been desperate to land this one crown which had eluded them. Twice they had reached the final only to lose in a play-off. Eventually, in 1986, they were successful. So determined was coach Bambino Veira that he fielded his reserve team in the league to keep his stars fresh and fit for the Libertadores.

Passions can run that high for fans, too. The Brazilian referee, Jose Roberto Wright, was lucky to escape with his life when a Bolivian crowd chased him from the pitch in the middle of a match after he disallowed a local equaliser. Wright jumped in a taxi outside the stadium to complete his getaway.

Boca Juniors missed out in the 1981 competition despite having Diego Maradona as their number ten. He left them the following year for Barcelona.

Even Brazilian involvement has not been all skill and invention. When Flamengo faced their fellow Brazilians of Atletico Mineiro in a first round play-off in 1981, the game was abandoned after 35 minutes because five Mineiro players had been sent off.

Ecuador, one of the countries whose clubs have never made an impression on the Cup, can at least boast the most effective marksman in the Cup's history. He was Pedro Alberto Spencer, a powerful striker who scored more than 50 goals in competition (South American statistics are notoriously inexact) for Peñarol. The best one-season tally was 17 goals by River Plate's Daniel Onega in 1966. But then, River did play a record 'high' of 21 matches that season before the competition was streamlined.

The country to watch in future Libertadores competition is Colombia. America of Cali were beaten finalists in 1985, 1986 and 1987. But such is the current financial strength of Colombia's top clubs that it should not be long before America or perhaps even the infamous Millionarios join the honours list.

Winners: 1960 Peñarol (Uru). 1961 Peñarol. 1962 Santos (Brz). 1963 Santos. 1964 Independiente (Arg). 1965 Independiente. 1966 Peñarol. 1967 Racing Club (Arg). 1968 Estudiantes de La Plata (Arg). 1969 Estudiantes de La Plata. 1970 Estudiantes de La Plata. 1971 Nacional (Uru). 1972 Independiente. 1973 Independiente. 1974 Independiente. 1975 Independiente. 1976 Cruzeiro (Brz). 1977 Boca Juniors (Arg). 1978 Boca Juniors. 1979 Olimpia (Par). 1980 Nacional. 1981 Flamengo (Brz). 1982 Peñarol. 1983 Gremio (Brz). 1984 Independiente. 1985 Argentinos Juniors. 1986 River Plate (Arg). 1987 Peñarol. 1988 Nacional.

Overall: Independiente 7; Peñarol 5; Estudiantes and Nacional 3 each; Boca Juniors and Santos 2 each; Argentinos Juniors, Cruzeiro, Flamengo, Gremio, Olimpia, Racing, River Plate all 1 each.

WORLD CLUB CUP

It took the advent of Japanese sponsorship to provide a most unlikely rescue act for the most tarnished of the game's high-prestige events.

The lowest point was reached in the late 1960s, first when six players were ordered off in a play-off between Racing of Argentina and Celtic, then when Estudiantes de La Plata brought a malevolent cynicism to their clashes with Manchester United, Milan and Feyenoord.

The World Club Cup is more important in terms of prestige and cash to the South Americans than the Europeans. That is why Uruguay's Nacional, Argentina's Independiente and Boca Juniors and Paraguay's Olimpia insisted on playing the European runners-up in the 1970s and when Ajax, Bayern Munich, Liverpool and Nottingham Forest all found their fixture lists too conveniently crowded to risk World Club battle.

Then along came the Japanese car firm, Toyota, with the financial support which converted the final into a one-off annual event in Tokyo to promote soccer in Japan. Nacional won the first final of the new era, beating Nottingham Forest 1–0 to maintain the general pattern of South American superiority.

The most dramatic recent final was Juventus' victory over Argentinos Juniors on penalties in 1985, but the best display of pure football was laid on by Zico's Flamengo in their delicate 3–0 demolition of Liverpool in 1981.

Winners: 1960 Real Madrid. 1961 Peñarol (Uru). 1962 Santos (Brz). 1963 Santos. 1964 Internazionale (It). 1965 Internazionale. 1966 Peñarol. 1967 Racing (Arg). 1968 Estudiantes de La Plata (Arg). 1969 Milan. 1970 Feyenoord (Hol). 1971 Nacional (Uru). 1972 Ajax Amsterdam. 1973 Independiente (Arg). 1974 Atletico Madrid. 1975 No competition. 1976 Bayern Munich. 1977 Boca Juniors (Arg). 1978 No competition. 1979 Olimpia (Par). 1980 Nacional. 1981 Flamengo (Brz). 1982 Peñarol. 1983 Gremio (Brz). 1984 Independiente. 1985 Juventus (It). 1986 River Plate (Arg). 1987 FC Porto (Por). 1988 Nacional. Most wins: Nacional and Peñarol 3 each.

Even Liverpool were outclassed by Flamengo of Brazil in 1981. Nunez scores the second in a 3-0 win.

THE EUROPEAN CHAMPIONSHIP

1960 in France
Final: U.S.S.R. 2 Yugoslavia 1 (after extra-time)

The European Nations' Cup, as it was first called, began in 1958 with 17 countries taking part in home and away knockout matches on the European Cup model, before the four semi-finalists adjourned to France.

As with the World Cup, though with even less excuse, Britain remained aloof. The Republic of Ireland took part, (as they had in all but the first World Cup) and on 5 May 1969 defeated Czechoslovakia 2–0 in one of the first Nations' Cup matches played. Only five days later, Czechoslovakia won the return leg 4–0 in Bratislava and later went on to reach the semi-final, losing to the U.S.S.R. 3–0 in Marseille.

The other semi-final was a thrilling game in which Yugoslavia spoiled the chances of a 'home' victory in the inaugural tournament by defeating France 5–4. Even without Raymond Kopa and Just Fontaine from their exciting 1958 World Cup team, France scored 21 goals in five matches, knocking out Greece and Austria along the way.

The crowd for the final in Paris on 10 July 1960 was understandably modest in France's absence, but the 18,000 present saw a close game which went to extra-time before Ponedelnik struck the winning goal.

Khussainov (U.S.S.R.) and Calleja (Spain) in 1964 final.

Yachin clears Yugoslavia attack in first final.

1964 in Spain
Final: Spain 2 U.S.S.R. 1

Twenty-nine countries were sufficiently impressed to enter the second competition, though Scotland, were not among them. The other British countries made little impact. England lost 5–2 away to France in Alf Ramsey's first match as manager; Wales went out to Hungary and it was Northern Ireland who carried the flag most effectively. They had two fine wins over Poland (the 2–0 victory in Belfast was Danny Blanchflower's last international) and then held Spain in Bilbao before losing 1–0 at home.

Unlike the World Cup, the host country was not (until 1980) automatically given a place in the finals. The organisers were therefore grateful that Spain had scraped through.

They had an easier passage in the quarter-final against the Republic of Ireland (5–1, 2–0) and good fortune too in the finals. The wins against Hungary in the semi-final and the holders in the final both came from very late goals.

A crowd of 120,000 watched the climax in Madrid, illustrating the competition's potential.

1968 in Italy
Final: Italy 1 Yugoslavia 1 (after extra-time)
Italy 2 Yugoslavia 0

A group system was introduced for the first time to accommodate the 31 entries for a competition now known as offically as the European Championship. The results of the Home International Championship over two seasons determined one of the groups, which England eventually won, despite losing to Scotland at Wembley in April 1967 – their first defeat since winning the World Cup.

World Cup runners-up West Germany were the victims of a shock when they could only draw 0–0 in Albania, allowing Yugoslavia to qualify.

Italy, the host country, having won their group easily, only just beat Bulgaria (2–3, 2–0). The U.S.S.R., Yugoslavia and England also qualified for what were to be the eminently forgettable final stages.

Alan Mullery became the first England player sent off in an international as his team went down 1–0 to Yugoslavia in Florence and Italy won the other semi-final on the toss of a coin (!) after a goalless draw with the U.S.S.R.

Yugoslavia, for whom Dragan Dzajic was outstanding, deserved to win the final but were denied by a late equaliser and lost the replay two days later.

1972 in Belgium
Final: West Germany 3 U.S.S.R. 0

The competition came of age with the 1972 finals, thanks to West Germany. With Günter Netzer in midfield added to the best of Bayern Munich's emerging side, they were the outstanding team of the moment: Holland, who would challenge them later, had not yet produced a team to match that of Europe's champion club Ajax.

One of the Germans' most difficult games was their first group match, a 1–1 draw at home to Turkey! They grew more impressive, Netzer destroying England at Wembley before Ramsey chose to save face with a depressingly negative performance in Berlin.

Italy's second goal in 1968 replay against Yugoslavia.

Belgium helped towards the success of the finals by knocking out the holders Italy in the quarter-final, then running the Germans close before going down 2–1 to them in Antwerp. With that match shown live on televison, fewer than 4,000 turned up for the other semi-final, in which the U.S.S.R. beat Hungary.

The Soviets, so much more consistent in this competition than in the World Cup, were still no match for a vibrant German side, which won the final with goals from Gerd Müller (2) and Herbert Wimmer.

West Germany's outstanding mid-Seventies team (in green) against England in 1972.

1976: Antonin Panenka's penalty wins a thrilling tournament for Czechoslovakia.

1976 in Yugoslavia

Final: Czechoslovakia 2 West Germany 2 (Czechoslovakia won on penalties)

For the first time, a major international final series was played in Eastern Europe, where the Yugoslav spectators were treated to a magnificent tournament, every game of which went to extra-time.

The only sadness was that penalties should be used to decide that Czechoslovakia prevented West Germany from adding to their successes in the previous European Championship and World Cup

Ironically, the Czechs' campaign began almost two years earlier with a clear-cut 3–0 defeat by England in Don Revie's first match as manager. Their 2–1 victory in Bratislava, however, meant that England, like Scotland, failed to qualify.

Wales unexpectedly won their group, then lost over two wild quarter-finals to Yugoslavia. Holland got through despite a heavy defeat in Poland and were expected to meet West Germany in a repeat of the World Cup final. But the Czechs beat them 3–1 in the semi-final, then held the Germans 2–2 before converting their penalties more accurately.

It was clearly the best Czech team since 1962, but one which peaked with that winning penalty and failed even to qualify for the next World Cup finals, losing to both Wales and Scotland.

1980 in Italy

Final: West Germany 2 Belgium 1

The hosts were now given an automatic passage to the final stages, for which seven group winners were to join them. But the final stages were disappointingly dull, with much negative football and few goals for the generally small crowds.

England, having qualified emphatically by dropping only one point in eight matches, travelled with high hopes, which were dented early on. Belgium held on for a 1–1 draw against them in Turin, a match marred by crowd trouble. England then lost 1–0 to Italy after Ron Greenwood had dropped Trevor Brooking and thrown Garry Birtles in for an unsuccessful full international debut.

A 2–1 victory over Spain was not enough, though Belgium kept the host country out of the final with another boring 0–0 draw. Italy's three group matches had produced just one goal to either side, the one Marco Tardelli scored against England.

West Germany, with Bernd Schuster an outstanding play-maker, won a group containing Holland (3–2), Czechoslovakia (1–0) and Greece (0–0). Now two goals by the powerful, if unsophisticated Hamburg striker Horst Hrübesch, won them the Cup for what would have been a third time in succession but for those missed penalties in 1976.

Horst Hrübesch celebrates West German goal in 1980.

1984 in France
Final: France 2 Spain 0

After the disappointment of Italy came a tournament to revive memories of 1976. This time there were two outstanding teams, France and Denmark, who met, sadly, in a group match but not the final.

The French, although short of a class striker, had a superb midfield of Jean Tigana, Alain Giresse, Fernandez and, above all, Michel Platini, who had to take on the role of chief goalscorer. He claimed the goal which beat Denmark in the opening match, then hat-tricks against Belgium (5–0) and Yugoslavia (3–2).

In the other group West Germany failed for once, edged out by Spain and reviving Portugal, who then took France to the brink in one semi-final. It went to extra-time before Platini, inevitably, won it.

That should have set up the dream final but in the other semi-final a tired Denmark could only draw with Spain, who beat them on penalties. The final was something of an anti-climax but at least produced the right victors, as Platini maintained his record of having scored in every game.

England had been eliminated in the qualifying groups, bemoaning a home defeat by Denmark, though the failure to beat Greece at Wembley was equally costly. Wales and Northern Ireland were extremely unlucky not to get through (the Irish having won in West Germany) but Scotland were an inglorious fourth in the group won by their bogey team Belgium.

1988 in West Germany
Final: Holland 2 USSR 0

West Germany's home advantage made them narrow favourites to win the tournament, even when they came up against Holland in the semi-final. It proved to be a thrilling game, decided in the last minute when Marco Van Basten swivelled to send a fine shot past the fingertips of goalkeeper Eike Immel.

Holland had played the better football and they did so again in the final, when it was fitting that the goals should be scored by Ruud Gullit, the complete modern footballer, and Van Basten.

Van Basten's brilliantly taken hat-trick had effectively eliminated England, who finished without a point after losing to the Republic of Ireland (1–0) and the USSR (3–1). Ireland made plenty of friends at their first major championship, which could not be said for the wilder supporters of England or West Germany. More than 1200 arrests were made in all, even though there were no incidents actually within the stadia.

The Soviets surprised many people with their pace and mobility and defeated Holland 1–0 in a group match before coming up against the Dutch side again in the final.

A typical Michel Platini free-kick puts France ahead in the 1984 final against Spain.

Ruud Gullit climbs above the Soviet defence as Holland win the 1988 title.

SOUTH AMERICAN CHAMPIONSHIP

The South American Championship is the oldest major international event in world football: 13 years older than the World Cup, and 43 years senior to the 'fledgling' European Championship.

It was the product of a meeting in Buenos Aires between officials from Argentina, Brazil, Chile and Uruguay to found a South American confederation. With only three exceptions the format has involved all matches being played in a few weeks in one host country.

In recent years problems over player release meant countries such as Brazil and Argentina did not field their strongest teams. It was only in 1987 that a determined attempt was made, with sponsorship support, to revive the event's prestige. Argentina, the hosts and captained by Diego Maradona, were favourites. But in the end it was Uruguay who came through to beat Chile in the final, despite having star forward Enzo Francescoli sent off in the first half.

Argentina's most memorable years were in the 1950s, culminating in their 1957 success with a team built round an inside-forward trio of Humberto Maschio, Antonio Valentin Angelillo and Omar Sivori. The manner of their victory prompted forecasts of a first Argentine World Cup victory in Sweden the following year. But by then Maschio, Angelillo and Sivori had all left for Italy and Argentina's hopes went with them.

Winners (official tournaments only): 1917 Uruguay. 1919 Brazil. 1920 Uruguay. 1921 Argentina. 1922 Brazil. 1923 Uruguay. 1924 Uruguay. 1925 Argentina. 1926 Uruguay. 1927 Argentina. 1929 Argentina. 1937 Argentina. 1939 Peru. 1942 Uruguay. 1947 Argentina. 1949 Brazil. 1953 Paraguay, 1955 Argentina. 1957 Argentina. 1959 Argentina. 1963 Bolivia. 1967 Uruguay. 1975 Peru. 1979 Paraguay. 1983 Uruguay. 1987 Uruguay.

Overall: Uruguay and Argentina 9 each; Brazil 3; Paraguay and Peru 2 each; Bolivia one.

Zico, the great Brazilian forward, scores for his club side Fluminense.

WORLD CUP

1930 in Uruguay

Final: Uruguay 4 Argentina 2
Leading scorer: Stabile (Argentina) 8.

Uruguay, as Olympic champions, had the honour of staging the first World Cup tournament, played for the Jules Rimet Trophy. It was no great surprise that Argentina came through to meet them in a repeat of the 1928 Olympics final.

That match had needed a replay, which Uruguay won 2–1; now, with seven of the same team, they again defeated their neighbours, who had led 2–1 at half-time.

Europe's challenge was a muted one. The British countries had resigned from F.I.F.A. and would not compete until 1950. Only Belgium, France, Rumania and Yugoslavia were prepared to make the three-week sea crossing to Montevideo. Three were eliminated in the qualifying groups, while Yugoslavia lost their semi-final 6–1 to Argentina.

Above: *Jules Rimet presents the trophy which bore his name to the Uruguayan FA president after the first World Cup final.*

Below: *Giuseppe Meazza shakes hands with Sarosi before the exciting 1938 final in Paris.*

1934 in Italy

Final: Italy 2 Czechoslovakia 1 (after extra-time)
Leading scorer: Conen (Germany), Nejedly (Czechoslovakia), Schiavio (Italy) 4

The initial competition had proved a great success and 34 countries entered the second: though not the holders. Uruguay, who had been peeved by Europe's lack of enthusiasm in 1930, stayed at home and watched their American rivals flounder.

All eight quarter-finalists were Europeans, who set about each other in some over-physical matches.

Vittorio Pozzo's Italy and Hugo Meisl's Austria, the favourites, met in a mud-bath of a semi-final which the Italians, despite having to play their third match in four days, won 1–0. The final was again an exciting one as the skilful Czechs went ahead through Puc, only for Raimondo Orsi to equalise after 82 minutes, and Angelo Schiavio to win the Cup in extra-time.

1938 in France

Final: Italy 4 Hungary 2
Leading scorer: Leonidas da Silva (Brazil) 8.

For the first time, victory eluded the home country, France going out in the quarter-final to Italy, who had struggled unexpectedly against Norway in the preceding round. But the Italians grew more assured, beating Brazil, who inexplicably left out the competition's leading scorer, Leonidas, and then Hungary in another good final.

A knockout format was again employed, after the 36 entries had been reduced to 16. One of those qualifiers, Austria, had to withdraw after Hitler annexed their country, Germany taking four of their players but losing to Switzerland in a first round replay.

England refused an invitation to replace Austria, and with it the opportunity to test their standing in world football.

Hungary get a shock in the 1954 final as Morlock (white shirt) reduces their early 2-0 lead.

Below: *A star is born. Pele, 17 years old, scores against Sweden in the 1958 final.*

1950 in Brazil
Final: Uruguay 2 Brazil 1
Leading scorer: Ademir (Brazil) 9

The deciding match of the first post-War competition was not a 'final' in the strictest sense. F.I.F.A. had gone from one extreme to the other, changing from a knockout competition to a group system, not only in the early stages but right to the end.

And so Brazil, having beaten Sweden 7–1 and Spain 6–1 in the final pool of four teams, needed only a draw against Uruguay, who had dropped a point against Spain. The 200,000 who had forced their way into the Maracana stadium began celebrating in earnest when Brazil took the lead, but were devastated as Uruguay fought back to win with goals by Juan Schiaffino and Alcides Ghiggia.

Earlier England, agreeing to compete at last, had been even more demoralised by a 1–0 defeat against the U.S.A.

1954 in Switzerland
Final: West Germany 3 Hungary 2
Leading scorer: Kocsis (Hungary) 11.

Neither Brazil nor Uruguay were fancied, on European soil, to end Hungary's extraordinary unbeaten run, which dated back to 1950. The Hungarians duly defeated both on their imperious way to the final, scoring 25 goals in four matches.

Eight of those came in a group match against West Germany, who were saving themselves for a play-off against Turkey, which they won 7–2, later demolishing Austria 6–1 in this highest-scoring of all World Cups.

In another dramatic final, Hungary, still hot favourites, led two-nil after eight minutes. But Morlock and Helmut Rahn pulled the Germans level and five minutes from time Rahn added another goal to snatch the cup away from the half-fit Ferenc Puskas's team.

1958 in Sweden
Final: Brazil 5 Sweden 2
Leading scorer: Fontaine (France) 13.

England and Scotland, both beaten by Uruguay four years earlier, qualified again, but were overshadowed by Northern Ireland and Wales, both of whom won group play-offs to reach the quarter-final.

Northern Ireland succumbed to an exciting French team, which included Just Fontaine and Raymond Kopa while Wales went out, by only 1–0, to Brazil.

In the semi-finals, the 17-year-old Pele's hat-trick destroyed France, and Sweden, their five Italian-based players outstanding, put out West Germany. The hosts took the lead against Brazil, but were overcome as Pele and Vava scored.

1962 in Chile
Final: Brazil 3 Czechoslovakia 1
Leading scorer: Jerkovic (Yugoslavia) 5.

Although the exuberant Brazilians retained their trophy, the era of more functional football beginning elsewhere was reflected in a dull and occasionally violent tournament.

Spain, like Italy, played 'catenaccio': both were eliminated before the quarter-finals, at which stage England went out to Brazil. Chile, who had effectively knocked out Italy in the Battle of Santiago, caused another surprise in the quarter-final by beating the U.S.S.R.

Their semi-final saw Garrincha (Brazil) and Landa (Chile) sent off but Garrincha was allowed to play in the final, in which the Czechs scored first through the admirable Josef Masopust, only to be overrun by goals from Pele's deputy Amarildo, Zito and Vava.

1966 in England
Final: England 4 West Germany 2 (after extra-time)
Leading scorer: Eusebio (Portugal) 9.

Back on their own territory, the Europeans dominated again, providing all four semi-finalists. Brazil, victims of brutal treatment by Portugal and Bulgaria, did not even reach the last eight.

North Korea astonishingly defeated Italy at Middlesbrough and even more remarkably led the talented Portuguese 3–0 in the quarter-final before Eusebio took hold of the game, scoring four and making a fifth. In the semi-final his team became the first to score against England, without managing to stop them.

West Germany found that scoring first in the final was still a kiss of death. Even though Wolfgang Weber forced a dramatic late equaliser after goals by West Ham's Geoff Hurst and Martin Peters, Hurst went on to complete the first hat-trick in a World Cup final.

1970 in Mexico
Final: Brazil 4 Italy 1
Leading scorer: Müller (W. Germany) 10.

High altitude and the midday sun took its toll of the Europeans, who produced no more than four of the eight quarter-finalists. There, England, having lost a fine group match to Brazil 1–0, met West Germany, who extracted revenge for 1966 by coming from 0–2 down to win 3–2 in extra-time.

The Germans were forced into extra-time in their semi-final as well and, with Franz Beckenbauer handicapped by injury, Italy finished the stronger, taking another extraordinary game 4–3. Brazil's reborn attacking spirit and a forward line of Jairzinho, Tostao, Pele and Roberto Rivelino carried all before them, emphatically defeating Peru, Uruguay and then Italy 4–1 in the final.

1962 and Brazil are again unstoppable. Zito (19) celebrates his goal in the final against Czechoslovakia.

England celebrate victory in 1966: Peters, Hurst, Moore and an emotional Bobby Charlton.

Holland relaxed too much after opening the scoring with this first-minute penalty by Johan Neeskens and lost 2-1 to West Germany in 1974.

1974 in West Germany

Final: West Germany 2 Holland 1
Leading scorer: Lato (Poland) 7.

Having won their third World Cup in Mexico, Brazil kept the original Jules Rimet trophy. Sadly, they tried to win the new one with what they perceived to be European power-football, the emphasis on solid defence.

The best of the Europeans, Holland and West Germany, had in fact grown much more sophisticated and although Poland, who had prevented England from qualifying, surprised many people, the best two teams unquestionably met in the final.

The Dutch, after scoring from a penalty in the game's first attack, dominated the first quarter. But another penalty, by Paul Breitner, and then Gerd Müller's sweeping shot as he fell brought victory to the hosts.

1978 in Argentina

Final: Argentina 3 Holland 1 (after extra-time)
Leading scorer: Kempes (Argentina) 6.

Argentina, hitherto producing some talented but temperamentally suspect teams, withstood the pressures of being host country and made good use of all its advantages.

Beaten by Italy in a group match, they needed a dubious penalty against France to reach the second stage, which as in 1974 comprised two mini-leagues. This time, in order to finish above Brazil, they needed to beat Peru by four goals – and scored six!

Holland had scraped through their group despite losing to Scotland, who had again qualified for the finals when England had not. Like West Germany, the Dutch were weaker than four years earlier, but could still have won the final, Rob Rensenbrink hitting a post when the score was 1–1 just before the end of normal time.

Holland again lose a final to the host country, in 1978. Daniel Bertoni scores Argentina's third.

1982 in Spain
Final: Italy 3 West Germany 1
Leading scorer: Rossi (Italy) 6.

Another new format allowed for an extension to 24 countries, among them England, Scotland and Northern Ireland. The Scots fell in a difficult group won splendidly by Brazil; England reached the second stage, only to fail in goalless draws against West Germany and Spain; Northern Ireland did just as creditably before going out to France, also in the second stage.

The outstanding second round group was between holders Argentina, favourites Brazil, and Italy – who overcame both of them, drawing enough confidence from a marvellous 3–2 win over the Brazilians to go on and win the trophy.

The final was against the Germans, whose semi-final against the exciting French, won on penalties, was another memorable occasion.

At the last stage, though, the Germans disappointed.

Above: *England started well in 1982, Trevor Francis scoring in an early group match against Czechoslovakia, but failed in goalless second-stage games against West Germany and Spain.*

Left: *Fulvio Collovati flies in against German striker Horst Hrübesch in a challenge typifying the 1982 final.*

Lothar Matthäus (8) was never far away from Diego Maradona in the 1986 final. But, like so many before him, he came off second-best.

1986 in Mexico
Final: Argentina 3 West Germany 2
Leading scorer: Lineker (England) 6

Mexico, to general surprise, were awarded a second World Cup in the space of 16 years when Colombia dropped out, and almost had to withdraw as well after an earthquake struck the capital city.

A generally enjoyable tournament followed, once the 24 teams had been reduced to 16, who then met in straightforward knockout matches. Almost straightforward, anyway: three of the four quarter-finals had to be decided on penalties, with France (after a classic match), West Germany and Belgium keeping their nerve better than Brazil, Mexico and Spain respectively.

Only Argentina went through in normal time, after one illegal goal and one superlative one by Diego Maradona against England. Maradona undid Belgium in one semi-final while a tired French team went down to West Germany, who showed their resilience again. Argentina were hauled back from 2–0 to 2–2 before Maradona made the winner for Burruchaga.

German goalkeeper Toni Schumacher is hopelessly stranded as Jose Luis Brown heads Argentina's first goal.

INDEX